AMISH AMNESIA

The Covert Police Detective Unit Series

BOOK 3

Ashley Emma

GET 4 OF ASHLEY EMMA'S AMISH EBOOKS FOR FREE

www.AshleyEmmaAuthor.com

Download free Amish eBooks at www.AshleyEmmaAuthor.com, including the exclusive, secret prequel to Undercover Amish!

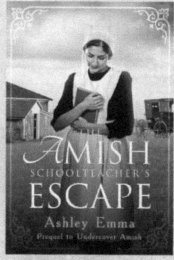

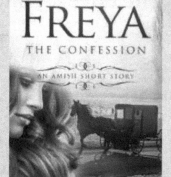

HOW TO ACCESS YOUR FREE BONUS:

Use this secret link to instantly access your 3 free Ex-Amish Interview videos!

http://ashleyemmaauthor.com/free-videos-entry/

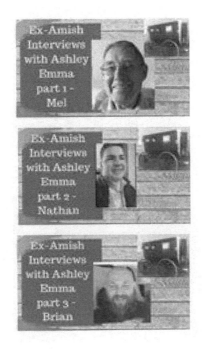

Check out my author Facebook page to see rare photos from when I lived with the Amish in Unity, Maine.

https://www.facebook.com/ashleyemmaauthor/

Join my free Facebook group The Amish Book Club where I share free Amish books weekly!

https://www.facebook.com/groups/theamishbookclub/

Looking for something new to read? Check out my other books!

Check out other books by Ashley Emma on Amazon

The characters and events in this book are the creation of the author, and any resemblance to actual persons or events are purely coincidental.

CONTENTS

ACKNOWLEDGMENTS

Thank you so much to the following people for helping me with research, proofreading, and beta reading! (Last names left out for privacy.)

Scott E.

Abigail W.

Erica E.

Janene

Pat J.

Gail S.

Kit D.

Lisa L.

Julie

Erin C.

And my entire production team.

I couldn't have done this without you, and you all helped make this book so much better. Thank you!

-Ashley

CHAPTER ONE

Jefferson Martin reached his hands towards the campfire, inhaling the woodsy, smoky scent as he looked at the stars through the skeletal maze of branches above. After returning home from Afghanistan a few days ago, Jeff planned on spending his time off doing nothing but enjoying nature in Maine.

"Dad would have loved this," he told his sister, Estella.

"Oh yeah. He'd be making s'mores right now." Estella tossed her blonde hair over her shoulder, then smacked her forehead with a chuckle. "That's what we forgot! Stuff to make s'mores."

"Wow. I haven't had one of those since I was a kid." Jeff looked at her, grinning like the mischievous boy he used to be. "We should go to the store right now and get some in honor of Dad."

"You mean you should go. I'll stay here and watch the fire." Estella smiled as she stoked the flames with the stick in her hand and pulled the blanket tighter around her shoulders. The night air was beginning to get chilly. "Get some coffee while you're at it, okay?"

"Okay." Jeff was already walking down the short path through the woods towards his car in the gravel parking lot near the restrooms. He figured it wouldn't take him more than a few minutes to drive to the small store a couple of miles down the road. Pausing at a stop sign, he drove down the lane towards the main road.

He peered through the darkness at a dark colored sedan parked on the side of the road. He heard shouting from inside the car, and the hairs on the back of his neck rose instantly. The passenger door opened and a girl who looked like she was in her late teens tumbled out of the vehicle. Even from this far away, she looked terrified and confused. Stumbling across the street, she looked back at the car over her shoulder. The ragged clothing she wore hung loosely on her thin body.

The male driver shouted profanities out the window at the girl. The first thing that came to Jeff's mind was that it was probably a fight between a couple, possibly a violent one. He'd seen it before many times in his line of work. His police and military training kicked in.

He was reaching for his door handle when the sedan veered out onto the street at about ten or fifteen miles an hour toward the girl. The driver clearly wanted to hurt her, not kill her. Jeff watched in horror as the car struck her, knocking her over. She landed awkwardly and lay motionless on the street. The sedan stopped when it hit her and backed up.

Jeff slammed his foot on the gas and sped toward the woman. The sedan quickly veered off in the opposite direction. With no street lights to offset the darkness, Jeff couldn't get a good look at the plates or the driver.

Anger flared inside Jeff's chest, and he shouted as the car tore off. Pounding the steering wheel in indignation, he wanted nothing more than to chase the attacker down and force him to answer for his crimes. But this girl needed his help right now.

He pulled his car across the road between the girl and potential oncoming cars and jumped out, glancing again at his cell phone. No service. Of course. They were in the middle of nowhere.

Shoving the phone back in his pocket, he took another look at the girl, surprised when he saw she was older than he'd first thought, maybe late teens or early twenties. He checked her vital signs, relieved when he found a steady but very weak pulse. She was still breathing, barely. Her pretty face had old and fresh bruising and some small cuts. She was abnormally thin and pale. Her clothing was worn and too big, and she wasn't wearing shoes. Angry red lines from a rope or some other restraint were wrapped around her wrists. She didn't seem to have any broken bones, but she was banged up pretty badly.

What had happened to this woman? Who had done this to her?

Rage coursed through Jeff's veins, and his protective instincts kicked in to overdrive. He would find that guy, or whoever did this to her and make him pay. He wanted to hunt him down and do to him whatever he had done to her, but Jeff wouldn't be allowed to do that, and it wouldn't be right.

He gently scooped the woman up into his arms and brought her to his car, laying her on the back seat and awkwardly buckling her in. Jeff slammed the car door and flew down the road at record speed.

Luckily, Estella had brought her own car to the campsite, so Jeff would try calling her once he got cell phone reception. She had a different cell phone service provider and usually got better reception than he did. If that didn't work, he'd have the police notify her of what had happened. But first, he needed to call the local police about this woman.

He periodically held his phone up again. Still no service.

Out in the woods near the campsite, a hospital wasn't exactly close by. Jeff didn't know how long he had been driving, but it seemed like hours later when he rolled into the hospital parking lot. He pulled into the emergency room entrance and carried the still unconscious woman inside.

"Help! She was hit by a car," Jeff called out. A few nurses rushed towards him with a gurney, and he laid her on it gently, instinctively smoothing her dark hair back from her face before they wheeled her down the hall. Jeff began to follow, but a tired-looking nurse held up her hand. Jeff had to stumble to a stop so he wouldn't slam into her.

"You can't come in while we treat her, sir. Are you family?" She adjusted her rectangle glasses.

"No. I found her at the scene. I witnessed her being assaulted and hit by a car."

"Okay. You can wait out here or leave your contact information at the front desk. Then we can let you know how she is doing later on." With that, she hurried down the hall to where the other nurses had taken the woman.

Jeff let out a deep breath. There wasn't much he could do at this point except park his car and wait until he could speak to her.

Now that he finally had cell phone reception, he called the local police station to report the crime, which he instinctively classified as attempted murder and a possible kidnapping. He finally reached Estella, who was at the store and had better reception when he made the call, so he'd called just at the right time. He finally reached Estella who had gone to the store, where there was better reception, after realizing there were more things they had forgotten.

Well, his vacation would have to wait. After over a year of searching for terrorists in the desert, he'd been looking forward to time off at the Kennebunkport beach house he and his sister had inherited. He needed to recover from a year's worth of dust, bullets, scorching sun, and the haunting memories that kept him awake at night. This time off was supposed to be for mourning the recent death of his father before he returned to work at his old unit, the Covert Police Detectives Unit, also known as CPDU. But his father would have wanted taking care of this woman to take priority. He would wait here all night if he had to until he found out how she was doing.

It looked like they weren't going to be having coffee and s'mores after all.

CHAPTER TWO

The woman tried to open her eyes. It felt like lead weights had been placed on top of them. Finally getting them open, she found herself in an unfamiliar white room with strange machines. A dull pain throbbed rhythmically in her head, ribs, and legs. Every part of her body hurt, and it felt like she was being weighed down.

Where am I? How did I get here? she wondered, frowning at the thin tube that snaked from her hand to the I.V. bag hanging over her bed. In the distance, she heard voices and tried to lift her head to see who it was, but eventually gave up and rested her head on the pillow. Hearing the sound of her door being opened, she sighed in relief. She was finally going to get some answers, and she needed a lot of those.

Two nurses approached her bed.

"Hey, how are you feeling?" one nurse asked.

"Like I was hit by a truck," the woman said.

"You've been through a lot, haven't you?" the other nurse said as she checked the IV bag.

The woman said nothing, still too disoriented to make sense of what they were saying. Her head hurt, and her whole body felt stiff.

"Don't worry," the first nurse said. "It's okay if you don't feel like talking yet. Rest and take it easy, okay?"

"Where am I? How did I get here?" the woman asked.

The two nurses exchanged a look before they turned to face the woman.

"Actually, we were hoping you could help us with that. What do you remember about the incident?"

The woman frowned. "What incident?"

Again, the nurses exchanged the same look before they looked at the woman again.

"What's your name?"

"My name...? My name is..." The woman paused, her mouth hanging open for a few seconds. No name formed in her mouth or brain. "I... I don't know," she whispered.

This time there was a little bit of concern in the look the nurses shared.

"Do you know what year it is? Or who the president is?"

She shook her head, then immediately regretted doing that. It hurt.

"Do you know where you are from? Anything you can remember that you can tell us?" the nurses asked.

The woman squinted her eyes shut and tried to focus. She wondered what had happened to her and why she couldn't remember anything about her past. Did she have a life before this moment?

If she did, she remembered none of it. Except...a room. A small room with books and a tiny window.

She opened her eyes. "No, I don't remember anything. Just a small room with some books. I'm sorry."

"That's okay, dear. Do you remember anything else about the room?"

"The floor was dirty. There was a window. A small window."

"What was outside the window?"

"I don't know. It was hard to see through the window."

"Why?" the nurse asked. "Why couldn't you see through the window?"

"Well, the ground and rocks prevented me from seeing much. I guess I was underground, maybe in a basement? And the window—it was partially boarded up."

They looked at each other, then at her.

She looked down at her hands. The red lines around her wrists brought back a vague memory of someone tying her hands together, but all she got was a deep throbbing headache when she tried to recollect that memory. "What happened to me?"

"Just relax," one of the nurses tried to reassure her. "You'll be fine. I'll go get the doctor."

*

"Martin?" Officer Horton from the local police station walked toward Jeff and extended his hand. "Branson told me you returned home from Afghanistan and you're a sergeant in the Marine Corps now. We're glad to have you back. Thank you for your service."

Jeff shrugged awkwardly, never knowing what to say to people who thanked him for his almost five years of service in the military. "Thanks for saying that, sir. And you can just call me Jeff. I'm not back on duty yet for CPDU."

"That's what I heard. I'm sorry about your father."

Jeff nodded. "Thank you."

"I'll be leading this investigation. You're the one who brought in the young woman?"

"Yes."

"Tell me, what exactly did you see when you found her? What happened?" Officer Horton asked.

Jeff explained in detail how the man in the car had yelled at the young woman, then hit her with his car.

"The weird thing was the speed of the car. I'm guessing the driver was going about ten miles an hour. Maybe he didn't want to kill her. Maybe he just wanted to hurt her, but not too seriously, because she didn't break any bones. It seemed like he wanted to get a message across. They'd had an argument, so maybe he was trying to show her he was in control."

"Interesting." Officer Horton scribbled something on a notepad. "I already sent some of my officers to examine the tire tracks from the crime scene so we might get an idea of the type of car, but as you know, it might not give us much to go on. Is there anything else you'd like to add? Any information can help, as you know."

"That's all. If I think of anything else, I'll definitely let you know."

"Thank you."

The officer asked a few more questions, and when they finished, Jeff walked down the hallway toward the woman's room, a bouquet of pink flowers in his hand from the gift shop downstairs. A doctor saw him and met him in the hall.

"Hello, I'm Dr. Roswell," she said, shaking Jeff's hand. "I understand you're the one who found her and brought her in."

"Yes, ma'am. How is she?" Jeff asked, glancing inside the room. A curtain was drawn, and all he could see was the end of her bed.

"That's why I wanted to talk to you. We have no family to contact with her medical information. That's why she consented

10

to have you be notified of her medical information since you found her. Which means I can tell you what is really going on here, now that the police have talked to you," the doctor told him, shifting her weight. "Mr. Martin, this woman has amnesia. She can't remember anything at all, except for a few things she told us. She remembers vaguely that a man hurt her, but she can't remember who."

Several questions assaulted Jeff's head. "Woman? She looks like she's in high school."

"That's the other thing. We ran multiple tests. From what we can see so far, we think that she is actually in her mid-twenties and that she looks like a teenager because of malnutrition. She looks years younger than she really is. Did you notice how pale she is? She's been locked away somewhere for a long time. When she told us what she does remember, that confirmed it."

"What does she remember?" Jeff looked over the doctor's shoulder into the room again. The woman's feet fidgeted on the hospital bed.

"She told us about a small room with a dirty floor and lots of books, and a window that was boarded up so she couldn't get out. She thinks the room was underground. That's all she remembers," Dr. Roswell said, rubbing her tired eyes. Who knew how many hours she had already been working or how many patients she had cared for on this shift?

"Sounds like she was kidnapped."

She looked back at Jeff. "It seems that way, but we aren't sure yet. Anyway. Since, as you said, the car that hit her wasn't going very fast, her injuries are not too bad. Bruising, and a mild concussion. She also has older injuries that are healing. It looks like someone abused her for a long time. Look, be careful around her. No sudden movements. She's extremely jumpy and doesn't trust anyone. She's very timid. She's probably suffered a lot of trauma. Also, she is acting as if she has never seen very many electronics before, like the monitors in her room. It is all very strange."

Jeff knocked on the already open door and walked in slowly. A forty-something nurse was shuffling around behind the curtain but came out when she heard him.

"I'm done here for now," she said with a smile. When she got closer to him, she said, "Wow. You make me wish I was the patient here so you could bring me some flowers."

Jeff felt his cheeks grow instantly hot in embarrassment and was relieved when the nurse scampered out the door. Shaking off the awkwardness, he walked past the curtain.

The nameless woman's eyes widened, then darted around. She pulled the sheets to her chest frantically, looking as if she wanted to run out the door. Now that her face wasn't smudged with dirt anymore, he realized how beautiful she was, even with her bruises. He probably would have noticed before, but he had been so focused on just getting her here safely. Her long hair the color of dark chocolate cascaded down past her waist, resting on the hospital sheets.

"It's okay. I was the one who found you and brought you here. You were hit by a car. I brought you these flowers." He gently set them on the tray beside her bed, and she jumped as though pots and pans had clattered to the floor. She reached out and touched the pink tulips gently as if they could shatter.

She whispered something in what sounded like German, then looked at him, eyes filling with tears and stories of scarring memories that may never be told. "Thank you. I think this might be the nicest thing anyone has ever done for me."

CHAPTER THREE

Jeff's heart filled with sympathy for the woman, and also a fierce desire to protect her. Her dark eyes darted away from his, and whatever connection he was feeling quickly ended when his sister bounded into the room.

"I got here as quickly as I could. Do you know how hard it is to disassemble a tent by yourself? Especially with no coffee? Sheesh," she said with a dramatic sigh, flipping her hair as the bracelets on her arm jangled.

Jane Doe's eyes widened again at the ruckus Estella was making.

Jeff wanted to roll his eyes. Instead, he motioned for her to quiet down. "Simmer down, Estella." He had told his sister on the phone during her drive to the hospital to be quiet and make no sudden movements. Had she already forgotten?

Estella stopped, then practically tiptoed towards them. "How is she?" she whispered.

"You don't have to whisper. Just keep it down, okay? And she seems pretty good, considering the circumstances," Jeff said, then turned to the woman on the hospital bed. "My sister is here. She wants to meet you, okay? She's obnoxious, but she's actually really nice. I promise." Jeff chuckled at his own lame joke, and half expected the woman to crack a smile, but she just watched the curtain, waiting for Estella to step out from behind it.

"Okay, Estella." Jeff motioned for her to come forward, and she approached the hospital bed. Jeff couldn't help but cringe, half expecting the woman to panic in response to Estella's bubbly, loud personality.

"Hi. I'm Estella. I'm this guy's sister. It's very nice to meet you," Estella said with a big grin.

The woman stared at her for several seconds, then smiled. "Hi."

"As soon as you get better, I'm taking you shopping. A girl needs a wardrobe, right? You can't walk around town in that hospital gown."

Jeff grabbed Estella's sleeve and pulled her to the other side of the curtain. "Don't go making her promises. I have no idea what's going to happen to her after she gets better," he whispered. "She's not a puppy we can adopt."

"Sorry. She doesn't have any clothes. We don't have to adopt her. Can't I just take her shopping?"

"I don't want you getting attached."

"It's shopping. I'm not giving her my kidney. She doesn't need a kidney, does she? Because I have two and only need one, you know."

"No. She doesn't need a kidney, but thanks anyway."

"Estella?" the woman said softly on the other side of the curtain. Estella stepped towards her carefully.

"Yes?"

"I know nobody knows my name, but I would like to have a name more than anything. Would you help me think of one?"

"Of course!" Estella chirped and plopped herself on the end of the patient's bed. Jeff was about to remind her to make no sudden movements, but the woman smiled at Estella. So far, it seemed like Estella was the only person this woman actually felt comfortable around.

"Well, they keep calling me Jane Doe." The woman sighed.

"That's just a name people use when they don't know someone's real name."

"Well, I like the name Jane."

"Okay. We can call you Jane. It's not really original though. I mean, what about something more unique like Cordelia?"

Jeff scoffed. "You just want to give her a name that's weirder than yours so you're not the one with the weirdest name in the room."

Estella bared her teeth at her brother playfully before turning back to the woman on the bed. "But if you want us to call you Jane, then no problem."

Estella's phone rang, and Jane jumped.

"What was that sound?"

Estella silenced it. "My cell phone. Ever seen one?"

"I'm not sure. I don't know. But I don't think I've ever held one before. Can I hold it?"

"Sure." Estella handed Jane the phone. Jane gasped when she touched the screen, and it lit up, displaying a picture of a few of Estella's friends.

"Woah. How did a photograph get on there?"

"Well, the phone is also a camera." Estella gently took it back. "Would you like me to take your picture?"

"I don't think that's such a good—" Jeff began.

Jane shook her head and held up a hand. "No. I can't have my picture taken. It's prideful."

Jeff and Estella glanced at each other in confusion for a brief moment. Prideful? How was having your photo taken prideful?

"Sorry, we have to run a few more tests," a nurse said, bustling into the room. She added in a low voice, "The doctor also wants her visiting time limited for now. You should go home."

"I want to make sure she's okay." Jeff smiled at Jane. She almost smiled back, the corners of her mouth lifting a bit. Uneasiness settled into his stomach. Whoever had hurt her might be looking for her. If she had been kidnapped, her kidnapper would definitely not be happy that she escaped. Hospitals might be the first place he'd look.

"She is safe here?" he asked.

"Well, considering her situation, a police officer is staying all night to watch over her. I promise, she will be safe," the nurse answered.

"We'll be back soon, Jane. Come on, Jeff, you heard her. Let's go." Estella playfully shoved Jeff out the door.

Chapter Four

Fatigue swept over Jane as the nurses finally left her alone for more than a half hour. She knew they would be back to check her vitals throughout the rest of the night, so she closed her eyes and tried to get some rest.

In the early hours of the morning, while it was still dark, she had finally started to drift off when she heard someone enter her room. Wearily, she opened her eyes and saw a doctor wearing a medical cap on his head and a white mask covering his nose and mouth. "I'm sorry to bother you. I wanted to check on you before I finished my rounds," he said.

"I'm fine. Thank you. I am very tired."

"Of course. Here, let me fix your pillows so you can have a good rest."

Something in his eyes made Jane's stomach turn. Something in the way he stepped closer to her, pausing slightly as he stood over her. He took her pillow out from behind her gently, which surprised her.

"I'll fluff it for you," he said. She couldn't see his mouth, but she knew he wasn't smiling. What was happening? Was she being paranoid?

"No, it's okay. Really, I am already comfortable."

"I insist," he hissed, then he shoved the pillow down onto her face. Panic exploded into her bloodstream, and she clawed at him and kicked and tried to scream, but barely any sound made it past the pillow. Her heart pounded in her ears, and she wondered if it would be the last sound she'd ever hear. Her hands moved from his face to the table beside her bed, feeling around for anything she could use as a weapon. She felt something cool, the vase that held the flowers Jeff had given her. She grabbed it and flung it as hard as she could toward him. It smashed into his skull before falling to the floor and shattering.

He screamed out in pain, stumbling back and removing the pillow, and she gasped in sweet oxygen. She screamed for help as he backed away.

As he ran out of the room, nurses rushed in, followed by the police officer. No one tried to stop him.

"Stop that doctor! He attacked me!" she shouted. "He tried to suffocate me with this pillow."

The police officer ran back out of the room. What if he wasn't caught? He looked like all the other doctors in the building.

"Hold still, dear. What happened?" a nurse demanded.

"I told you. He tried to kill me with the pillow, so I hit him with the vase to make him stop. He was suffocating me," Jane cried as the nurses exchanged glances. Did they believe her, or did they think she was insane?

"I'm telling the truth! He had a mask over his face. He wanted to kill me!" Jane slammed her fist down onto the mattress. She wanted to take what was left of the vase and hurl it towards the wall. Time was wasting, and he could be getting away.

The nurse bandaged a small cut on Jane's hand she'd received from the shattered vase. After what seemed like forever, but was really only about twenty minutes or so, the officer returned. "We could not find him, but we will continue to look for him. Other officers are looking for the man who attacked you. Try to relax and remember everything you can about him. I know you said he had on a mask, but do you remember anything else about what he looked like?"

Jane closed her eyes. His figure loomed in her mind like a bad omen. "He had dark hair. Curly, I think. He also had a medical head covering on."

The officer scribbled something on a notepad. "Okay, great. Anything else?"

"Dark eyes."

"Was he Caucasian?"

"Yes."

"Is there anything else you remember? Even a small detail can help."

Jane opened her eyes. "No. I mean, all I remember is that he was scary, but that won't help you. It all happened so fast. He already had the mask on when I saw him, so I didn't see his face. I'm sorry."

"You did great. Now, I'm going to stay here with you. I'm calling in another officer to come and look at the security footage." He pulled out his phone and made the call.

One of the nurses finished bandaging Jane's cut hand. "That was some quick thinking, dear. I don't think I would have thought of that in a situation like that. I would have panicked."

"I almost did, but I didn't want to die. I had to do something."

The nurse nodded. "Try to relax. Everything is okay now. I am sure they will find that guy. You're safe now."

They kept telling her that, but as Jane watched the nurse walk away, she felt in her bones that the danger was only just beginning. Someone wanted her dead, and from the flaming look of rage Jane saw in his eyes, he didn't seem like the kind who would easily get caught or give up.

CHAPTER FIVE

Jeff slammed his phone down a little too hard on the counter after ending a call with the hospital.

Estella jumped. "What? What happened?" She pulled a carton of orange juice out of the fridge.

"I sure would like to have a word with the so-called police officer who was supposed to be guarding Jane. The incompetent idiot let the attacker waltz right past him and into Jane's room early this morning, just because he was dressed as a doctor. What, are they letting anyone graduate the police academies these days?"

"Jeff, come on. Don't be so harsh. He obviously thought he was a doctor checking on her. Are they supposed to ID every doctor and nurse going in and out of that room? That would take forever and slow everyone down."

"Yes! They should!" Jeff let his head fall into his hands and he rubbed his temples. "At least they have security tapes. Maybe we'll find something on there."

"Did you sleep at all?" Estella cracked some eggs into a skillet and put bread in the toaster. The solid pine cabinets and cream-colored countertops had been picked out by their late mother when they had renovated this place about ten years ago. Nautical décor and several shades of white and blue graced most of the house.

Jeff would normally have enjoyed the view of the huge rocks and the ocean, with the sun just barely peeking out over the ocean, but he barely noticed it as he plopped into one of the sturdy chairs at the rustic kitchen table. The tabletop wasn't smooth like most tables, and he usually appreciated how the natural grooves of the wood remained. Memories flooded back to him when he looked out onto that oceanic scene, like kite flying with Estella or fishing with Dad on his boat, The Sea Hag.

He pushed the thoughts away. All he could think about now was how terrified and alone Jane must feel.

"Jeff."

"Hmm?" he grunted, not looking up.

"Did you sleep?"

"Nope. Not really. I knew I should have stayed there with her. None of this would have happened."

"That's true. You would have knocked that guy out before he even stepped out of the elevator. Over easy?"

"What?" Now he looked up.

"Your eggs." She jabbed her spatula towards the skillet. Then he realized how hungry he was.

"Sure. Thanks." He looked out the window again, watching the waves roll onto the rocks. In the distance, a sailboat bobbed on the water. Jane would like it here, he bet.

"She should come here. She'd be much safer if I watched over her around the clock," Jeff mumbled. Estella set a plate in front of him with toast and eggs. "No bacon?" He looked at her with a mock sad face.

"Don't push it. You know I would burn it. You should appreciate this masterpiece." She gestured dramatically towards the eggs.

"Sorry. Yes, thank you very much, my wonderful sister."

"Don't get used to it. So, who should come here? Jane?"

"Staying here would be ideal for her. I could protect her, and she could live here until her kidnapper, or whoever hurt her, is caught. I just spent over a year hunting terrorists in Afghanistan. I have the training. Might as well use it to help her. The police force here is small because it's a small town. They probably can't spare officers to protect her twenty-four seven. Plus, with her amnesia, she could use friends like us, right?"

"Yeah, because you're all sunshine and rainbows. Remember, I'm the fun one. I'd love to have her live here. This will be so fun. I can take her shopping and we can do fun girl stuff. The best part is you'll have to follow us everywhere we go." Estella smiled deviously and Jeff wanted to groan. He squirmed at the idea of going to the mall and waiting while they got pedicures. "Problem is, you're supposed to be having time off for Dad's death."

Jeff threw his hands up. "Who cares? This is more important. Wherever you make me go with you two, it would be worth it to protect Jane. Besides, it could be fun showing her around and introducing her to technology. Do you remember the way she reacted to your cell phone? Who knows where she's been the last several years? I'll call Branson at CPDU to ask for more time off."

Jeff dialed his boss's phone number in Portland, Maine, and the captain answered in his usual gruff voice. "Branson here. Martin?"

"Yes, it's me."

"Glad you're back. We all thank you for your service. I hope you're enjoying your time off, considering the circumstances. I'm sorry to hear about your father."

"Thank you. Well, actually, I'm calling about my time off. Something's come up and I might need to extend my break before I come back to work." He explained Jane's situation.

Branson listened without interrupting. When Jeff finished, he said, "Martin, you've been through a lot in Afghanistan and now with losing your father. You know I thought you should take a longer break anyway. I know your training, and you're a good option for this woman. Just take care of her, keep me updated, and do what you need to do. Take the time you need."

"Thank you, sir."

After hanging up, he called Officer Horton. "I just heard the perp walked right into Jane Doe's hospital room and assaulted her. Right past your officer."

"I'm sorry. He's been replaced. The man was dressed as a doctor, but still, he should have been more vigilant."

"What, did you have your newest rookie posted there to watch her?"

"Actually," Officer Horton said with a sigh, "he was all we could spare. We've had most of our officers working on a string of burglaries downtown. Unfortunately, we really can't spare much manpower right now. This isn't Portland or Augusta. We're a lot smaller than CPDU. We're understaffed, and we don't have the budget to hire anyone else right now."

"I'm sorry." Jeff pinched the bridge of his nose and squeezed his eyes shut. "Look, I didn't call to complain. I'm calling because I want to personally protect Jane at my house. My sister is here too, and she can keep her company. I just called Captain Branson, and he told me to take the time I need before returning to work. So, since you don't have the manpower, let me help you guys out."

"Branson has told me before about you and about your training. You know he's an old friend of mine. Don't tell him I said this, but he's said a few times you're one of the best officers at CPDU."

Jeff smiled a little. Branson would never tell Jeff that to his face.

"I know you also had advanced training in the Marines. If you're willing to watch over her day and night until we catch this guy, then we won't stop you. Now, you don't work for the town's police station, so this would be a non-paying job. Strictly in a volunteer capacity, you understand. We don't have the funding to make it official. You're willing to volunteer your time to this?"

"I knew that. Yes."

"Okay. And we will drive by as much as we can to check on you. Thank you. Really, thank you."

After ending his call, Jeff and Estella drove to the hospital and went up to Jane's room. The nurse told Jane they had arrived, and they stepped around to the other side of the curtain.

"Oh, you poor thing. Are you okay?" Estella asked, sitting right down on the bed.

"I'm okay now." Jane held up her bandaged hand. "Sorry, but I broke the vase you gave me when I hit the attacker with it."

Jeff couldn't believe she was apologizing for doing what she had to do to defend herself. "There's no need to apologize. It was just a vase I got downstairs. We are glad you are okay. We are so sorry this happened to you. I should have been here. I wouldn't have let this happen." Heated anger filled Jeff once more at the thought of Jane being attacked while under guard, but he took a deep breath to calm himself. "That is why we're here. We want to ask you something."

"You are going to come live with us! If you want to," Estella burst out, and Jane finally smiled.

"Really?" Jane looked at Jeff expectantly, her big brown eyes melting his heart.

"Yes." He couldn't help but smile. "Let's just say I have advanced military training. I'm going to protect you. The local police station is understaffed, so I'm volunteering. I promise, no one will hurt you on my watch. You're safe with us. Estella will take good care of you...and spoil you."

"That's the idea!" Estella said with a grin, then became serious. "But if you don't want to, you will still be taken care of. Once you are completely better, the state would take care of you for a while."

Jane shrank back. "I don't know... It is a nice offer, but I am not sure yet. I should think about it."

Of course, she wanted to think about it. She didn't know them, so why would she trust them enough to let them take her to their house to stay with them? After all she had been through, he didn't blame her for her hesitation.

Jane looked from Jeff to Estella as thoughts scrambled in her brain. Should she go live with these people who had rescued her? Where else could she go? To a place where she didn't know anyone? Jeff and Estella understood her situation, and she felt very comfortable around them.

These two people had dropped everything to bring her here and stay by her side as she recuperated, and made her feel wanted. They actually cared about her, and for all she knew, they were the only two people on the planet who really did.

Jane's eyes filled with tears.

"What's wrong?" Estella asked, patting Jane's good hand.

"I am so happy. I am so happy that I get to live with the both of you. You have been so kind to me." Jane swiped away a tear and smiled. "Thank you."

Now Estella was tearing up, and Jeff looked as though even he was holding back tears.

He cleared his throat. "Look, Jane, we care about you. We wouldn't want you to stay anywhere else but with us. We'd love to have you as soon as the doctors say you can come home."

Chapter Six

About a week later, Jeff wheeled Jane out into the parking lot in a wheelchair after checking her out of the hospital. Estella followed right behind them.

He had been so moved when Jane had accepted their offer to live with them. When he saw those tears of gratitude in her eyes, Jeff hated to admit it, but he had felt a lump forming in his throat. This woman continued to amaze him. After all she had been through, she was so grateful and sweet.

"You know, I can walk," Jane said quietly. The week of recovery and her improved nutrition had done wonders for her body, and the doctor and nurses said she was healing nicely.

"I know. This is standard procedure," Jeff told her. They reached his car, and he opened the back door for her. "Do you need help getting in?"

"I don't think so." She wobbled, realizing she had stood too quickly after lying in a hospital bed for so long.

Jeff instantly reached out and steadied her, gently but firmly taking hold of her shoulder and waist. "You okay?"

She nodded, avoiding his eyes as shyness and embarrassment overcame her. She felt her cheeks heat and she turned away, ducking as she slid onto the back seat ungracefully. "I'm fine, thanks."

Well, that sure had been dignified.

"Don't feel bad. You're hurt, malnourished and feeling weak, so it's understandable. You'll get your strength back before you know it," Estella piped in, opening the other back door and sitting next to Jane in the back seat.

Jane nodded. Jeff took the wheelchair back to the hospital, and they left the parking lot. Jane stared out the window the entire drive.

"Wow! We are going so fast! This is so fun!" she gushed, watching in amazement as trees and buildings flew past the window.

"Do you think you've ever ridden in a car before?" Estella asked.

"I don't know."

"It sure seems new to you."

"You are so lucky you get to ride in this all the time."

"It's no big deal to us," Estella explained.

About an hour later, the car drove onto a quaint street lined with shops. In the middle of the square stood a tall, wide pine tree.

"This is Dock Square. At Christmas they decorate and light up that tree over there, and it is so pretty. They actually put lobster decorations on it, because this area is known for our lobsters. There's Alison's, one of my favorite restaurants, and an ice cream shop back there, and a bunch of gift shops. When you start feeling better, I will take you out and show you around," Estella said excitedly, pointing out the window.

Jane pressed her nose against the glass, taking in the sights as the lovely shops went by. Then they drove onto a bridge. A seafood restaurant sat near the water. The ocean seemed to go on forever and ever into the horizon. Where did it end? She wanted to swim in it, but fear clutched her throat at the thought.

"There's so much that I have planned for us to do. You just wait and see," Estella said with a smile. A few minutes later, they drove down a street lined with huge, beautiful houses. Some of them were mansions. They turned a corner, and there was the ocean up close, lapping at the shore and shining in the sun. Jeff drove into the driveway of a house right in front of the water.

"You live here?"

"Yes. Our parents died and left us this house. Our mom died a few years ago and dad just died recently of a brain tumor," Estella explained softly. "We used this as a summer home that we rented out for the rest of the year, and we came here a few weeks in the summertime with our parents growing up. Now we're leaving our apartments and moving here. I work a few towns over in Portland at an insurance company, but I'm on vacation right now. Jeff was working in Portland too at the Covert Police Detectives Unit until he reenlisted in the military."

"But now I have time off for a while until I go back to work at CPDU in Portland." Jeff opened Jane's door. "Let me walk you into the house."

"Let's show her the ocean first!" Estella said cheerfully.

Jeff offered Jane his arm, and not wanting to offend him, she looped her arm around Jeff's elbow. They walked past the white gate and down the wooden walkway to the beach that was surrounded by tall, swaying dune grass. The expanse of water sparkled as the water lapped onto the shore.

A small tan colored fishing boat bobbed in the water with the words *Sea Hag* labeled proudly on the side in black letters.

"The Sea Hag?" Jane held back a laugh.

"Not the most dignified name, is it?" Estella asked, smirking. "It's okay; you can laugh."

"Our dad had quite the odd sense of humor," Jeff said, letting go of Jane's arm awkwardly.

"Can we go for a ride?" Estella asked.

"No… I'd rather not. I don't think I'd like deep water, and I don't think I can swim." Jane crossed her arms and looked out over the water with apprehension.

"That's okay. I could teach you to swim. Riding in the boat is so fun! You'd love it. Maybe eventually—" Estella began hopefully.

"One thing at a time, Estella. Let's not push it. For now, let's get inside and get settled in." Jeff turned to walk back to the house and offered Jane his arm again. She wasn't sure if it was because he thought she might fall or if he was just being polite, but she took it anyway.

Jane stared at the majestic house as they approached. It was three stories tall, gray with white trim, and had large windows.

When Jeff opened the door, Jane gasped. The entryway had a cathedral ceiling with a huge chandelier made of candles and driftwood. "How do you reach way up there to light all those candles?"

"They are electric, so we hit the switch. See?" Estella flipped the light switch on the wall and the chandelier lit up, casting a warm glow on the light blue walls.

"I bet this is the most beautiful house I have ever seen." Jane left Jeff's side and wandered further into the house, into the kitchen. A large island sat in the middle of the room, with two ovens and a huge dining room table. The best part was the huge window with a view of the ocean. Jane couldn't help but sigh. She was going to love it here.

"Oh, I would love to cook in this kitchen," she murmured.

"Can you cook?" Jeff asked. "Because we sure can't."

"Of course. You don't know how to cook?"

The two shook their heads. "Mom taught us how, but we are both terrible at it," Estella said.

"Oh, it just takes practice. I would love to make you dinner," Jane said, walking into the next room.

"Really, you don't have to do that."

Jane barely heard what Jeff said as she stepped into the living room, with two big couches and a large black television on the wall. She only knew what that was because there had been one in her hospital room.

"Want to see your room?" Estella asked. Jane's eyes widened as Estella led her up the stairs, where there were four bedrooms. Estella opened one of the doors and Jane walked in. "Here it is. Your new temporary home."

"This is beautiful," Jane said, taking in the sea blue walls, white bedspread, fluffy pillows, and vintage wicker furniture. The best part was the window seat overlooking the ocean. From here she could see the entire cove, boats in the distance and people walking along the beach. She wished she could stay forever. "Thank you so much again for letting me stay here."

"We're glad that you're here." Estella pointed to a bag on the floor. "Those are some things I bought you at the store before we went to pick you up. Just some basic things like a toothbrush, underwear, a hairbrush, stuff like that. For now you can borrow my clothes, but I'm going to take you shopping soon so you can pick out your own."

"Oh, thank you. But really, you don't have to."

"I want to! What are friends for?" Estella grinned, and Jane's insides warmed.

Had she ever had a best friend before? Either way, Jane was excited to get to know Estella better.

Estella patted Jane's arm. "Now, I'm going to make dinner. Or try to, anyway. Maybe we should order pizza."

"Can I help you cook?"

"No, no, that's okay. You should rest." Estella waved away her offer and gestured towards the white bed.

"I've spent enough time resting in the hospital. I feel fine. Let me help."

"Okay. If you're sure."

As they went back downstairs, Jane asked, "What were you planning on cooking?"

"Well, I was going to try to make this chicken, rice, cheese and broccoli casserole recipe I found. I wasn't sure if I could do it."

"Don't worry. I'll help you. It'll turn out great."

After they'd finished making the casserole, Estella slid it into the oven to bake. Jane leaned against the countertop. "What about dessert?"

"There's a box of cookies in the cabinet, I think." Estella shrugged.

Jane smiled and shook her head. "No, no. Store-bought cookies are for the birds. Let me make you some homemade chocolate chip cookies instead. May I?" She pointed to the cabinets.

"I went grocery shopping for all the essentials. I think we have everything you need. I try to bake, but I'm bad at it. Knock yourself out." Estella moved over to give Jane room.

"What?"

"I mean, not literally. Go ahead and let me know if you need help."

Jane chuckled. "Thanks."

Jane pulled out flour, baking soda, baking powder, salt, butter, eggs, chocolate chips, and cream cheese from the fridge.

"Cream cheese?" Estella asked. "In chocolate chip cookies?"

"Trust me. It's really good."

"How do you know this recipe by heart? How can you remember it?"

"The doctor told me that some things are like muscle memory. If I did something repeatedly, especially during my childhood, I would know how to keep doing it. So, this must be one of those things. Do you have a mixing bowl?"

"Oh, we can use this big electric mixer." Estella pointed to a large robin's egg blue standing mixer on the counter.

"What is that?"

"You pour your ingredients in the bowl and press the button and it mixes it for you. Like this." She pressed the button on the mixer and Jane jumped.

"Wow! That is fascinating." Jane stared at it, then carefully put in the butter and sugar. They poured in the rest of the ingredients including the chocolate chips. When it was mixed, they scooped little mounds of batter onto the baking sheet and put it in the oven.

Jeff came into the kitchen. "I just checked all the surveillance equipment and security system. Mom and Dad never really used it, but I wanted to make sure it was all working. It needs a few updates, so I'm having someone come and fix it first thing in the morning. What smells so good in here?"

"A casserole and homemade cookies," Estella said proudly with her chin in the air. "We made it. Well, Jane did most of the work, and I watched and helped her open things."

"You didn't have to cook, Jane," Jeff said and inhaled the scent of the food in the oven. "Though I'm glad you did. Really, don't feel like you have to cook for us."

"I love cooking. I don't mind at all," Jane said, putting some dishes in the sink. When the timer went off, the three sat down at the dining room table to eat.

After putting a scoop of casserole on her plate, Jane bowed her head and closed her eyes for a few seconds to pray.

"Let's all pray together," Estella said once Jane looked up.

"Oh, yes." Jane smiled. "It must be one of those muscle memory habits I still remember. Let's pray."

She took their hands, and they all bowed their heads.

Estella prayed, "Dear Lord, thank you for bringing Jane into our lives. Thank you for this food, and please keep us all safe. In Your name, Amen."

Jeff hadn't prayed in a while, not since he'd been in Afghanistan. He kind of missed it.

After a few bites, he exclaimed, "This is amazing! Wow, Jane, you're a great cook. I mean, Estella is good too—"

"No, I'm not, and I know it." Estella laughed.

"I'd be happy to teach you how to cook, Estella," Jane offered.

"Yes! I wish I was better at it. I wonder how you learned to cook so well."

"I don't know. I have a feeling I could follow pretty much any recipe."

"In that case, I will make you a list of my favorite foods," Jeff said with a chuckle. A few minutes later, the oven timer beeped again, and after the cookies cooled, they ate their dessert with glasses of milk.

"Wow! These are amazing. Thank you so much, Jane. This dinner was great." Jeff devoured six cookies, knowing he shouldn't eat so many, but he couldn't help himself.

After dinner, the three of them cleaned quickly and Estella took Jane back upstairs, into Estella's room.

"Wow, your room is lovely," Jane said in awe, staring at the dusty pink walls, antique furniture and white canopy bed.

"Thanks. My mom decorated this entire house. She always wanted to be an interior decorator, but I guess life got in the way and she never did it. Instead, she homeschooled me and my brother and took really good care of us. She used to say being a mom was enough for her and made her happy."

"Sounds like she really loved you."

"She did. Jeff and I were really close to our parents." Estella sighed, rifling through her dresser and pulling out a set of pajamas, then handed them to Jane. "This is for you to borrow for tonight. Tomorrow, if you feel up to it, I'm taking you shopping. Okay?"

"Okay. Are you sure? Once I get a job, I can pay you back."

"No, no. Don't worry about that. Our parents left us some money, and we want to help you out. I'll take you to the Maine Mall tomorrow, and it will be really fun, I promise." Estella's eyes twinkled at the mention of shopping.

Jane couldn't stop the smile from spreading across her face. "Okay. It does sound fun. I don't know if I've ever been to a mall before."

"Well, make sure you get enough rest tonight. Do you want to watch a movie before bed?"

"A movie? I don't know… I'm not sure about that." Jane's face scrunched up, uneasiness in her eyes.

"Don't tell me you don't think you've ever watched a movie before," Estella said. "It'll be fun. You'll like it."

"Well, okay. I guess so."

"Okay. Let's go make popcorn." Estella took her back downstairs and put a popcorn bag in the microwave.

"Oh my! What's that noise? What's happening?" Jane stared into the microwave.

"The microwave is cooking the kernels, and they are popping to make the popcorn."

"But there is no fire. How is it cooking?"

"Um, I don't know how to explain it, but somehow the microwave heats it up." Estella shrugged. "The magic of technology."

"It's magic?" Jane jumped back from the microwave with wide eyes.

"What are you telling her?" Jeff asked, coming into the kitchen. "It's not magic. The microwaves are vibrating so fast that they are heating the food. I think that's a good way to explain it. Microwaves are so tiny you can't see them."

"That is amazing," Jane murmured, practically pressing her nose against the microwave door.

"Take a step back, Jane. My mom used to say standing close to a microwave causes cancer." Estella gently tugged on her arm.

Jane jumped back from the microwave. "Really?"

"She used to say a lot of things. We don't really know if that is true," Jeff said. The microwave beeped, and Jane jumped once more.

"What does that mean?"

"It means it's done cooking." Estella couldn't help but giggle at Jane's reactions. She pulled the bag of popcorn out carefully and poured it into a bowl. "Let's go pick a movie. Want to watch one with us, Jeff?"

"Sure."

They went into the living room and opened the cabinet full of DVDs. "Wow! You have a lot!" Jane exclaimed.

"Our parents loved movies. We collected a lot over the years. Do you want to pick one?" Jeff offered.

"Oh, I have no idea. They're all the same to me. You two pick." Jane shrugged and stared at the movie collection.

"How about a funny one?" Estella pulled a DVD off the shelf. "I think you'd like this one."

They started the movie and got comfortable on the couch. Jane sat between Jeff and Estella, and Jeff was very aware of how close she was to him and how she didn't seem to mind at all. As soon as the movie started, Jane was enthralled, literally sitting on the edge of her seat even during the opening credits. She laughed hysterically at all the funny parts, even at parts that weren't supposed to be funny. Estella giggled right along with her. Or at her. Jeff wasn't sure.

He smiled at Jane's joyfulness, how everything was so new to her, and how it all amazed her. Her dinner sure had amazed him. Maybe he was used to Estella's terrible cooking, but Jane's cooking seemed out of this world. He wouldn't mind having her live here at all.

"That was a great movie!" Jane jumped up, pieces of popcorn falling off her and onto the floor. She didn't seem to notice. "Let's watch another one."

Estella glanced at her phone. "It's getting late, and you have your therapist appointment tomorrow. We should go to bed so we get enough sleep for tomorrow. I have a lot planned for us. Oh, you'll come, right, Jeff? We are going shopping at the mall, then I'm taking Jane to see the sights of Kennebunkport."

"The mall?" Jeff leaned his head back on the couch and groaned.

"You promised to come everywhere with us," Estella reminded him.

"I know. It's okay. I will survive."

"Of course, you will. Goodnight," Estella said before going upstairs with Jane.

*

A knock sounded on the door, and Jeff went to see who it was. When he looked through the peephole, he saw that it was Officer Horton with another officer.

Jeff opened the door. "Officer Horton, nice to see you. Come on in."

"Hi, Martin. I'm stopping by to check on you all. This is Officer Hendricks. He's a rookie, so I take him out with me. Hendricks, this is Jefferson Martin. He worked at CPDU as a police officer and a bodyguard, and he's a veteran and sergeant in the Marine Corps. He volunteered to watch over Jane Doe. You're planning on going back to work at CPDU after your time off, right, Jeff?"

"Yes, I am. Nice to meet you." Jeff shook the rookie's hand.

"Nice house you got here," Hendricks said.

"Thanks."

"So, how's everything going since you got here?" Officer Horton asked.

"Fine so far. They just went to bed."

"Good. We don't have a lot of manpower here, but we will still try to drive by as much as we can. This was really nice of you to offer to watch over Jane Doe during your time off."

"It's my pleasure. Estella and Jane are already best friends. We appreciate you checking in. Did you get anything useful from the tire tracks at the crime scene?"

"We didn't discover anything that we didn't already know before from what you told us. If we do find something, you'll be one of the first to know. If you need anything, you have my number."

"Thanks."

"Have a good night." The two officers left, and Jeff checked the security equipment twice. He cleaned his gun, loaded extra magazines, and looked out each window.

He sat in the living room recliner, cocked his Smith & Wesson 9mm, and set it on his lap. It was going to be a long night. He didn't plan on getting any sleep.

CHAPTER SEVEN

A high-pitched scream tore through the night. Jeff grabbed the gun from his lap and sprang off the recliner, his feet on the floor in a second. He bounded towards Jane's room and pushed the door open.

Jane's face was covered by her hands and her blankets, and sobs made her shoulders shudder as Estella sat on the bed beside her.

"It was a nightmare," Estella said.

Only a nightmare. Relief coursed through his veins.

"It's okay now. You're safe with us," Estella murmured, stroking Jane's hair.

Jane lifted her face and wiped away her tears. "I saw him in my dream."

"Who? The man who hurt you? Did you see his face?" Jeff blurted, and Estella gave him a look as if telling him to stop asking so many questions.

Jane sniffed and scrubbed the sheet across her damp eyes. "I couldn't see his face, but I know he was chasing me. I only saw the outline of a man, that's all."

Jeff knew this was just a dream, but maybe, somehow, she was remembering something through her dreams. "Was there anything else you remember about the dream? Like where you were, or if the man was heavyset or thin?"

"We were in the woods. Running through the woods. He was big. Heavyset. Very scary." Jane's lip quivered, and she covered her face with the sheet again. Estella rubbed her back, whispering comforting words.

"You can go, Jeff. I'll stay with her until she falls back asleep," Estella told him, and he went downstairs to the living room.

Once again he wracked his brain for more details about the car and the driver. It had all happened so fast, and he hadn't gotten a good look, even though the man had turned his head toward Jeff. It had been dark.

Maybe Jane had been held somewhere in the woods, but that didn't help him much. Neither did her saying that the man was heavyset. Over time, she would remember more.

Even if she had to have terrifying nightmares for that to happen.

*

"Rise and shine!"

A pillow hit Jeff in the face. He bolted upright in his recliner, about ready to fight back. Then he realized his attacker was Estella. Wanting to kick himself, he realized he must have fallen asleep at some point in the night.

"What the heck! Don't you know not to wake a sleeping Marine like that? I almost tackled you." He rubbed the fatigue out of his eyes.

"Sorry, sleepyhead. We're ready when you are. We'll go make some breakfast. Or, rather, Jane will and I'll help." Estella marched back out of the living room.

He needed some strong coffee.

As he got dressed, Jeff smelled something delicious cooking in the kitchen, chasing away his grogginess. What had Jane whipped up this time? He turned the light on in his bathroom. The bathroom contained a vintage sink, rustic-looking mirror, and starfish decorations on the wall. He ran a comb through his dark, disheveled hair, realizing he needed a haircut. He slapped on some gel and called it good, then wandered into the kitchen.

Estella was setting three plates on the table. "Jane made pancakes. From scratch. I don't think we've ever had that before."

Jeff smiled, then looked to the stove where Jane was standing, turned away from him. Her long hair cascading down to her waist in a braid. She turned to face him, wearing Estella's gray t-shirt and jeans. Jane's dark eyes darted away when she noticed him staring at her. She had looked as though she was going to say something, but now she was silent. He inwardly kicked himself for making her feel uncomfortable. But he couldn't help but sneak another glance at her. She looked beautiful.

Before he could make any more of a fool out of himself, he grabbed the orange juice from the fridge and the milk from the counter, along with three glasses. "Smells great," he said, trying to break the awkwardness in the air. Estella didn't seem to notice.

"Oh my gosh, I am so excited for today. First, we are going to the mall, then we can go to lunch and then come back here to see the sights, and go swimming at some point if we have time." Estella fluffed her hair, which had been curled. "Actually, I don't want to ruin my hair. We can go swimming another day."

"Whatever you want to do is fine with me." Jeff set the drinks on the table and collected silverware. Jane brought a plate of pancakes to the table, then a plate of fruit and sausage. "Wow, this looks amazing!" Jeff exclaimed.

"Nonsense. This sausage was in the freezer and you had lots of fruit on the counter. It's no big deal." Jane smiled shyly, sat down, and said, "Let's pray." They all held hands, and Jane bowed her head. She prayed, "Lord, thank you for this day, and thank you for this food. Please keep us safe and do your will. Amen."

"Jane," Jeff said in between bites after the prayer. "I've made an appointment with the local paper today. I want to run an ad, asking around if anyone can help us identify you. Maybe you have family who live around here and are looking for you. Maybe someone local would know them and get in contact with us."

She looked a little bit confused and Jeff was about to explain what he meant when she asked, "But that would cost money, right?"

"Sure, but not much. Look, you don't have to worry about that, alright?"

Jane nodded, then shook her head. "I don't know. I mean, you've been so good and kind to me and I don't know how to ever repay you."

Estella made a smacking sound from where she was sitting. "You cook this for breakfast for the next three days and I think we'll be the ones owing you."

Jeff glared at his sister before turning back to Jane. "You owe us nothing, Jane, and you don't ever have to worry about paying us back. We're glad to help you."

Jane nodded. "Then thank you so much for everything. It's like you are an angel sent by God to help me."

Estella snorted. "Jeff? An angel? Yeah, right."

Jeff had to chuckle. He definitely wasn't an angel.

After the delicious breakfast and washing the dishes, Estella said, "Well, we have to go. We can't be late for your therapist appointment." The three of them piled in the car, and Estella drove.

"What exactly is going to happen at this appointment?" Jane asked apprehensively. With everything that had been going on, she hadn't had time to even think about it.

"You're just going to talk. The therapist wants to help you remember your past so we can figure out who you are," Jeff explained.

"So, no needles?"

"No. No needles. Just talking. Don't worry if you can't remember anything or give her any answers. Just do your best."

Jane nodded, filling with hope. Maybe this therapist could help her remember something.

CHAPTER EIGHT

After the appointment, Jane walked out of the room, feeling defeated.

"How did it go?" Estella asked, leaping out of her chair in the waiting room, followed by Jeff.

"She did great," Dr. Wellington said, pushing her glasses further up her nose.

"No, I didn't. I didn't remember anything new," Jane said dejectedly, looking at the floor. "I thought I would."

"But we made great progress and we talked things through. This is your first appointment. Don't expect yourself to remember things right away. You're putting too much pressure on yourself. I want to help you cope with what has happened to you and work through your feelings. If you remember something as we're talking, that is great, but don't feel bad if you don't," Dr. Wellington said in a soothing voice. "One step at a time."

"Thank you, Dr. Wellington," Jane said. "You made me feel a lot better."

The doctor smiled. "I'll see you soon."

They made their next appointment, and Estella drove them to the Maine Mall in Portland.

"Don't worry, Jane. I'll cheer you up in no time. Shopping is the best therapy," Estella chirped.

Jeff rolled his eyes. "Yeah, until you look at your bank account. And your closet."

"Wow! This is a mall? It's all stores?" Jane asked as they got out of the car.

"Yup," Estella said.

"Why are there so many? Do people really need that many choices?"

"No, I guess not, but it's more fun that way. Come on," Estella said, tugging on Jane's sleeve. Jeff chuckled and followed closely behind them. They entered the food court, and Jane was amazed all over again.

"There are so many places to eat. I could never decide what to get. So many choices make my brain hurt." Jane laughed as they walked by Chinese food, a sushi place, and a pizza bar.

"I love having a lot of choices. Sometimes it does take me a while to decide. Let's go to the bathroom really quick before we shop, okay?" Estella said.

"I'll stand right outside the door," Jeff told them. Estella led Jane inside the bathroom.

Jane stopped when she saw all the bathroom stalls. "What are those?"

"Bathroom stalls. There are toilets in them." Estella opened one of the stall doors. "See?"

"There are cracks in the door! What if someone sees inside?" Jane squirmed at the thought.

"I know, there really shouldn't be cracks in the door, but there are. No one will look inside. Want me to wait here while you go?"

"Okay."

Jane hurried, and when she was done, she waited for Estella but got distracted by the automatic sinks and hand dryers. She couldn't help but stare at the women who were using them. The air magically came out of the wall to dry your hands? That was incredible.

She walked over to the sink and looked for a button to push for the soap dispenser, but once she put her hand under it, soap came out and dripped onto the countertop. Giggling, Jane put her hand under it again, the soap dropping into her hand. Water sprayed out of the faucet. "Oh, my."

Estella came out of her stall. "I see you found the sinks," she remarked, amused.

Jane put her hands in front of the hand dryer and laughed out loud as air blasted her hands dry. "This is amazing!" she shouted over the noise. Several women turned to look at her, but she didn't seem to notice or care.

Estella quickly washed her own hands, smiling at Jane's excitement. "You think that is great? That's nothing. Just wait until I show you the merry-go-round."

"The what?"

Estella led Jane out of the bathroom to where Jeff was waiting. "I could hear you from out here. You like the hand dryers, huh?" He chuckled.

Jane blushed.

"She got a little excited. Come on. Let's show her the merry-go-round," Estella said, and Jeff followed them to the other side of the food court.

"What is that?" Jane asked in awe, staring at the colorful ride going around in a circle.

"That's a merry-go-round. It's a ride. It's really fun. Want to go on it?" Estella asked.

"Oh, yes! Can we?" Jane clasped her hands together under her chin like a little girl, and Jeff couldn't help but grin as he handed them some cash.

"Go ahead," he said.

"No, you should come too. Come on!" Jane grabbed his sleeve and pulled him with a surprising amount of force towards the ride.

Jeff almost tripped, then caught his balance while trying to keep up with Jane as she dragged him along. He paid the bored-looking teenager running the ride, and they entered the fenced-in area around the merry-go-round.

"Which one should we pick?" Jane looked at all the different horses and other animals decorating the vibrant merry-go-round.

"Hurry and pick one before it starts," Estella told her with a smile as several children ran on to the merry-go-round.

Jane bounced back and forth between a few horses before climbing onto a white unicorn. Estella took a seahorse behind her. Jeff couldn't help but grin at Jane's childlike enthusiasm and excitement.

"Aren't you going to ride one?" Jane asked.

"Of course not. I'm here to watch over you, not to have fun and make a fool out of myself," he grumbled. "I'll just stand here."

"You are no fun. Do something spontaneous. Who knows, you might like it." Jane's eyes sparkled and a funny feeling bubbled in his stomach. What was happening? Of course, she was beautiful, anyone could see that, but why was it affecting him? And why was her joyfulness so contagious?

Estella prodded him. "She's right, Jeff. Sometimes you are all seriousness and no fun. Live a little. We won't laugh at you."

"Oh, fine. If someone I know walks by, I'm jumping right off." Jeff swung his leg over the horse next to Jane, hoping he wouldn't break it since it was intended for children.

After all the children were situated, the ride started, and Jane immediately started giggling, then outright laughing. Jeff couldn't stifle his own laughter. After their parents' deaths, it was nice to see someone be a friend to Estella and cheer her up. Now, Jane's joy was rubbing off on him.

He knew his job was serious and that he should be serious, but he couldn't help it at the moment. A laugh burst from his lips again and again, like a pot of boiling water bubbling over. He couldn't contain it at all.

Jane closed her eyes and tipped her head back, her long hair flowing behind her like a horse's mane. She was a picture of what it meant to be carefree, oblivious that someone was after her, endangering her life. Jeff stared at her, and for a moment, she made him forget, too. He found himself wishing that she was a normal young woman with a normal life, that she was safe.

He caught himself, then looked away, relieved to see that Estella hadn't noticed him watching Jane. She was also in a world of her own, looking all around and smiling.

He shouldn't have let himself get so distracted. All it takes is a split second for someone to attack, he reminded himself as he looked at the people passing by. Did anyone look suspicious, with a strange bag or an odd or nervous look about them? No, no one looked suspicious from what he could see.

As the ride slowed to a stop, Jane tossed a knowing grin his way. "Wasn't that fun?"

"Well, yes. Kind of. I shouldn't be doing stuff like that," he muttered and led them off the merry-go-round. Jane's look of disappointment made him regret his tone, but she needed to know he wasn't her buddy. He was supposed to be protecting her, even if it wasn't official. He couldn't get distracted. Estella could be her buddy, but not him. The personal attachment would compromise his performance and could endanger her.

"Where to next, ladies?" he asked.

"Let's go to my favorite clothing store. You will love it," Estella said to Jane. "It's this way."

They walked to a huge store full of women's clothes and accessories, and Jeff's head was already starting to hurt from all the colors, and music, and flashiness. He'd rather be in the woods or out on the ocean in his dad's boat than here. But he was glad to be helping Jane.

Estella helped Jane pick out several items, and he waited patiently near the dressing rooms as she tried them all on. This repeated at a few more stores, and what seemed like hours later, Estella was finally satisfied.

Jeff glanced at his watch. It really *was* a few hours later. "I'm famished," he announced, and bored out of his mind.

"We are, too. Let's go to the food court." Estella handed him several bags of clothing. "Would you be a doll and hold these?"

Jeff rolled his eyes at her choice of words. "Of course, darling." He took the bags, then added, "Did you buy out the whole store?"

"They had some great sales, and Jane needed a whole new wardrobe. We did not go overboard at all."

"Okay." He sighed, knowing there was no sense in arguing with his sister. They walked back to the food court.

"So, Jane, that Japanese place is my favorite, but we can go anywhere you want to go," Estella said, pointing.

Jane looked around. "Honestly, I have no idea what to try, so let's do that."

"Sounds good," Jeff agreed and followed them. As they waited in line, two high-school-age guys pointed, nodded and whistled at Estella and Jane. Jeff tensed, his hand automatically moving to the end of his concealed holstered gun beneath his jacket.

"Hey, babe, what's your name?" one called as they approached. "Did it hurt when you fell from heaven?"

Jeff turned to face them. "Walk away," he growled, walking toward them slowly.

When they saw his muscular frame towering over them, they both stopped abruptly and put their hands up. "Whoa, man, we were just having some fun."

"Sorry," the other guy said, and they scampered off like two frightened puppies.

"Sheesh, Jeff. You didn't have to scare them." Estella crossed her arms. Jane just raised her eyebrows at the scene.

"Hey, I don't like guys looking at you two like that. They were pigs. Come on. We're next in line."

After they finished eating, the three returned to Kennebunkport.

"Let's show her Dock Square. Then we can go to Turbat's Creek. Sound good?" Estella suggested to Jeff as she drove.

Jeff liked to sit in the passenger seat where he could see everything going on, like if someone was following them. "Whatever you say. I'm just along for the ride."

Estella parked on the street in front of an ice cream shop. "Anyone up for ice cream?"

"Always." Jeff smiled. The two of them looked at Jane in the back seat.

She shrugged. "I don't know if I've ever had it, but let's go for it."

At that, the three piled out and waited in line outside. Jane gawked at the long lists of different flavors and different things to order, like shakes and sundaes and cones. "I have no idea what to get. There are so many choices! How do you pick just one?"

"Well, Jeff always gets the same thing." Estella laughed and elbowed him in the side.

"I do not."

"Yeah, you do. He doesn't like trying new things. I, on the other hand, always try something different. I've had lots of things listed on the menu, and my favorites were strawberry ice cream and the marshmallow chocolate ice cream."

"How about you surprise me?" Jane asked, her eyes wide with excitement. Jeff held back a laugh at this never-ending supply of childlike enthusiasm and curiosity she possessed.

"Okay." When it was their turn, Estella stepped up to the window. "I'll have two small strawberry sundaes with chocolate sprinkles and a medium grasshopper pie sundae." She flashed Jeff a smile. She was right. He really did always order the same thing. It wasn't because he was afraid to try new things, though. If you like something the way it is, why try to change it with something new you might not like?

When Estella handed Jane her ice cream, she looked as though she wanted to jump up and down with excitement. "It's too pretty to eat," she said as they sat down at a picnic table.

"Nonsense. It's for eating." Estella was already a third done with hers.

Jane took a big bite. "This is amazing! What is this? You are so lucky that you've been here so many times. There is no way I have ever tried anything so delicious in my life."

Estella and Jeff chuckled. Jane had a few sprinkles on the corner of her mouth, but she was so adorable, he didn't say anything.

Adorable? His eyebrows shot up at the thought. That was a strong word.

"What?" Estella asked him.

"What do you mean, what? Nothing." He dug his spoon into his ice cream with more force than necessary.

His sister eyed him. "You had a weird look on your face."

"Eat your ice cream." He jabbed his spoon at her playfully.

After finishing up, they got back in the car and drove to Turbat's Creek.

They parked the car and walked down a pathway. Before them was a rocky cove surrounding a bit of the ocean. A small sailboat was anchored in the shallow water, and a family with two small children built a sandcastle on the shore. As usual, there were only a few people here, or none at all, because the tourists didn't know about it, only the locals.

Jane hurried toward the water. Jeff followed her, with Estella trailing behind.

"She can't swim, right?" Estella asked.

"We don't know. She's not sure. This water is pretty shallow though."

Jane reached the water, took off her new flip flops and waded in to her knees. When Jeff and Estella caught up to her, Estella also waded in, but Jeff stood on the sand.

"If you want, we can come back and go in the water when we have our swimsuits on. Maybe tomorrow, if it is a nice day."

"Okay, maybe," Jane said with hesitation. Something in her told her to stay away from the deep water.

Jeff pointed to the sand. "Look, there's a crab."

Estella and Jane turned, and Jane burst out laughing when Estella shrieked.

"It's just a little crab." Jane picked it up and held out the crab toward Estella, who screamed and ran away. Jeff laughed out loud as Jane chased Estella around the beach, and Estella acted as if she was afraid for her life.

Suddenly, Jane stopped, her face pale as she looked to where they had parked their car. Jeff followed her gaze and saw a stocky man in a black sweatshirt—an odd thing to wear in the summer—as he hurriedly turned and walked away. Most of him was hidden by the bushes and the hood, so she couldn't see his face.

"Jeff!" she cried, but Jeff was already sprinting towards the man, kicking up sand behind him. He had started running as soon as he had seen the look on her face, knowing something was wrong. He reached the parking lot where he had seen the man, but the only people in sight were the family members getting into their car.

"Did you see a man run by just now in a black hooded sweatshirt?" he asked the man and woman as they helped the kids in the car.

"Yeah. There was a man going that way," the woman said, pointing down the lane.

"Thanks," Jeff barely got out as he whipped around and bolted down the lane. He ran past large beach houses, frantically looking around, but the man was nowhere in sight. He reached the main road. Several cars drove by, but he didn't see the man in any of them.

Kicking the ground, he sent a pebble flying. How long had that man been following them? Was he the man who had hurt Jane? He could have been some tourist leaving in a hurry. There was no way of knowing.

Defeated, Jeff jogged back to the beach where Jane and Estella were waiting in the car. He opened the passenger door.

"What happened? Did you find him?" Estella demanded.

"No, I couldn't find him. It's like he vanished."

"When you took off, I brought her in here and locked the doors," Estella said as Jeff got in.

"Good thinking." He turned to Jane, who was in the back seat again. "Who was that man?"

"Well, I am not sure, but I really feel like I've seen him before. The way he was watching me gave me the creeps." She shivered at the thought. "He was standing there, staring right at me."

"Did you get a good look at his face?"

"No. He was pretty far away, and that hood was covering most of his head. Something about him was familiar." She paused.

"Do you think it was the same man from the hospital?" Jeff asked.

"I don't know... I mean, at the hospital it all happened so fast. All I remember is that man had dark, curly hair. I didn't see his face then either because he was wearing that doctor's mask and a lab coat. I couldn't tell how old he was or anything. I was so scared, and I should have paid more attention. I didn't get a good look at him. I'm sorry, Jeff."

"Jane, none of this is your fault. You don't have to be sorry for anything." He patted her hand, and she nodded. Jeff turned to Estella. "Did you get a look at him, Estella?"

"No, I didn't."

Jane's eyes dropped to the floor, a frown clouding her face.

Her obvious fear clawed at his heart, and he let out a sigh. "Jane, I won't let anyone hurt you. I promise you're safe with me. Okay? You don't have to worry. I've hunted terrorists in the deserts of Afghanistan. I've survived bombs and combat. If I can handle that, I can definitely handle this stalker."

She looked at him, hope now brightening her eyes.

"We both care about you a lot. We're both looking out for you," Estella interjected. Jeff knew Estella didn't know anything about firing a weapon or self-defense, so she wouldn't be able to protect Jane, but he knew she meant well. He should teach her how to use a gun, just in case.

"Let's take you home. We've had quite a full day," Estella said, starting the car and shifting it in to gear. Jeff carefully watched the entire parking lot as Estella drove out, and he even made Estella take a few random turns to make sure no one was following them. When he was satisfied that they weren't being tailed, he let her drive home.

Once they got to the beach house and brought in the bags, Estella asked, "Want to watch another movie? Or play a game?"

Jane sighed. "Honestly, I'm really tired. I could read for a while and go to sleep. Can I borrow a few of your books? I saw them, but didn't get a good look yet."

"Oh, yeah. Our mom loved books," Jeff said and brought her into the living room where several tall bookcases lined the walls. "Help yourself," he said.

"Oh, wow! You have all kinds." Jane's eyes lit up as she read through the titles. She picked a novel written in French. Jeff and Estella's mom had loved those; she had always been a hopeless romantic, though she'd never gotten to see either of her children marry.

"Wait, you speak French?" Estella asked.

"Yeah. Well, I can read it, I guess. Not sure if I could speak it or understand someone speaking it."

Jeff blinked and shook his head. "Wow. Can you speak any other languages? My mom spoke French because she was Canadian French. When you were in the hospital you mumbled something in German."

"I think I know German too, and Italian. As for knowing other languages, I don't think I would know until I saw other things written in other languages. I would recognize them. I can't think right now of what other languages I know. Is that weird?" Jane hugged the book to her chest like a schoolgirl, and he smiled at her innocence.

"No. Not at all. You'll figure this all out as you go."

She smiled. "You're right. Okay, well, I'll go upstairs now. Goodnight. Thanks for a fun day. Sorry if you were bored."

"You two kept me busy."

She smiled again and turned to walk up the stairs.

Chapter Nine

Jeff hung up after talking to Officer Horton on the phone to update him about seeing the man at the beach. About an hour later, Officer Horton and Officer Hendricks stopped by to take a look around the house and talk with Jeff.

"I need a second officer here. I can't be awake every hour of every day," Jeff said.

"You don't even know for sure if that was the man who attacked her at the hospital. All you know is Jane saw him and he gave her the creeps. He could have been an innocent guy enjoying a day at the beach wearing a hoodie. We don't have as much manpower here as they do in Augusta or Portland, so I can't send anyone over just because you think you saw her attacker," Officer Horton said.

"But what if it was him?" Jeff sighed in defeat. "I'll see if the Covert Police Detectives Unit in Portland or Augusta can send someone to help."

"Well, I heard CPDU is low on manpower right now too. Olivia and Isaac are up north investigating a serial killer, and Turner's been injured. Johnson is busy with most of the other guys by investigating a human trafficking ring," Officer Horton explained. "I'm sorry. I'll try to stop by more and check in on you."

After the officers left, Jeff checked the security equipment again. He called Captain Branson and updated him on the situation. "I need another officer here, Captain Branson. I know you're all busy with the trafficking ring, but can you spare anyone?"

Branson sighed. "I really can't, Martin. I really need all my people here on the trafficking case. But you know, Banks is still on vacation like you. You should give him a call."

"Well, I hate to bother him on his time off, but I guess I will. Thank you, sir."

Jeff hung up and called his best friend, Ben Banks, who had also recently returned from Afghanistan. They'd served together overseas and been through a lot together. Really, they were more like brothers now because of it.

Ben was also taking some time off to recover from the war mentally before returning to work at the Portland Covert Police Detectives Unit, where they'd met. This wasn't the best time to call his friend and ask for a favor, but Jeff was getting desperate.

"Hello? Jeff?" Ben answered the phone.

"Hey, man. I'm sorry to bug you on your time off. Where are you?"

"Nonsense! I'm in Florida. But I was getting bored around here by myself. I'm glad you called. There's only so many spy novels I can read in a week sitting on the beach. And only so much writing I can do."

"Working on writing a new novel?"

"Yeah. Well, trying. You know how it is. My mind wanders. Things aren't the same after coming home," Ben said.

Jeff nodded in understanding. "I know what you mean." He sighed. "So, I have something I need to ask of you."

"Anything, Jeff. After you pulled me from that rubble and took a bullet for me, I'd do anything for you. I owe you my life," Ben said, sincerity lining his voice.

Jeff rubbed his thigh where he'd been shot while pulling Ben free from a fallen beam after an explosion and during a firefight. Along with a few others, they had pulled as many out as they could, but they hadn't been able to save everyone. Visions of his fallen friends still haunted his nightmares. He shook his head as if to rid his mind of the sickening images. "You would have done the same for me."

"You know you did everything you could. I hope you're not still feeling guilty about the ones we lost."

Jeff stayed silent, his eyes stinging with tears that he'd been holding back a long time.

"Jeff... It's not your fault. You did everything you could. You've got to let it go."

Jeff scrubbed a hand over his face. "Well... I guess I'm trying to make up for it. Trying to make myself feel better about what happened by doing something good. There's this woman. She's in trouble, and I volunteered to protect her." Jeff explained her situation while Ben listened intently. "So, I hate to ask you while you're taking your time off but—"

"I told you, I'd do anything for you. Of course I'll come help you protect her."

"It's unpaid. You'd just be volunteering."

"I know. But I'm happy to do it."

"Thanks, man. I feel like I haven't slept in days."

They talked a while longer, and after Jeff hung up, he sat in his chair and stared at the ocean.

He hadn't realized it before talking to Ben, but Jeff had volunteered to protect Jane partly because he felt like he needed to redeem himself after not being able to save all his friends who'd died in the aftermath of the explosion. Yes, of course he deeply cared for Jane and wanted her to be safe, but deep down, did he think that if he took down her stalker and kept her safe that he'd feel better about what had happened? That he wouldn't feel so guilty anymore, and that their names, faces and families wouldn't fill his mind so much? And that he also would stop feeling guilty about the terrorists he'd shot and killed? Yes, they'd been terrorists, but they were human. Men whose lifeless faces he still remembered every day.

Maybe helping Jane get her life and memories back would help Jeff forget the lives he'd taken and lost.

Maybe.

He squeezed the bridge of his nose and let out a long breath as he leaned back in the large recliner in the living room.

"Jeff!"

Jeff's head snapped up. He'd fallen asleep in the chair.

"Jeff!"

It was Jane. He ran up the stairs, taking two at a time.

*

Jane read for about two hours before her eyes grew too heavy to keep open. She turned off her light and snuggled under her blankets, letting the peaceful feeling of sleep settle over her.

Sometime later on, something awoke her. A shuffling noise by the door. She wearily opened her eyes and waited for them to adjust to the darkness. In the dim light of the moon coming through the window, she saw the outline of a man take shape in the doorway. Her heart caught in her throat, and terror washed over her.

Something glinted in his hand as he raised it. A knife took shape as he raised it higher and higher. He took a step toward her, and she tried to scream for Jeff, but no noise would come out of her mouth. She tried to call for help again and again, but only soft whimpers escaped her lips. She tried to run, but her legs felt as weak as noodles.

"Jeff!" she choked out. "Help!" But she knew her calls weren't loud enough to wake him.

The man lunged forward and grabbed her shoulders, shaking her violently.

"Jane! Jane!" he shouted.

She kicked and fought, but nothing she did seemed to hurt him.

"Jane!"

Jane's eyes snapped open, and she looked at the concerned face of Jeff.

"Jeff? Where is he? Did you see him this time?" she cried, pulling her blankets around her as if they were a shield. She partially sat up. Estella was also in the room, and she sat on the bed.

"There's no one here. You had a nightmare. Everything is okay now," Jeff said. His hands were still on her shoulders, and his touch comforted her.

"You had a nightmare. It's totally normal. It's okay," Estella said.

"I'm so sorry I woke you up," Jane told them, frowning. "Again."

"Don't you worry about that. Did you see his face? Was it the man from the hospital or from earlier today?" Estella asked.

"I saw him, but not his face. Only the outline of him," Jane said glumly. "And even that was fuzzy."

Estella didn't bother hiding her disappointment.

Jeff told Jane, "It's okay. Not much time has passed yet. Who knows? You might not end up remembering what he looks like. That's not your fault."

"If I can't ever remember what he looks like, how will you find out who he is?" Jane's eyes widened.

"The police are already working on this. We will find him one way or another," Jeff assured her, but he wasn't so sure he should be making promises. With Jane's amnesia, they had almost nothing to go on.

Jane slowly nodded.

"Want me to stay with you again?" Estella offered.

Guilt rose up in Jane. "No, no. I'll be fine on my own. I know it is just a bad dream, after all." She gave a weak smile.

"Okay. Well, if you change your mind, I'm right over here. Okay?"

"Thanks."

Jeff and Estella backed out of the room. Jane tried to settle back down, but she kept seeing the image of the man with the knife in her mind. She turned on her light and read for a while, the words distracting her.

She fell asleep with the book on her chest.

Chapter Ten

The next morning, Jeff drank a cup of coffee as he watched the ocean out the big kitchen window. Estella stumbled in, wearing her hot pink robe and matching fuzzy slippers. Her blonde hair was mussed from sleep.

"Jane still sleeping?" he asked.

"Yeah. I peeked in her room. She fell asleep reading Mom's French book. Poor thing." She poured herself a cup of coffee and grabbed cereal out of the cabinet. "She must have had a hard time falling back asleep."

"Understandable," he muttered, staring at a boat in the distance. The ocean was calm today. It would be a good day to take Jane swimming.

"What's that supposed to mean?" Estella set a bowl, spoon, and milk on the table. "What's that face about?"

"I'm just thinking."

"You don't believe her? You think she only wants attention?"

"No, no. I do believe she is having nightmares. The thing is, when someone is scared for their life, they can become paranoid. See things or hear things that aren't there."

"She's not seeing things. Did you see her face at Turbat's Creek when she saw that man? Or how scared she looked after you woke her from that nightmare?" Estella poured cereal and almond milk into her bowl. "She's not delusional."

"I'm not saying she's delusional. I'm not so sure she saw the man who hurt or kidnapped her at the beach. Or maybe she saw a regular guy and was being paranoid. By the time I got over there, no one was there. I mean, I was running in sand, so I wasn't going as fast as I normally could have. A couple said they saw a man go by, but that could have been anyone."

"Jeff, she was terrified. After you ran after the guy, you should have seen how scared she was. That's why we hid in the car. She was afraid for her life. She did see whoever hurt her." Estella took a huge bite of cereal and said around it, "And he could have run away really fast before you got there."

"Of course, she was scared. Seriously, she doesn't remember what the man who hurt her looks like. She didn't get a good look at the guy at the beach. He could have been anybody. There could have been something about the man that was familiar, but anything could trigger a repressed memory for Jane. We could end up chasing shadows and accusing people with no evidence. The police looked at the hospital video footage and said they couldn't find anything suspicious. There were so many nurses, orderlies, and doctors walking around, and nothing stood out. We didn't see someone dressed as a doctor with a mask over his face," Jeff said.

"You think I'm making this all up?"

Jeff's stomach clenched at Jane's words as he and Estella whipped their heads towards the kitchen doorway. Jane stood there, staring at them.

"No, no. Of course not," Estella said, standing and walking towards her.

"Jane, I don't think you're making anything up. I was going to say—" Jeff began.

"I heard every word. I'm not making it up, and I'm not crazy!" She ran out of the kitchen, out of the house, towards the beach. Jeff bolted out of his chair and followed her.

She flung open the gate and ran down the boarded pathway to the sand, and stopping when she reached the end of it. She sat down, and he sat next to her.

"Leave me alone," she said quietly.

"I can't. I have to be near you at all times so I can protect you. I can't leave you alone out here." People passed by, jogging, walking their dogs, or playing with their kids. "Not with all these people around."

Jane brought up her knees and wrapped her arms around them.

"Look, I don't think you're crazy or making these things up. I was exploring all the options. I'm really sorry you heard that. Really. I shouldn't have been thinking out loud like that," he said, and he meant it. "That was unprofessional and careless of me."

Jane rested her chin on her crossed arms, staring at the waves lapping the shore.

"What I was going to say was that you said the man was dressed as a doctor and had a mask over his face, but he might have taken the mask off before leaving the room so he wouldn't stick out. Maybe he took off his white jacket too and had scrubs on underneath. He was probably smart enough to know where the security cameras were and looked away, or nonchalantly hid his face from them. I believe you, Jane. I was thinking of all the things he could have done to get out of there without anyone seeing him."

"Okay. Sorry I overreacted. I guess I shouldn't have jumped to conclusions."

"It's okay, Jane. Don't give it another thought."

"And I'm really sorry about the nightmares. I hope I don't keep waking you both every night like that," Jane said.

"Don't feel bad. Besides, the nightmares might help you remember something. We are your friends now, and we care about you and want to help you. That's what friends do for each other."

She turned her head towards him, looking at him a little sideways, and smiled. "I don't think I have had a friend in a long time."

Jeff instinctively reached out and put his arm around her shoulders. "I mean it, Jane. We're here for you. Whatever you need." She rested her head on his shoulder for a few brief seconds, then stood abruptly before he could fully comprehend what was happening.

"You know what else friends do? Have fun!" she shouted and made a beeline for the water. He laughed out loud and ran after her. She ran into the water up to her knees and splashed him as he reached the shore. He splashed her back and she shrieked. He laughed so hard his side hurt. They splashed each other back and forth, giggling like little kids. Jane bent over, laughing.

"Okay, stop! My stomach hurts from laughing!" she cried. Jeff tried to stop laughing, but he couldn't. Jane straightened and flashed him a smile. She looked beautiful in her new shorts and t-shirt. Her hair was wet with salt water, already starting to curl.

"We can go swimming later today if you want," he said. "Or we can go now!" Jeff grabbed Jane, picked her up and started wading into the water. The waves crashed against them, spraying Jane's face and hair.

"Put me down!" she shouted, still laughing.

He waded deeper in and pretended like he was going to toss her in, but he had no intentions of actually doing it. "One, two—"

"No! Wait! I can't swim!" she cried out, now in all seriousness. She pounded on his back. "Please, put me down!"

"Okay. Sorry, Jane," Jeff said sheepishly, returning to the shore. As Jeff lowered her to the sand, Jane put a hand to her forehead.

"I'm sorry," he said, guilt wracking him again. "I'm sorry if I scared you. I was just kidding. That was stupid of me. Are you okay?" He inwardly kicked himself for getting so caught up in the fun of the moment.

"I... I remembered something. I was standing near a pond. I was young, just a kid. A little boy ran to me and tried to push me in the water, but I yelled at him, saying I couldn't swim."

"Do you remember where the pond was? What was around it?"

Jane slowly shook her head. "I think a farm was nearby... I don't know. That's all I remembered."

"It's okay. You'll remember. I'm so sorry," he said again.

"It's okay. You were just joking around. I guess I really am scared of deep water," she said, looking out over the waves. "Don't know why, of course."

"Come on," he said, walking towards the house. "I'll make it up to you by cooking you breakfast. Can't promise it'll be nearly as good as yours."

Jane laughed softly. "This will be interesting."

They walked back into the house, Jeff and Jane both dripping wet. Estella stared at them as they came in the door. "What happened?" she said with a laugh.

"I remembered something. Not much. I was standing near a pond."

"That's great, Jane! It's progress," Estella said.

Jeff said, "Okay, I'm going to put on dry clothes."

"Me too," Jane said, turning away from Estella, who stood there confused.

"Okay," she said with a shrug.

Jane stifled a smile as she twisted her damp hair around her fingers and hurried up the stairs. The thought of the way she had felt in Jeff's arms with her hands clasped around his neck as they'd waded into the water made a blush cover her cheeks. She stepped into her room, closed the door and leaned against it.

She couldn't deny it. Though she had been terrified of the water, somehow, she'd also felt safe and secure in his arms, if that even made sense. She didn't understand it, but she liked the feeling.

Her smile lingered as she pulled on a casual dress and dried her hair. She began braiding it, then glanced at herself in the mirror and suddenly felt foolish.

I shouldn't be feeling like this. I should be focusing on my own safety, she thought.

She stopped playing with her hair and shook her head before walking back downstairs.

CHAPTER ELEVEN

Jeff put on a dry shirt and shorts and went to the kitchen to make some eggs and toast for Jane. He burned the toast a little and the egg stuck to the pan, but it was the best he could do. He put it all on a plate, and by the time he set it on the table, Jane had come into the kitchen. She had on an orange and pink sundress, and her hair had been towel-dried. She looked great.

Estella carried an Italian book as she came into the kitchen. "I knew I smelled something burning."

He pulled out chairs for both of them. "Sorry, it didn't come out so great. This is actually better than how I usually cook."

"That's okay. I don't mind," Jane said, sitting down. "Thanks for doing this."

"It's the least I could do." He sat and ate an egg he had made for himself. He had made sure to give Jane the better one that had fallen apart less in the pan.

"This looks...delicious," Estella said, obviously lying, poking the eggs with her fork skeptically as if to see if they were rock solid. "You deserve an A for effort, Jeff."

"Ha. Thanks."

Jane took the first bite of her egg. Jeff cringed, waiting for her to tell him it was gross, or that there were shells in it, but she didn't. He took a bite of his; it looked worse than it tasted.

"Come on. Where did we leave off?" Jane opened some Italian books then she and Estella read as they ate, practicing their Italian.

Jeff's phone vibrated, and a text from Ben Banks lit up the screen. *I'm here.*

Oh, good. Now that his friend had arrived, maybe he would see something Jeff missed and help him out. Jeff hurried to the door and let him in.

"Hey. How have you been? I'm really sorry about your dad, man," Ben said and threw his big arms around Jeff, giving him a manly pat on the back. "I jumped on a plane home from Florida and got here as soon as I could."

"I'm just so grateful for you coming here. I can't believe you left Florida early to come help us out."

"Seriously, man, it's the least I can do for you. I'm honestly happy to help. Have you slept at all this week? Because you look like death."

"Thanks a lot." Jeff punched him playfully in the arm. "Come and meet Jane and Estella."

The two men walked into the kitchen where the two women were huddled over some books on the kitchen table.

"Jane, Estella, this is Ben Banks."

Estella and Jane both stood up.

"Jane is teaching me Italian." Estella cleared her throat and said something unrecognizable, and Jane giggled. "What, I didn't say it right?"

"No... Sorry!" Jane shook her head, laughing again.

"Jane is quite the genius. I was trying to say 'nice to meet you' in Italian. I'm not very good yet. Anyway, it is nice to meet you, Mr. Banks." Estella extended her hand for him to shake.

He grasped it. "Please. You can both call me Ben. I'm here to help in any way I can."

Jeff saw the way Estella smiled at Ben. It was a little obvious that she thought he was handsome, and Jeff had already told her

Ben was single. Estella had always been bad at hiding her feelings.

"And it's nice to meet you, Jane," Ben said, shaking her hand as well.

"Come on, I'll give you the grand tour," Estella said to Ben, and the two of them left the room.

"So, do you go to church? Or do you know of any good churches around here?" Jane asked.

"Estella goes more than me. There's a little church down the road. I haven't been much since my mom died. Not at all since my dad died."

"Why is that? I'd think one would need the Lord more than ever when going through a hard time. Are you mad at God for taking your parents?"

Jeff was taken aback by her blunt question. "Well, I wouldn't say I'm mad at God. I guess I lost the desire to go to church and to pray." Jeff shrugged and looked out the window.

"He hasn't lost the desire to be close to you, you know." Jane looked him in the eye. "You should go to church with me tomorrow morning."

"Well, I have to go, unless I send Ben in my place. But it's best if we all go."

It wasn't like he didn't want to go. He'd just been unmotivated. But something about what Jane had said made him reconsider.

A few minutes later, Ben and Estella came back.

"We're going to church tomorrow," Jane told them.

"Really? He said yes to you? You have no idea how many times I have tried to convince him to go with me. This will be great. Thanks for convincing him," Estella said, elbowing Jane playfully. "So, are we going to go swimming today? And I don't mean whatever you guys did this morning. I mean actually swimming."

"Yeah. It's definitely hot enough outside. Sure, we can go," Jeff said.

"I've got some emails and phone calls to catch up on for work. How about if we go after that?" Estella asked.

"Sounds good." Jane stood up, finished with her breakfast. Jeff hoped it hadn't tasted too bad, but Jane had seemed to enjoy it. She took their plates and put them in the sink, and Jeff thanked her. She then proceeded to wash the dishes, against Jeff's and Estella's protests.

After a long and fun day at the beach and eating dinner, Jeff, Estella and Jane watched another movie together on the couch while Ben kept watch.

For the first half, Jane laughed and giggled, but Jeff noticed her eyes getting heavy after a while. She probably hadn't had much sleep the past two nights because of her nightmares. She settled back onto the couch, leaning her head back, and closed her eyes. After a few minutes, her head rolled to the side and rested on Jeff's shoulder.

It doesn't mean anything, he told himself. *She's asleep and doesn't know what she's doing.*

But she had also put her head on his shoulder earlier that day when he had apologized on the beach. Was this her way of showing him that she trusted him? That she felt safe with him? Or was it something more?

Or did it mean nothing at all?

Jeff frowned. Of course, it meant nothing. Jane was a naïve, impressionable young woman and certainly not the flirtatious type. He was reading way too much into this.

Before he knew it, the movie was over, and Jane wasn't moving.

Estella turned to look at her and smiled. "Aw, poor thing. She must be exhausted from last night and after the full day we had."

"Should I wake her?" Jeff whispered.

"She could sleep here on the couch. I'll go get some blankets." Estella went upstairs.

Jeff carefully moved Jane and scooted off the couch as he laid her down. He looked at her and couldn't help but smile. She looked so peaceful. Maybe tonight she wouldn't have any terrifying nightmares.

She looked so deep in sleep that he couldn't bear to wake her, and he didn't want to leave her down here to sleep on the couch. She needed a good night's rest in her own bed. He gently scooped her up in his arms and walked towards the stairway, then carried her up the stairs. When he reached her room, he set her down on the bed, and pulled her blankets up over her, reaching down and slowly brushing a piece of hair out of her face.

Not wanting to disturb her, he quickly backed out of the room, but not before stealing one more glance. With the moonlight on her face and her hear flowing over the pillow, she truly looked like an angel.

He smiled, then softly closed the door.

*

The next morning, Jane gazed at the tall, white steeple as families congregated from the parking lot to the church's open red doors. She ran her hands over her dress, self-conscious of her bruises, as they walked into the church.

Jane looked around at all the people who were in the church as they made their way into the sanctuary. She hadn't been around so many people in what felt like a long time. Did she look okay? She straightened out her dress again and fidgeted with her hair. Could people tell that she didn't know how to act or what to say?

A hand touched her shoulder. "You look great. They'll love you. Stop worrying," Jeff whispered in her ear.

A shiver snaked down her neck when she felt his breath on her, and her cheeks heated up. Was she that obvious? She clasped her hands in front of her to keep them from fiddling with her clothes and hair as a couple walked up to them.

"Good morning!" a woman with big blonde hair chirped, eyeing Jane's bruises. "Who are your friends?" she asked Jeff and Estella.

"This is Jane, and this is Ben. They are friends staying with us," Estella said. "Jane, this is Eileen and her husband Bill. They've been coming here since forever."

"We've known these two since they were babies! You are so blessed to be staying with them," the man, Bill, said.

"So, where are you from, Jane?" Eileen asked. "And what happened to you? How did you get all those bruises?"

Well, that was blunt.

Jane opened her mouth, then realized she didn't know what to say.

Jeff cut in. "Jane was in a car accident and has amnesia, so she doesn't know where she's from," he said quietly, leaning towards them.

"Oh." Eileen covered her mouth with perfectly manicured red nails. "I'm so sorry. That is tragic."

"Well, you're in good hands with these two," Bill assured her.

Jane smiled and nodded, wanting to hide under a pew. She saw the pity in their eyes. Would everyone she met feel bad for her? Or think she was odd when her shyness overcame her?

"We should find a seat. It is starting soon," Estella said, guiding Jane and Ben away. "See you later."

Relieved, Jane let Estella lead her to their seats in the back. "Thanks. I didn't know what to say. What should I say when people ask me things I don't remember?"

"I could tell you were uncomfortable. Sorry, she was kind of nosey. I have to say I didn't think about this before we came. I guess you should tell them the truth. You were in an accident and you don't remember."

"They'll think I'm weird. Or feel bad for me." Jane crossed her arms over her body as if to protect herself, slouching lower into her seat.

"Who cares what people think?" Jeff chimed in. "Yeah, people might feel bad for you. Don't worry. Everyone is going to love you. Soon you'll feel right at home here. I always did love this church. I shouldn't have stopped coming."

The pastor stepped up to the podium.

He expected her to feel at home here? What did he mean by that? Did he want her to stay?

The pastor welcomed the congregation, then the worship began. A drummer, bass player, guitar player, and pianist created beautiful and upbeat music that had Jane swaying and tapping her toes. They sang both hymns and contemporary songs, and as she worshipped, she felt more at home than she had since she had lost her memory.

Something niggled in the back of her mind, telling her that playing instruments was prideful, but she didn't agree.

Suddenly a vision entered her mind of a room full of people singing in a large room with wooden benches. The congregation sang with no instruments, but they sang beautifully. Somehow, she knew she was remembering a church she used to go to. What type of church was it?

Maybe it wasn't even a memory at all. Maybe she was imagining it. After all, it didn't seem like something from this century.

Jane shook off the vision and tried to focus on the worship. The cheerful music lifted her spirits, and soon she forgot all about her insecurities and worries. She loved going to church, loved to worship God. As the music segued into the sermon, she followed along in one of the church's Bibles and finally felt in her element. This was what she understood. As the congregation prayed, she closed her eyes and felt her heart become calm.

Lord, please help me fit in here. If it is Your will, please let me stay here a while. If I have a family, please help us find them, but if I don't, would it be too much to ask if I could stay here? She prayed.

There was something strange and yet familiar about being here in church. The passages the pastor read felt comforting, and when she closed her eyes to pray, it was the first time she felt at real peace that she could remember.

After the sermon, a few more people greeted them, but Estella whisked her out the door as quickly as she could.

"It's okay. I feel a lot better now. We don't have to avoid everyone," Jane said softly.

"Well, I didn't want to overwhelm you. I bet Eileen already spread the word about you, and we didn't want people asking questions."

"Yeah. Word travels fast around here," Ben added. "It's a small town."

"What do you say we go out to lunch?" Jeff asked. He leaned in closer to Jane and added quietly, "And I don't mind avoiding the chatty Eileen at all, to be honest."

Jane giggled.

"How about The Clam Shack?" Estella suggested.

"Seafood? I'm in," Ben said.

"Sure. Haven't been there in a long time. Since..." Jeff gazed off into the distance.

"Since Mom and Dad were alive. It was one of Dad's favorite restaurants." Estella sighed, then smiled at Jane. "You'll love it. It's a nice place."

"Sounds great."

"Okay. Let's go!" Estella said cheerfully, and they got back in the car.

Jane said, "When we were singing, I think I remembered something else. I was in a church with wooden benches and we were singing, but there were no instruments."

Estella looked at her intently. "Seems a little odd. Benches instead of chairs?"

"It does seem odd," Ben said. "You know, when I was in the Amish community in Unity investigating a human trafficking ring, the Amish church there didn't have instruments. And they had benches instead of chairs."

"I don't know. It could be a coincidence. Maybe it wasn't even a memory, just something I imagined that seemed real, like from a book I read," Jane said, looking glumly out the window.

Estella patted her hand. "Just give it time, Jane. You'll remember more."

CHAPTER TWELVE

The restaurant had been beautiful, and Jeff had insisted that Jane order whatever she wanted. The foods on the menu were unfamiliar to her, so she ended up ordering the same dish that Estella always ordered: chicken alfredo. It had been divine. Ben had ordered a lobster, and Jane had watched with wide eyes as Ben ate it, wondering how it could possibly taste good. She couldn't get past the googly eyes and the red claws.

After lunch, they returned to the house to get their swimsuits and go for a swim at the beach. Jane went to her room to grab her swimsuit and flip-flops. She sank down on her bed for a moment, soaking in the day.

Why was she so fortunate? She was having the time of her life, as far as she knew, with Estella and Jeff. They were so kind to her, and this house was so beautiful. It had only been a short time, but she really was feeling at home here.

She sighed and gazed out the window at the cluster of trees and bushes near the house swaying in the gentle breeze. She saw something move, then the figure of a man in dark clothing slinked through the trees.

"Jeff! Ben!" she cried, running down the stairs and into the kitchen. "There's a man outside in the trees!"

"Ben, stay with them." Jeff slammed his coffee mug on the counter and bolted out the back door as Estella ran into the kitchen.

Ben drew his Smith & Wesson 9mm and looked out the window.

"If someone's out there, Jeff will catch him," Estella promised, pulling Jane into a hug. Jane then sat at the table, watching the clock on the wall as the seconds crawled by. A minute later, Jeff came back inside.

"I think it was our neighbor Mr. Jenkins doing yard work," he said. "He's wearing dark clothing."

"No. It was the man from the creek."

"Come here," Jeff said, standing by the door. "Look at him and tell me if it is him."

Jane peered out the back door. An elderly man in jeans and a dark blue shirt was trimming hedges. "No. The man I saw had all black clothing."

"Are you sure?" Jeff asked, looking in her eyes. Suddenly she was aware of how close he was standing. She could smell his cologne and aftershave, a woodsy smell. She ignored it and stepped away.

"I'm sure."

"I asked Mr. Jenkins if he was working in the trees and shrubs near our house, and he said no. But honestly, his wife has been saying that he is not remembering things lately. So, he might have been in our bushes and doesn't recall. They are right there, not far from where he is working now."

"I know what I saw."

Jeff sighed. "Look, you know I'm looking out for you. And I'll check the security camera footage."

"We'll ask the other neighbors if they saw anything," Ben added.

"Okay. Thanks," Jane said solemnly, getting the feeling that Jeff didn't believe her. Did he think that the trauma she had gone through was making her see things?

"Well, do you guys still want to go to the beach?" Estella asked.

"Yeah." Jane smiled. She didn't know if Jeff believed her or not, but she didn't want her doubts to ruin this beautiful day. "Let's go."

*

Guilt niggled at Jeff as they walked down the boardwalk to the beach. He'd checked the security footage but hadn't found anything. He had seen the hurt look on Jane's face when he had asked her if she was sure about what she had seen. He was trying to gather all the information he could.

Dune grass covered the ground, lining the boardwalk the closer they got to the water. He opened the creaky little wooden gate, and they stepped onto the beach.

Ben carried the cooler, and Estella carried the umbrella to a spot on the sand where she began to set up. Jeff and Jane walked a bit behind them.

"Jane?" Jeff said.

Jane turned to Jeff, her long hair blowing in the breeze. She was wearing an orange and pink sundress over her bathing suit, and she looked incredible.

"Listen, I'm sorry if I gave you the wrong impression back there," he said.

She just looked at him, pain in her eyes.

He continued, "I do believe you. I was trying to get all the facts. I don't think you're seeing things or anything like that. I want you to know that. I'm sorry if I made you think otherwise."

The corners of her mouth tugged upwards a bit, and a smile crept onto her face.

"Come on. I'll teach you how to make a great sandcastle," Jeff said.

Jane grinned. "Sounds fun."

That night, they walked back to the house, laughing and tired after a long day of playing in the sand and the water. Since Jane was afraid of the water, they hadn't gone in very deep, but they had splashed each other enough to get cooled off.

Jeff walked ahead to open the door for the two ladies, then stopped short when he saw something taped to the door.

"Is that what I think it is?" Ben said to Jeff.

It definitely was not a note from a friend, saying they were sorry they missed Jeff and Estella while they were out. One glance told him that this note was a threat. The big block letters gave it away. He stepped closer to read the words more clearly.

I'M WATCHING HER.

A sickening feeling settled in his stomach as Jane approached. "What's wrong, Jeff? You look a little pale." She followed Jeff's eyes and saw the note, then her own face whitened as her smile fell to the ground.

"What is it?" Estella huffed, trudging a little behind, carrying bags of towels and food. She followed their gazes. "Oh no. This happened while we were gone? He was here?" She dropped the bags and covered her mouth. "The thought makes me sick."

Jane still held the umbrella she was carrying, staring at the menacing paper.

That was enough. Jeff opened the door and ushered them inside. "Don't touch it. I'll send it to CPDU to run it for prints. It'll probably be quicker than the local police station, and the lab is definitely more advanced. Maybe this guy was sloppy and we'll get something." He briefly touched Jane's arm as they entered the kitchen. "I've got to go call Officer Horton and CPDU. Don't worry, Jane. You're still going to be safe."

"Clearly she's not as safe as you thought," Estella grumbled, heaving the bags onto the counter. "Or else he wouldn't have been here. Look, we have security cameras installed. If someone was here, we'll find out who he was."

"Well, not necessarily. If this is the same guy from the hospital, he knows how to hide his face from the cameras, especially in the dark. In that case, all we'll be able to do is verify if someone was here and when they were here, and compare footage to the hospital footage. At least it's something," Ben explained.

"Exactly." With determination in his step, Jeff pivoted on his heel and walked upstairs to make some calls. "I'll need to go make a copy of the security tapes to give to the police."

Jeff finished his phone calls quickly. He walked back into the kitchen where the other three were sitting at the table talking. Jeff's phone buzzed. When Jeff looked at the screen, his heart felt as though it had dropped into his stomach.

He had a text from an unknown number: *Hope you guys had fun at the beach. Sorry I missed you. Did you get my note?*

"What's wrong?" Estella asked when she saw his face.

"Nothing. That was Branson asking for an update," he lied.

Before they could question him further, he walked out of the room. Now the stalker had Jeff's phone number? Jane didn't have a cell phone, so he was getting the texts. Anger burned through his veins and a determination to keep Jane and Estella safe. He stalked off to watch the security camera footage and see if he could nail this guy.

Over an hour later, while poring over security footage from when they were at the beach, Jeff sat up straighter when the image on the screen finally showed what had happened while they were gone. Jeff watched as a man wearing dark clothing with a hood covering his face left the note on the door. He must have walked because there was no vehicle in the driveway. Maybe he had been smart and parked down the lane.

There was no hope in finding footprints because he had walked along a well-traveled pathway to their house. Jeff could see that he had been wearing gloves.

Jeff called all his neighbors, but none of them had seen the man in the dark clothing. He dropped his head in his hands as he sat at the desk in the living room.

"Any progress?" Ben asked, coming into the room.

"I called all the neighbors, and no one saw the guy. He was wearing a hood and dark clothing, so he was hard to see at night. He had gloves on, so he probably left no prints. He did it late at night, and people don't stay out late around here. I'll have the note run for prints, but I doubt we will find anything. He walked here or left his car further down the lane. We have nothing to go on."

CHAPTER THIRTEEN

The next morning, the four went to Jane's follow-up medical appointment. Jane was healing well, and the doctor was happy with how well she was doing physically. They made another appointment, then went back to the house.

At the kitchen table, Estella gave a heavy sigh, slamming down her Italian book as she and Jane practiced new words. She leaned toward Jane and whispered, "Hey, don't you think Ben is cute?"

"Cute? What do you mean?"

"You know, good looking."

Jane laughed. "And I suppose you do? I thought I saw a funny look on your face when you two first met."

"Was I that obvious?" Redness crept over Estella's face. "Well, he is, isn't he?"

Jane smiled and nodded. "I won't deny that."

"And..." Estella sat back down. "My brother is also pretty good looking, isn't he?"

"Why are you asking me all these questions?" Jane slammed shut the Italian book a little too hard and stood up, gathering the rest of Estella's mother's books.

"Oh, come on. Don't tell me you haven't noticed." Estella followed Jane into the living room, where they put the books back on the shelf.

"If I have, it doesn't mean anything." Jane shoved the last book onto the shelf, wishing Estella would drop the subject. She was obviously a hopeless romantic.

"Wow, this is like one long double date!" Estella was practically giddy with excitement.

"No, it's not. They are protecting us, and that is all. You're reading way too much into this."

"Well, it is an awfully romantic idea."

Jane shook her head, smiling a little.

"Jane, Estella!" Jeff came barreling into the room. "We saw a man on the security camera looking in the windows just now. Go upstairs and lock yourselves in a room. We're going to get this guy."

"What?" Estella cried, freezing up.

"Do it! Now!" Jeff shouted, then ran to the other room, weapon drawn.

"Come on. You heard him." Jane grabbed Estella's arm and yanked her toward the staircase.

"No, wait. I have a better idea. Let's go to the boat. If something happens to Jeff and Ben, we're on our own, and a locked door won't protect us long. The boat will get us far away fast."

"But Jeff told us to lock ourselves in a room. If he wanted us to go on the boat, he would have told us to."

"He's panicking. Maybe he didn't think of it. Plus, he thinks I'm not good at driving it, but I am. Now enough arguing; let's go!"

Ben poked his head around the corner. "Get upstairs right now," he demanded, then disappeared.

"Come on." Estella dragged Jane out the back door, and they ran to the boat.

"I still think this is a really bad idea. You sure you know how to drive this thing?" Jane asked.

"Of course. And it'll be a lot better than being trapped in a room upstairs when the stalker kicks the door down." Estella got in, then helped Jane in. "My dad took me out on this boat when I was a kid too, not just Jeff." Estella revved the engine and they sped out of the cove.

Jane pulled on a life jacket and buckled it, and so did Estella. Jane peered at the water, her palms sweating at the sight, even though she was wearing a life jacket.

Estella slowed the boat down. "We're taking on water," she said as she turned off the engine. "I thought it was the water that was already in the boat, but it's increasing. Do you see where the leak is?"

Jane's heart raced in a panic, her nerves leaping. "A leak? Are we going to sink?"

"No. Look, I have the bilge pump. Let's try to find the leak. Here, dump water out of the boat." Estella tossed her a tin and Jane started scooping out the water. "I'll run the bilge pump."

"Here! Looks like someone made a hole intentionally. It's high enough that water didn't start coming in until we got in and weighed the boat down lower into the water. It looks like there was some type of adhesive covering it! But the water keeps coming in, and it's wearing away more and more!" Jane said.

Estella and Jane exchanged looks. "You think he did this?" Estella asked.

"Probably. What do we do? We can't go back there, and we can't stay here."

"Actually, once Jeff sees the boat gone, he'll figure out what we did and come looking for us."

"But what if he and Ben can't come look for us? What if... What if—?"

"Don't say it." Estella looked closely at the bilge pump. "This isn't working. Why isn't it working?" Estella's voice rose in frustration.

"The stalker probably tampered with that too."

"Ugh! Okay, fine. I'll try the epoxy glue to fix the hole." Estella opened a compartment, then another one, then a box. "Where is it? Jeff always keeps it in there." She pointed to the first compartment she looked in.

"He probably took it so we can't fix the leak. This is all your fault. This was your idea! We never should have gotten on this boat."

"I was trying to protect you!" Estella shot back, grabbing a tin and scooping up water.

"We should have done what Jeff said and locked ourselves in a room upstairs." Jane furiously bailed water out over the side of the boat.

"Who knows what would have happened to us if we had done that? We could be dead right now." Estella sighed. "Okay, you're right. This is my fault. Jeff's going to kill me. This was Dad's boat. I know it was important to him. He and dad spent a lot of time on this boat together."

Jane looked at her sympathetically. "I'm sorry I snapped at you."

"It's okay. We'll be okay," Estella said, noticing her discomfort, briefly patted her arm gently before continuing to bail more water. "At least we have life jackets on. Okay, enough talking. We need to find the radio so we can call for help." Estella rifled through the compartments on the boat, and Jane helped her. They looked in every container, box and crevice on the boat.

"He took the radio, didn't he?" Jane asked, defeated.

"Jeff always kept it next to the epoxy glue. I'm so sorry, Jane."

Jane's eyes filled with tears.

"We aren't far from the shore. Someone will come get us," Estella said.

Estella's words didn't comfort Jane. Any calm feelings had evaporated. She felt as though someone was squeezing her lungs tighter and tighter as she fought to just take a breath. The water poured in faster and faster as it pooled around her feet. It climbed higher, covering her ankles and rising to the bottom of her shins. Estella continued speaking, but her words became garbled as the sound of the trickling water grew into a deafening roar in her ears.

They were going to sink. Jane imagined herself sinking down to the bottom of the ocean, lungs screaming for air as she kicked for the surface, only to plunge deeper and deeper. Would the life jacket really save her? What if it came off? What if the stalker had tampered with it as well?

Jane couldn't help the panicked cry from escaping her lips.

Estella put her arm around Jane. "You look pale. I know you're afraid of the water, but the life jacket will keep you floating. You can't drown if you have it on."

Jane swallowed back bile. "I'm still afraid. I've never worn one before. How does it work? Will it really keep me floating?"

"Yes, of course."

The water flowed into the boat faster and faster, making their efforts to dump water out futile. "It's no use. There's no way we can keep up with the flow of water," Jane said.

"We have to try. Let's make as much noise as we can. Maybe someone from the shore will hear us," Estella said. "And if they get here in time, maybe we can save the boat."

Jane looked at her skeptically. "We're not that close to shore."

"I don't know, sometimes sound carries far. It's worth a shot."

"Help! Help!" they both shouted as loud as they could, waving their arms.

After a few minutes, Jane stopped. "Estella, no one can hear us. The boat's going to sink."

"It's okay. Even if you can't swim, the life jacket will keep you floating until someone comes by and rescues us."

Panic renewed within Jane, stealing her breath. "Until someone comes? How long could that take?" She tried to focus on her eyes, but she couldn't help from looking at the water all around them. The marina was in sight, but it seemed like it was a hundred miles away.

"It's a nice day. I'm sure someone will come by soon."

How long would they be in the water for? Water swirled around Jane's legs, making her stomach churn with anxiety.

"Let's jump out before it goes under," Estella said, standing up. She held out her hand, and Jane grasped it. They stood at the edge of the boat. "Come on. I'll jump in with you. On three. One, two, three."

She sucked in a breath and they jumped in together, hand in hand. Jane's body fully submerged in the cold water and shocked her, and panic shot through her. She was sinking!

Then her head bobbed above the surface like a buoy, and she looked around.

The life jacket held her up as Estella said it would. "Okay, this isn't so bad," she said. The water wasn't so bad after a few moments.

"See? I told you. No big deal," Estella said, then looked at the boat with a frown. "Except for Dad's boat."

One end dipped under the water's surface, and the rest followed, then the water bubbled as the ocean swallowed it whole.

"Come on. Let's swim back to shore. Look, kick your legs like this." Estella showed Jane how to swim like her, and in a moment, Jane caught on quickly.

A few minutes later, a small red boat appeared in the distance, and Jane and Estella waved. The small boat turned towards them and zoomed over.

The driver, a hefty man in his fifties with a mustache, asked, "You all okay?"

"We are fine, but our boat sank," Estella said.

"Sank?"

"Long story. Can we get a ride back to shore?"

"By all means! Climb on in," the man said. "Lucky I came by this way. Everyone's over at the beach this time of day."

"Thanks." Jane kicked her feet and was surprised by how quickly she moved towards the boat. She swam up to the ladder on the back of the boat and climbed on to the boat.

"Well, happy to help. My name's Frank. I'll get you back in a jiffy," Frank said and turned the engine back on. As they sped away, Jane noticed Estella staring at the spot where her father's boat had sunk. Her heart ached for Estella and Jeff.

They reached the shore, and Frank pulled the boat to the dock.

"Thanks so much for giving us a ride," Estella said. "We really appreciate it."

"Just glad I could help," Frank said, bobbing his head so his bald spot showed for a second.

"You live around here?" Estella asked.

"Just vacationing here for a few weeks. Nice place, huh?" Frank looked around, gesturing towards the quaint village near the clear, sparkling ocean. "Though, who knows? Maybe I'll stick around longer than I planned. You never know."

The women stepped onto the dock. "Well, thanks again," Jane said.

"No problem. Have a nice day," Frank said before speeding off.

"Jane! Estella!" Jeff shouted, running out of the house, followed by Ben. "Where were you? And why are you both soaked? I told you to go upstairs and lock yourselves in a room. We thought you were still there until a minute ago."

"I'm so sorry, Jeff. This is all my fault," Estella said, her eyes filling with tears. "I feel terrible for what happened."

Jeff looked around the cove. "Where's Dad's boat?"

"Well..." Estella began.

"Never mind. Come on. We need to get you both in the house, and then we can talk," Jeff said. "At least you're both still alive."

Once they got inside, Ben grabbed them two towels.

"Okay. Now, what happened out there? Where's the boat?" Jeff's voice quavered a bit on the last word. "Estella, please tell me the boat is okay."

"I'm sorry, Jeff. It's gone." Estella wiped tears from her eyes. "This is my fault. It's my fault it sank."

"What happened?" Jeff asked slowly between clenched teeth.

Estella explained, "Well, I know you told us to go upstairs, but I thought it would be safer for us to get away on the boat. Jane was totally against it, but I talked her into it."

"Well, I could have put up more of a fight," Jane added. "But to be honest, it did sound safer than locking ourselves in a bedroom."

"It doesn't matter. We got on, and we were in such a hurry that I didn't check for leaks, and I didn't check to make sure the bilge pump or the epoxy glue was on board, or the radio. There was a big leak. The bilge pump had been tampered with, and the epoxy glue and radio were gone. We tried bailing as much as we could, but the leak took over and it sank. At least we had the life jackets."

"Wait. So the stalker tampered with everything else to purposely sink the boat but didn't take the life jackets?" Jeff said, scrunching up his eyebrows. "Seems odd."

"Maybe he wanted to scare you by sinking the boat, but didn't want to kill or hurt you," Ben offered. "He is one sick and twisted person."

"He just wants to make me miserable. He probably knows I can't swim, so that must be why he left the lifejackets. But how did he know Estella and I would go on the boat alone?" Jane asked.

Ben shrugged. "Could have been a lucky guess, or maybe he wasn't even counting on that. Even if we had been there with you, the boat might have still gone under. Either way, it still would have scared you, and that's what he wants."

"What a psycho." Estella crossed her arms and turned to Jeff. "Jane said we should have done what you told us to do. She said if you wanted us to go on the boat that you would have told us to, but I didn't listen to her. I thought you didn't tell us because you thought I didn't know how to drive. It was stupid. This is all my fault." Estella broke down into tears and fell into Jeff's arms. "I'm so sorry, Jeff."

Jeff's hard expression softened, and he stroked Estella's soaked hair. "You're both safe now, and that's all that matters."

Jane studied Jeff. Even though he tried to appear unaffected by the loss of his father's boat, Jane could still see the sorrow in his eyes.

"It's just a boat," he added. "It's replaceable. You two are not."

"So... What happened here?" Jane asked, turning to Ben.

"It was a false alarm. One of the residents from the nursing home down the street wandered to our house. He's only in his fifties or sixties, but he must have either dementia, Alzheimer's, or some other type of memory loss. I'm not sure. Well, he got lost and came here to ask for directions. He tried opening the front door, but it was locked, so he looked in the windows. We called the nursing home and they came to pick him up. He was wearing dark clothing, a dark baseball cap, and sunglasses, so we thought he was a threat. He was anything but," Ben explained.

"Poor man," Estella said. "You must have terrified him."

"Well, we feel bad for scaring him. We were about to arrest him. It seems kind of silly now, but we can't be too careful." Jeff sighed, scrubbing a hand over his face. "I need to go and question

95

the neighbors even if they didn't see anything. Then I'll go call Officer Horton." He looked at Estella, then Jane. "Thank God you're both okay."

As he left the room, guilt and sorrow filled Jane's chest. Jeff had lost one of his last connections to his father, and she felt as if it was all her fault.

CHAPTER FOURTEEN

As Estella and Jane went upstairs to change, Jeff remembered all the times he had gone fishing with his father on the old Sea Hag as a kid. That had been their thing. Those were the times when he'd seen his dad smile and laugh the most, finally taking a break from work to spend time together.

After Dad died, Jeff felt personally responsible for taking care of that boat, and now it was gone.

Anger bubbled up within him. Why were people so cruel? The desire for justice grew within him like a roaring flame. If the stalker had tampered with the life jackets, Jane could have possibly drowned, since she couldn't swim. Things could have gone a lot worse.

Why didn't they tamper with the life jackets? Why sink the boat when it wouldn't harm them in any way? He clearly hadn't been trying to kill them. Was he showing his power? Or was it just payback?

Maybe the assailant didn't want Jane dead at all. Maybe he wanted to make her life miserable in return for leaving his captivity.

Until he could get her back.

Jane came back downstairs, dressed in a t-shirt and jeans. Jeff noticed Jane frowning, a remorseful look in her eyes as she towel-dried her hair.

"You okay?" he asked.

She looked up at him. "I'm fine. The question is, are you okay?"

He shrugged. "It was just a boat, right? I'm glad you're both safe."

"It's not just a boat to you. I can tell you're sad."

"I don't want you feeling bad about this. Okay?"

She looked at the floor. "That boat was obviously important to you."

"My dad used to take me fishing in that boat, so it was special to me, yes. It's just an object. Your safety is so much more important."

Jane looked away. "I'm so sorry. I feel like this is all my fault."

"No. No way. This is not your fault. Why would you think it's your fault?"

"If I wasn't staying with you, this never would have happened."

He took two long strides and stood directly in front of her, putting a hand on her arm. He touched her chin gently with his other hand to get her to look him in the eye. "Don't think that for a second. It's that creep's fault. Now he's made it personal. I bet he knew that boat used to be our dad's and that it was special to us."

His hands captured one of her own, and he leaned forward. His dark eyes stared into her own intensely. "I promise, Jane, I will find who did this. I'll find the stalker, and he'll never hurt you again."

Jane looked away, her eyes still filled with sadness.

"It's his fault, not yours. That criminal is going to pay for everything he's done to you. It kills me to see you feeling guilty about something you can't control. I wouldn't want you staying anywhere else but here. I wouldn't trust anyone else besides Ben and me to protect you. So don't feel bad about it, okay? Don't feel guilty about any of this."

A slow smile spread across her face. "I won't. Thank you. I'm glad I'm here."

"Good."

Jane nodded and headed upstairs.

He shook his head slowly. She truly was a sweetheart. Observant and compassionate...

He cleared his throat when Estella walked in.

"What's that look for?" she asked with one raised eyebrow.

"What look?"

"That crooked smile, dreamy-eyed look. What just happened?" She cocked her head to the side.

"Nothing."

"It was Jane, wasn't it? Did you two have a moment?"

"A moment? No. There was no moment. What do you think this is, one of your romance novels?"

She made a face.

"Look," Jeff said. "She could be married for all we know. We don't know anything about her. That's why, at least until we figure out who she is, there can't be anything going on between us. She doesn't need that. Besides, I don't want emotions clouding my judgment or distracting me. I can't think about this right now. I need to go get some extra security equipment to set up." He let out a frustrated sigh and stomped out of the kitchen.

His feelings were already distracting him.

"Nothing personal. Yeah, right," he heard Estella mutter behind him.

Was he that obvious? He needed to get his feelings in check and make sure he hid them better.

CHAPTER FIFTEEN

Jeff was still half asleep when he stumbled down the stairs and into the kitchen. He'd been up late installing the new security equipment, which he'd done during Ben's shift when Jeff should have been sleeping.

He wasn't completely surprised to see Jane hard at work at the stove. After a night spent tossing and turning as he reflected on the events of the day, he had finally fallen into a restless sleep around two in the morning, only to be woken up a few hours later by the glorious smell of Jane's cooking. What surprised him, though, was the view of the various dishes on the counter. There was bacon, sausages, bread and eggs.

As for the cook responsible for all of this, she was humming something by the stove as she worked, still unaware that she was no longer alone. Jane turned around to place the plate of eggs she had finished preparing on the counter.

"Jeff!" she exclaimed, clearly shocked to see him in the kitchen.

"Morning, Jane," he said with a small smile.

"Uh," she stammered, looking clearly confused to see him. "You woke up earlier than usual today. I was kind of hoping to be done with all of this before all of you got up. I was going to keep them warm on the stove."

"You should have closed the kitchen doors then," Jeff replied with a smile as he walked to the island and took a seat. "The smell of the food woke me up."

"Oh, I'm sorry about that."

"No, no," Jeff quickly stopped her. "I'm definitely not complaining. I mean, I wasn't really sleeping."

"Neither was I," Jane said as she dropped the eggs on the counter and turned around to face him. She opened her mouth to say something and then seemed to change her mind before finally talking again. "I couldn't sleep so I decided I'd come down and make breakfast for all of us."

Jeff smiled. "I think you made more than breakfast. For a moment I thought it was your birthday."

"My birthday?" Jane looked confused. "No. Well, I don't know when my birthday is anyway."

Jane turned away from him and began to fill the coffeepot, sadness shadowing her face.

Jeff frowned. "Please don't tell me you're still feeling guilty about the boat."

She didn't respond, busying herself with the coffee pot.

"Jane," Jeff said in a quiet voice as he joined her at the counter.

Jane turned around slowly, the look in her eyes unmistakable. "I heard what you said, Jeff, but I also know what I saw, and I know how much it hurt you to lose your dad's boat. Don't try to say it's not my fault because you and I both know that the only reason why that boat sank is because I'm here."

Jeff opened his mouth to deny her claim and then stopped. Sighing, he stood right in front of her, looking down at her with a gentle smile on his face. "I guess it makes no sense for me to deny that it truly hurts me to lose that boat. I may have given you the impression that losing the boat was the major reason for my gloomy attitude last night. But the truth is that I was pretty angry with myself for—"

"Angry with *yourself?*" Jane sounded shocked by his admission.

Jeff continued talking. "...angry with myself for putting you in danger, Jane. I should have made sure you were upstairs and not in the boat."

"But you didn't put me in danger!" Jane cried, taking one step closer to him and looking at him with a fierce look that questioned his statement.

"What if the life jackets had been tampered with? You could have drowned, Jane, and I would never have forgiven myself."

Now Jane looked angry, and to Jeff's shock, her anger was directed at him. "Okay, enough of that...nonsense talk," she finally said. "None of this was your fault and it's mighty arrogant of you, Jefferson Martin, to think you can control everything in the world. You were busy handling a situation. You thought the stalker was looking in the windows. Of course, you had all your attention on that. Also, you told us to do something and we should have done what you said."

"I should have checked on you..." Jeff said in a remorseful tone. "Or I could have sent Ben upstairs to check."

"Hush," Jane snapped at him, her hands resting on her hips as she stared at him. "We made a bad decision, and we're fine now. You keep telling me not to blame myself for any of this. Well, how would I not blame myself when you blame yourself?"

"I guess you have a point," Jeff said as he took her hand. "A well-made point too. I don't think I've heard you say my full name before."

Jane smiled shyly, blushing. "I needed to make sure you heard what I had to say."

"I definitely heard what you had to say."

He was still holding her hand. Jeff was reluctant to let go of it, his eyes on hers. There was an undeniable attraction there, and even though he knew it was a very bad idea to act on it, in that moment he seemed very unwilling to fight it. He should tug his hand out of hers. His hold on it was so light, all it would take was a slight motion and she would be free. He liked the warmth of the contact too much to end it. The pounding in his heart, the way she was looking up at him—he should not like it, but he did.

This wasn't right. He shouldn't be feeling this way about someone he was protecting. It had already become a distraction. What if she really was married?

"Jane," Jeff whispered her name, a question on his lips.

Suddenly the sound of a door opening and then closing jarred them back to reality. Jane jumped back, her hand moving to the counter to steady herself. They had mere seconds to compose themselves before Ben walked into the kitchen.

"Jeff," Ben said, stopping in the doorway and looking at them strangely.

Jane quickly turned around and busied herself with the dishes.

"Morning, Ben," Jeff said in a voice that sounded somewhat gruff.

"Morning," Ben replied stiffly as he stood in the doorway. "Jeff, can I see you?"

"Sure," he replied, looking at Jane before moving towards Ben.

Ben looked to the counter as if seeing the food for the first time. "So, was that what I was smelling?"

Jeff smiled. "Apparently, Jane woke up in a cooking mood this morning."

Jane chuckled as she watched them leave the room. Telling herself that whatever was happening between her and Jeff in the few moments before Ben had walked into the kitchen was nothing, she walked to the fridge to get the orange juice.

"I was walking around the property this morning and I found..." Ben stopped and looked at the kitchen door to see if Jane could hear him. After he was sure she could not, he continued. "I found this outside the perimeter of the fence."

Jeff looked down at what Ben was holding in his hand. It was a piece of paper.

"What is that?" he asked quietly, looking back at Ben with a confused expression.

"A note," Ben turned it around and held it out so Jeff could read it. "It was held down with a piece of rock."

Ben looked back at the note and realized Jeff was holding it at the edges. He focused on the words printed on the paper and as he read, fear and anger slowly crept up his spine.

It said, *SHE BELONGS WITH ME. SHE'S NOTHING WITHOUT ME.*

CHAPTER SIXTEEN

"Where did you find this?" Jeff asked.

"Just outside the fence, in one of the blind spots of the security cameras. Maybe the camera caught him as he walked away."

"All the camera will probably show is a guy in a mask and gloves, but let's check. We can't let Jane see it," Jeff said fiercely, his head swiveling to the kitchen to make sure Jane was not listening.

"Let Jane see what?"

Jeff and Ben both whirled around as Estella walked in, her hand moving to cover a yawn. "What are we hiding from Jane, and will someone please get me a bite of whatever it is that smells this heavenly?"

Ben hid the note behind his back as they both faced Estella.

"Good morning," Jeff said with a forced smile he hoped look natural. From the look she was giving him, it was clear he did not fool her one bit.

"Okay, what's going on?" she asked Jeff. He knew she wasn't going to drop it until he answered.

Ben hesitantly showed Estella the note. "I found this outside the fence a few minutes ago," he informed her as she read the note. "It's a—"

"Another note from the stalker," Estella finished for him, her expression almost the same as Jeff's after he finished reading the note. "What about Jane?" Estella looked at both men in turn.

Jeff said, "What do you mean?"

"Are you going to tell her about it?"

"I don't think we should. What would telling her about it accomplish?" Jeff asked. "Except make her worry more."

"She's not a child. She won't be too happy if she finds out later that you hid something like this from her."

Jeff couldn't deny that Estella was right. Still, the thought of telling her that her stalker had found a new way to torment her left a bitter taste in his mouth. He remembered the way she had smiled this morning, the beauty and innocence of it. That was what he wanted for her.

"Jeff!" Estella called out his name, and he turned around to look at her.

"Shh! Keep it down. All right, we'll tell her about the note. But not right now. Later." He glanced toward the kitchen where Jane could still be heard puttering around. "She put a lot of work into making breakfast for us, and I'd like to let her enjoy that before we spoil the mood with this news."

Right on cue, Jane poked her head out of the kitchen and looked at the group standing in the living room. "I'm all done here, and I don't know how long you guys are going to be, but if you could wrap it up before the food gets cold..."

"Of course, Jane," Ben said with a smile. "We're all done here."

The three of them moved towards the kitchen, and a few minutes later they were sitting at the table, laughing as they ate breakfast together.

Ben and Jeff sat Jane down later that day to talk about the note. As they had talked, Jane first felt fear. That fear quickly turned to anger. She looked at them, sitting in front of her, concern in their eyes.

The mood turned dark, and Jane broke the silence and stood up. "I have to go get ready for my therapy appointment."

"Right. We'll leave in about twenty minutes," Jeff said.

Jane nodded and walked upstairs. As soon as talk of the stalker and the note had come up, the atmosphere of cheer in the room had dissipated.

Her memories were gone, and her freedom had been taken away, and no one knew how many years her kidnapper had stolen from her. As she walked up the stairs, she vowed to herself that she would not let her joy be stolen.

*

Later that night as Jane prepared for bed, she heard a small knock on her door and checked to make sure she was dressed modestly. Tying the belt of her robe, she wondered if it was Jeff at the door, and her eyes went to the mirror above the dressing table before she shook her head, reminding herself of the danger of vanity.

"Come in," she said.

"Hey," Estella pushed the door opened and poked her head inside.

Jane told herself it was not disappointment she felt as she waved the other woman inside. "Hey."

Estella walked in and closed the door behind her. "Just wanted to check in on you and make sure you were okay."

"I don't know, Estella," Jane admitted as she sat down on the bed and twisted her fingers in her lap nervously. "It seems like every day this assailant finds new ways to make my life miserable. The worst part is that I seem to have drawn you, Ben, and Jeff into this with me. And they're not even being paid to protect me. I owe you all so much."

"Jane," Estella had a stern expression on her face. "They're doing this because they care about you. Don't tell me you're still worried about that after how much Jeff and I have told you not to."

"Hard not to worry about it when it is the truth."

"No. The truth is that you're a sweet, gentle, and amazing woman who has had the misfortune of being targeted by this sicko. He keeps trying to make you miserable. And he will, but only if you let him." Estella moved closer to Jane and took her hands. "For a moment there, I was happy when I saw you play and laugh, even after you saw that note. I was happy because despite the note you still found a way to be happy. That is something the stalker can't take away from you. Jeff and Ben are here now, and you can rest assured they will protect you. The only thing you have to concentrate on is living your life to the fullest."

Jane opened her mouth to talk, then shut it and smiled instead. "Why do I feel like I just listened to a sermon?"

Estella chuckled.

"I guess you're right. I wish I remembered something useful. Maybe that would help Jeff and Ben in catching him faster."

Estella glanced at Jane cautiously. "Still no new update on your memories?"

Jane shook her head. "Not really. Sometimes I get dreams and then wake up and only remember bits and pieces that don't really make sense. I'm not sure if it's real or if I imagined it."

Jane sounded frustrated, and Estella understood the emotion. "Don't worry. Remember the doctors said that as long as you take it easy then you may start to remember things."

Jane nodded, then looked at Estella with a smile. "How was your trip with Ben to the docks to carry out investigative work?"

Estella rolled her eyes. "It would have been boring, but Ben made it fun. It's not as exciting as in detective novels. Did you know Ben writes novels?"

"He does?" Jane asked in surprise.

"Yes." Estella nodded. "Well, he writes crime novels and is quite successful. I'm thinking of reading one, but I don't know if I should."

"Why not?" Jane asked perplexed. "I definitely would."

Estella shrugged and looked bashful for a moment. "I don't know if I'd like it, and I really want to like it. I mean, it's Ben, so I know it's going to be awesome. We were talking today, and he was telling me stories from his past. He's kind of incredible."

There was a soft look in Estella's eyes as she talked about Ben, and Jane knew what that look meant. It was clear that Estella was attracted to Ben, but Jane had no idea if he liked her too. Not that she had actually been looking since it was none of her business. It seemed like she was going through the same thing. Shaking her head and telling herself that what she felt for Jeff was nothing more than gratitude. She pushed that part of her emotions down and turned her attention back to Estella.

Chapter Seventeen

Jeff stared at Jane's hair as she stared down at the book in her lap, sitting in a porch chair. The dark waves cascaded over her shoulder and down her back. As she absentmindedly tucked a few strands behind her ear, the way the sun shone on it reminded him of how the sun glittered on the ocean waves.

"Stare much?" Estella whispered as she joined them outside.

Jeff glared at her. He had left her at the kitchen table with Ben. She'd been making moony eyes at his friend. He wasn't sure how he'd feel if the two of them became an item. It was weird to even think about it.

"Hey, Estella," Jane closed the book in her lap, an expectant and questioning expression on her face.

"Nothing today," Estella said with a shake of her head.

There was a visible sign of relief in Jane's eyes that made Jeff clench his fist in anger. It had been a week since the first note had arrived. Three more paper notes had arrived. Jeff had sent them to CPDU Portland for analysis, and apart from confirming things they already knew, they offered no new information. In all this, Jane had somehow managed not to lose her spirit. This in itself was a source of inspiration to Jeff.

The three of them sat looking at the skies above them. It was still early in the morning, the sun not yet hot and the skies a pretty shade of blue. Jane pointed to two butterflies flying across the landscape as they flew from one flower to another.

"We may have to visit the library in town. I want to pick out some more books," Jane said.

"Don't tell me you've read all the books in the house," Jeff said, aghast.

"Well, no, but I would love to go to the library and have more of a variety. I also want to get a journal, if possible."

"Of course," Jeff replied. "Just let me know when you are ready."

"Actually, I'm ready now if you are." Jane pushed herself to her feet. "Estella, are you coming with us?"

"Uh, no. No, I think I'll stay here with Ben. You and Jeff go ahead."

"Okay," Jane said. "Let's go."

Jeff kept his right hand on the steering wheel and his left hanging out the window as he drove Jane to the library. He glanced at her, not surprised to see her staring out the window with a wide smile on her face, her head darting back and forth as if trying to take in as much of the sight as she could before it disappeared out of view. There was a childlike innocence to her curiosity.

"When we were young," he said, pointing to a small path that led off the road, "Dad used to take Estella and me down that road. A few miles in, there is a small stream of water with a little bridge. See, because of the woods, only the locals knew how to get there so it was often quiet and empty. Dad, Estella, and I had many good times there."

Jane looked at the path he was pointing to, noting how it was flanked by the thick foliage that lined the roads on both sides.

"Weren't you scared?"

"Scared?" Jeff sounded surprised by the question. "Why would we be scared when our dad was with us? Dad made sure we always stayed on the path he had marked out for us. I got lost once," he remembered with a smile on his face.

"You did?" Jane sounded surprised as she turned in her seat to look at him.

Jeff smiled back, glancing at her as he switched hands on the wheel. "I sure did. Saw a rabbit and chased it off into the woods when Dad and Estella went to inspect a fallen log for mushrooms and salamanders. I remember following this rabbit until it ran too fast for me to keep up. When I turned around to go back to Estella and Dad, I couldn't find the path I had taken."

"You must have been scared then," Jane said, unable to help herself from smiling at the thought of a young Jeff lost in the woods. Mostly because it was hard to imagine someone like him lost. He always seemed sure of himself.

"That time I was. I remembered what Dad had said. He'd told me to stay where I was if I ever got lost and to start screaming as loud as I could. So I did, and in a few minutes, I could hear Dad and Estella calling my name back. Those minutes felt like years back then," he recalled, remembering it clearly.

"Good thing you remembered what your dad taught you back there. I bet Estella was scared for you when she realized you were lost."

Jeff chuckled at Jane's statement. "Sure, until my dad found me. Then she gave me a long lecture about not wandering off."

Jane looked out her window, a sad expression crossing her face before she hid it. Jeff had already noticed it.

"What is it, Jane?" he asked gently.

"Nothing; it's nothing."

"You sure?" he asked, looking at her but noticing she was refusing to meet his gaze. "If you don't want to say anything, that's fine. I want you to know that I am here for you."

"When I hear you and Estella talk about this exciting childhood you had, I wonder if mine was anything like that. If it was happy at all. If I had a family who loved me and if I still do."

"Jane..." Jeff said, compassion in his eyes as he glanced at her.

She turned in her seat yet again to look at him. "Sometimes I'll see something or think of something, and this strange sense of déjà vu washes over me. It's as if my memories are locked somewhere in my head and I can't find the key. I'm just searching."

She sounded frustrated and angry, and Jeff couldn't blame her. All he could do was offer his support and help her through it until she got her memories back like the doctor had said could happen.

"Jane..." He paused, not knowing what to say. He wanted to reach for her hand, but refrained. "Look, I can imagine how it feels to think back and not remember anything about my past. Remember the doctor said your memories should come back in time and that you shouldn't stress yourself trying to remember."

"I know." Jane nodded in agreement. "And I guess I should focus on my blessings instead. Like the fact that it was you and Estella who found me. I don't know what I would have done without the both of you, and Ben, too."

"Somehow I think you would have found a way," Jeff said with a smile. "In all my life, I've never seen someone as strong and smart as you. You cook the most delicious meals, you can speak French, German, and Italian, and you love reading."

"Now you're just trying to make my head swell."

Jeff snorted. "As if that were possible."

"Thank you, Jeff, for everything you've done for me. I guess if it were you taking me through the woods I wouldn't be scared because I would know that if I got lost, you'd find me."

He smiled, his heart warmed by her words. Now he really wanted to reach for her hand, but he couldn't. "We're here," he said as he pulled up to the front of the library.

Jane's eyes lightened in anticipation as she stared at the big brick building that housed her favorite things in the world.

"This is going to be fun," she said as she reached for her door.

Jeff chuckled. "Only you would think a library is one of the places the word fun was meant for."

"I bet there is a book in there that you'd like too, written in English of course," she added, wrinkling her nose as she tried not to smile.

"That is one bet I won't mind taking," he said. Smiling, Jeff followed her into the library, his eyes scanning the people around them to make sure there was no threat to the woman who seemed to be burrowing deeper into his heart with each passing day.

*

Estella walked into the living room to see Ben sitting at the kitchen island and making notes into a small black journal.

"Ideas for a novel?" she asked as she walked to the fridge to get a jar of peanut butter, then grabbed a loaf of bread.

"Something like that," he said with a smile. "But for now, let's just say it is more like an idea of an idea and not an actual idea yet."

She raised her eyebrows. "Okay then. I'm making a peanut butter sandwich. Want one?"

"Sure," he said, closing the book and standing up from his chair.

Ben grabbed some dishes from the counter and brought them over. Standing beside him, Estella felt the heat from his body, and when she turned around to look at him he towered over her. Yet his gaze was soft.

She dropped a sandwich on one of the plates he brought over and turned around to make another.

"Sorry it's just a PB sandwich," she said apologetically when she turned around to put the second sandwich on the second plate he had brought.

He walked to the fridge and took out two bottles of water, and they sat down to eat at the kitchen island.

"When I was little, my mom used to make me a PB and J sandwich for lunch. Every day. Of course, as a kid, I hated always having to eat the same thing at lunch every day."

Estella absentmindedly took a bite of her sandwich, all her attention on Ben as he told his story.

Ben's lips curved in the barest hint of a smile. "Then one day mom fell really sick and had to spend about two weeks at the hospital, which meant my dad was now in charge of lunch. Between his work and my mom in the hospital, my dad didn't have time to make me lunch every day. He always gave me money to buy lunch at the cafeteria. Now I could eat whatever I wanted. But I hated every single moment of it. When my mom came home and started making me peanut butter sandwiches again, I was so happy. I had taken her for granted. I never complained again when Mom handed my lunch bag to me."

By the time Ben finished telling his story, Estella was smiling.

"I don't know how, but somehow you made the fact that I'm not a good cook sound like a good thing. You know, for someone who pops up a lot in my brother's stories, I'm surprised we haven't met before. If Jeff's stories are anything to go by, you're like Superman, Batman and Spiderman all rolled into one."

Ben burst into laughter, unable to help himself, and Estella beamed at him, proud she could make the often quiet and reserved man laugh like that. When he looked at her again, there was a small twinkle in his eyes.

"If that is true, then Jeff must know two Bens, or he is a better storyteller than I know him to be."

"Then why don't you tell me about yourself then?" Estella asked, astounded by how easy it was to talk to him.

"You sure you want to hear about me? Would hate for the myth to become a mere man."

Estella's eyes went soft as she looked at him. "I think the man would prove even more interesting than the myth."

Ben paused before a slow smile crossed his lips. "What can I tell you about myself that may sound even the least bit interesting? Well… Did Jeff ever tell you about the case of stalking and human trafficking we investigated in an Amish community?"

"He's mentioned it, but you know him. He doesn't like to talk about his work much."

"That case will stay with me forever. We protected a woman named Maria, and actually, we are good friends now with her and her husband Derek, who used to work with us at CPDU. Actually, I went out on a few dates with one of the Amish women."

"What?" Estella laughed. "How scandalous! Do tell."

"It wasn't really. And nothing came out of it. Her name was Anna, and she was a midwife there, but she left the Amish to become a nurse. She was really busy after those few dates with finding a place to live and applying to schools, so we lost touch. She was nice, but I didn't really feel a connection with her. We didn't have much in common. Sometimes when you meet people, you can just tell you have a connection, you know?" He smiled at her, and Estella's stomach flipped.

Was he referring to her?

A half hour later of swapping stories, including embarrassing ones about Jeff as a kid, they turned around to see Jeff and Jane walking in, both of them laughing about something.

"How was the library?" Estella asked Jane, who held a bag filled with books in front of her.

"Fine," she replied with a smile. "And Jeff has something to tell you guys."

Jeff scowled at her before taking a step into the room. "Everyone, you will be happy to know that due to a bet I lost to Jane, I'll be in charge of preparing dinner tonight. No, Estella, before you ask, takeout is not an option." Then he turned to Ben with a betrayed look on his face. "Why didn't you tell me there are PI novels even more interesting than PI movies?"

"What?" Ben asked, confused as Jane burst into laughter.

Estella looked down at her forgotten sandwich, picked it up and started eating. Ben had already eaten his, but she'd been so focused on talking to him, she'd barely touched hers. With Jeff in charge of dinner, lunch had suddenly become the most important meal of that day.

Chapter Eighteen

"Check," Estella said, forcing Jeff to rethink his strategy.

It was late in the afternoon, and they were playing chess in the living room while Jane sat on one of the couches reading a book. In her lap was the journal she had gotten and every so often she would stop and scribble something on it before continuing. Ben had gone out to run some personal errands. Apart from the clink of the chess pieces and the occasional words from Jeff and Estella, the house was quiet.

Too quiet.

However, several times a day a police car would drive by, and Jane found it comforting.

She glanced at Jeff and Estella, smiling when she saw the furrowed look on Estella's face.

"Checkmate," Jeff said.

"You know," Estella was saying as she studied the board, "sometimes I think you're cheating. I haven't figured out how yet."

Jeff laughed at her. "You don't want to believe I'm better than you."

"Because you're not," Estella retorted. "And I'll prove it to you. Come on, let's play another game," she said as she began to rearrange the pieces.

"Your wish, your loss." Jeff waved his hand theatrically.

Jane couldn't help herself as she chuckled from where she sat. She wondered if she had siblings. If she did, she hoped they loved one another half as much as these two did.

The phone suddenly rang, and she glanced at the phone on the coffee table. She froze as she stared at it, remembering the phone calls to Jeff's phone. Then she shook her head.

This was the house phone, not Jeff's line. It could be Ben calling to ask something. Before Jeff could get to it, she reached out and grabbed the phone.

"Hello," she said, a small thread of anxiety in her voice. Her face paled.

At first, she heard nothing but the sound of someone breathing heavily on the other side. Jane turned to motion to Jeff, but he must have seen the look on her face and was already using equipment to record the call. He listened in on one of the other landline phones.

"Who is this?" she asked the person on the phone, anxiety slowly giving way to impatience.

Then the voice spoke, heavy and thick. "Don't tell me you've forgotten the sound of my voice, Cecilia."

Jane met Jeff's eyes as she froze in fear, her face turning white as she gripped the phone. "Who are you?" she asked in a shaky voice.

"Keep him talking," Jeff whispered, motioning for her to go on.

"Well, well," the voice said in mock disapproval. "You can't even tell who I am by my voice. I miss you, Cecilia. Don't you miss our farm?"

"Farm? What farm?"

"Oh, don't tell me you've forgotten your room with that window you always used to stare out of."

"Actually, I do remember that room. You locked me in there, didn't you?" she cried. "What kind of person does that?"

"Cecilia, I was good to you. When you were good, I gave you freedom to go outside. You loved the farm, and the animals, and the pond."

The memory of a pond returned to her mind again, and this time, she remembered what surrounded it. A farm with an old red barn, an old farmhouse, and that room downstairs where he'd locked her away for days at a time. She'd stared out that tiny window, praying for freedom, for some way to escape that place. She tried to keep herself distracted by reading the college textbooks and the novels that were there, but time still seemed to pass so slowly in that small room.

"Don't worry, Cecilia," the voice on the phone rasped, sending chills slithering down her spine. "I'm coming for you. I'm going to take you home with me where you belong. You're mine and I'm going to get you back again."

"I am not yours," Jane said slowly through clenched teeth. "You don't own me."

"You're nothing without me. If I can't get you back, I'll kill you."

"Who is this?" Jeff demanded into the other phone he was holding, slamming his fist onto the coffee table. "You coward!"

But all he got in reply was the dial tone when the call was ended.

Jane stood still, shock on her face as she stared at Jeff. "He wants to kill me," she said in a strangled whisper. "But what he said made me remember the farm a little. All I remember was an old red barn, an old farmhouse, and that room he locked me in. That room I remembered at the hospital. That's it. It could be any farm anywhere in the country. It tells us nothing."

Estella quickly ran over and wrapped her hands around Jane's shoulders. "So, Jeff, can you trace the call?"

"Police can't trace a number. We can request a ping that will give a location on a cell phone. It'll take between ten minutes and two hours to get a good location, so we might have to wait," Jeff explained. "Cell phones have settings that can be shut off, so the location will probably be limited to the cell tower that the phone was connected to. It could be a radius of several hundred to several thousand meters. If location data is turned on, the accuracy can be almost exact when the phone is near several towers, but this guy probably is smarter than that. If he was inside a building, it'll be less accurate."

Jane slumped with disappointment.

"Well, that's just great," Estella said.

Jeff patted Jane's arm. "Look, at least the call was recorded. Maybe CPDU can trace it faster than the local police here, since they're understaffed. CPDU has more advanced technology, and my friend there owes me a favor." Jeff picked up his phone. Dialing a number, he put the phone to his ear.

"Hey," he said as soon as the person on the other side picked up. "Sorry, Lawson, but this is kind of urgent." Jeff explained the situation to his coworker. "Any information you can get for me would be great, and don't worry, I'll clear it with Branson. Call me when you find out anything. I really need that information ASAP." He listened for a few seconds before nodding again. "Yes. Thank you, Lawson. I really appreciate it."

He ended the call, then called Officer Horton to update the local police. After he hung up, he looked over at where Estella was handing a cup of water to Jane who was trembling slightly. For a moment he closed his hand into a fist, wishing there was something nearby he could drive that fist into. Then he took a deep breath and made his way over to Jane.

"How are you feeling?" he asked, kneeling beside her.

"I'm fine," she replied with a shaky smile. Then sighed. "I hate that you're seeing me like this. I mean, it's just a phone call. I shouldn't be this scared."

"We're talking about someone that already tried to kill you," Estella countered immediately. "And threatened to again. Of course, you have every right to be scared."

Jeff nodded in agreement. "It's okay to be scared. It means you're cautious." He paused for a few seconds, trying to gauge how she was doing. He got to his feet and starting to pace the length of the room. "I feel so stupid. If only I had caught him..."

"No, Jeff," Estella warned him. "You did your best then."

Jane quickly nodded to show she didn't blame him at all.

Jeff scoffed. "If I had been more careful and paid more attention, we would have him by now."

"You can't blame yourself for that, Jeff," Jane replied. "There was no way you could have gotten him there. Too many people around that day, and he had a big head start since he was so far from us." She paused, hugging herself. "He called me Cecilia, and yet I know that is not my name."

"Are you sure?" Estella asked, glancing at Jeff.

"Yes." Jane nodded vigorously. "I hated the name immediately when I heard it. Not the name itself, but the fact that he called me that."

"Maybe a part of you associates something bad with that name," Jeff said. "Of course we'll never call you that. To us, you're still Jane."

"Thank you." Jane had no idea why she hated the idea of anyone calling her by the name the stalker had mentioned, other than the fact that he'd called her that.

The doorknob on the front door clicked and all three of them froze. Jeff was already reaching for his gun when the door swung open, and Ben walked in. Ben paused when he found the three of them staring at him strangely.

"What?" he asked, looking behind him. "Did I track mud into the house?"

"No," Estella said as everyone looked relieved.

"He called the house phone," Estella informed Ben as he strode into the room. "And he made Jane remember a farm, but all she remembered was a red barn and a house. Nothing specific."

"When did he call?"

"A few minutes ago," Jeff replied, looking at Ben.

"Have you tried to trace the call?"

"I called Lawson at CPDU and gave him the number. I should be hearing back from him anytime now."

"Who took the call?" Ben asked, looking at each of them in turn.

"I did," Jane said.

Ben paused, searching her face. "And what did he say?"

"Here, I'll play the recording for you." Jeff played it as Ben listened closely.

When it was done, Ben nodded. "I think he's starting to come unhinged. It means he is likely to make a mistake soon. It also means he is getting more and more dangerous. Jane, I think you should see a sketch artist. Maybe they can get a description from what you remember of his face from the creek."

124

"I didn't see his face really. He was far away and his face was hidden by his hood," Jane said with a frown as she tried to recollect the man she had seen at the creek.

"Don't worry," Ben reassured her. "You'd be surprised what those sketch artists can manage to do with a few things you can remember."

Jeff stepped forward too. "From now on, we need to be extra careful." He turned to face Ben. "I'll see if I can get round the clock protection for Jane until this whole debacle is over."

"I seriously doubt that'll happen with the size of their staff," Ben remarked.

"I know, but the least I can do is try. Hopefully, Lawson will have some good news for us about that phone number."

Jeff's phone rang and he lifted it to see that it was indeed Lawson calling. He put the phone to his ear, spending a few minutes talking. Finally, he ended the call to see the three of them looking at him expectantly.

"What did he say?" Ben asked.

"The phone was a burner so there is no way to know who it belonged to."

"Ugh. Of course it was. Could he find out where the phone is right now or where it made the last call?"

"Yes." Jeff nodded. "Only the phone is not giving off any service anymore. For now, we can assume the stalker has either destroyed the phone or taken the battery out of it. All we know is the signal used the local cell tower, but we already know he's around here, so that doesn't help. Either way, we have nothing."

Ben added, "Historical data may be available but would likely only be the cell tower the phone hit at the exact time of the call. Rarely, store video footage may be available of the purchase but would take quite a while of investigating to find that, and we have no clue which store he got it at."

"This guy is starting to annoy me," Estella said in a tone that forced a smile out of Jane.

"Who, Ben or the stalker?" Jeff joked, lightening the mood when Jane and Estella chuckled.

"I guess we were too quick to hope it would be that easy to get him," Jane said with a sigh.

Jeff glanced at Jane. He could still remember the look on her face after she received that call. He silently cursed himself for not getting there in time to pick up the call himself.

*

"You're blaming yourself for this again, aren't you?" Estella said to him a few minutes later in the other room, her voice quiet so it didn't get to Jane.

"Hard not to," Jeff answered.

"She's fine, you know. As hard as it may seem for you men to understand, women are not made of china. We won't break at the slightest touch." She smiled as she looked at her brother to see him still looking at Jane. "But you'll worry about her no matter what I say and we both know why."

"Because I care about her as a friend." Jeff turned to look at his sister. "Stop imagining things."

Estella chuckled. "She likes you too, you know."

"She what?" Jeff asked, his excitement belying his earlier statement. Then he got control of himself and assumed a cool expression. "Of course she likes me. Just as I like her. As friends. Now if you don't have anything better to do, how about you go make sure she's doing okay."

"Sure thing, boss," Estella said with a chuckle as she made her way back to Jane's side.

Jane looked up from the talk she was having with Ben, smiling a little when Estella squeezed herself onto the couch beside her.

"Before you ask, I'm fine now. Sorry I scared all of you like that," Jane said.

"Don't worry," Estella reassured her with an arm around her shoulders. "I knew you were going to be fine." Then she turned around to look at Jeff. "You hear that? She's fine so you can stop worrying now."

Jane laughed, her eyes twinkling, and for a moment it was almost impossible to believe that a few minutes earlier she had listened to someone threaten her.

CHAPTER NINETEEN

Jane was writing in her journal two nights later when she heard a noise at her door. She instantly froze in fear, staring at the door. Then she heard the sound again and realized it was someone knocking.

"Jane," Estella whispered from behind the door. "Are you asleep?"

Jane got down from the bed, placing her hand on her chest to still her pounding heart. She walked to the door and opened it to let Estella in.

"Why are you not asleep?" Estella asked.

Jane said nothing, just closed the door and walked back to the bed to join Estella, who had already climbed on and was now settling in the middle of it. Since it was a few minutes past midnight, Jane couldn't help but wonder what Estella wanted.

"What are you writing in there?" Estella asked, looking at her journal but not making any attempt to open it.

"Nothing," Jane quickly replied as she reached for the journal and drew it to her. Then she realized that it may look somehow rude to do that and offered an explanation. "I'm writing my thoughts down, like a diary. The doctors said it may help me with my memory."

"Okay," Estella shrugged in understanding. "I used to have a diary once. Didn't get how it worked though. Like, do you sit there and write everything you did during the day?"

A small smile crept upon Jane's lips. "You can write whatever you want. Your thoughts, ideas, your worries... That kind of thing. Then if something important happened during your day, you can also write about it and how it makes you feel."

"Then I wonder what you would have written about the phone call."

At Estella's words, Jane looked away. "I already told you, I'm fine."

"You say that, and I know a part of you wants to believe it for a while. I've seen you get jumpy at any sudden noises. You haven't gone outside the house in two days, ever since the call."

Jane still didn't meet Estella's eyes as she defended herself, crossing her arms "Because I don't have anything to do outside."

"Nonsense. You used to enjoy sitting in the garden, going to the beach, the sunshine and all that. It was your favorite part of the day." Estella leaned in close to Jane. "Look, I'm not saying I understand how you're feeling, but I honestly don't expect you to be totally fine and I think you hiding it isn't going to help you. What did your therapist say about it?"

Jane finally met Estella's gaze. "Okay, so I'm not totally fine. What do you expect? I'm being pursued by a madman who wants to kill me for reasons I don't know." She stopped, realizing she was crying and her voice had gotten loud. Wiping her hands across her face, she continued in a quiet voice. "I'm not trying to be ungrateful or anything. You know how much I appreciate what Jeff, Ben, and you have done for me. I know that without you all I would be dead by now..."

Estella reached for Jane's hand and held it.

Jane continued talking. "And I'm scared of that, Estella. I have dreams, things I want to do. I want to travel and be a novelist. If I'm not already married, I want to get married and have children. I have a past I'm still curious to discover and future plans I hope I can make happen. How do I do that when I'm always going to be scared that someone can come out and kill me when I'm out walking on the street? And don't say Jeff and Ben because you and I both know they can't protect me forever."

"I don't know about that. Jeff would want to if you give him the chance," Estella mumbled.

"What?" Jane said, not hearing what Estella had said.

"Nothing," Estella quickly said. She sighed and moved closer to Jane on the bed, hugging her and patting her on her back before separating. "Look, I understand that you're scared. Remember that they are also trying to catch this guy too and even though it seems unlikely, you'd be surprised what could happen in the next couple of days. This person, whoever he is, is human and bound to make a mistake. When he does, they will catch him. I'm not saying you should be reckless or anything like that. Not saying you don't have to be scared. Jeff and Ben are good at their jobs and there is no way that guy can pose any real threat when they are around."

Jane nodded. "I guess you're right. Maybe that phone call shook me up more than I was willing to admit."

"Totally understandable," Estella replied. "I'm mad at you that you didn't come talk to me. We're the only two women here and we should be able to tell each other everything. It's okay to be scared. And it's okay to not be okay. You don't have to act fine when you're not."

Jane gave her a half-smile and rested her head on Estella's shoulder, her eyes stinging with tears.

"No more secrets?" Estella said.

"No more secrets."

*

Estella stayed up with Jane, talking for almost two hours before finally leaving after covering Jane with blankets. She closed the door quietly behind her and was about to head for her room when she saw a light on downstairs.

Estella debated with herself for a split second about going to her room or heading down to find out what was going on before she found herself heading down the stairs.

When she got downstairs, she found Ben standing by the counter with a mug of coffee.

"Hey," she said.

He paused with the drink halfway to his mouth.

"Estella." He dropped the drink back on the counter, looking confused for a few seconds before clearing his throat. "Why are you up this late at night? The only reason I'm not sleeping is because it's my shift."

"Had to talk to Jane and make sure she was okay. She was still shaken up by the call and hearing her stalker's voice, but I let her know she doesn't have to pretend to be fine if she's not. Then we stayed up talking until she nodded off. I hope that was because it's late at night and not because she finds me boring."

Ben chuckled. "I really doubt she finds you boring. Want some coffee? It's still warm in the pot."

Estella smiled as she took a step forward. "Sure. Thanks. I probably won't be able to go to sleep after staying up this late anyway."

Ben reached behind him for another mug in the overhead cabinet. He turned back around and poured her some coffee, stopping when she lifted her hand.

"Cheers," she said as they clinked mugs.

For a few seconds after they drank, neither of them said anything. Then Ben cleared his throat. "I hope Jane's okay after what happened. I'm not really good at talking to people about their feelings..." He shuffled his feet uncomfortably. "I never know what to say to try to make someone feel better."

"Oh, come on. I have a hard time believing that."

"No, it's true. I end up just stuttering. I mean, I do care, I just can never find the right words. I guess it's easier to write words than say them sometimes." He nodded toward the stairs. "She's fine now? Has she said anything about the therapy helping?"

Estella shrugged. "Hard to tell, but I think yes. Although she raised some valid points when we talked. I mean, it's fine when you or Jeff are around. What happens if she's alone and something happens?"

"What if that happened to you? What if you were alone and you were attacked?"

"Me?" Estella glared at an imaginary foe. "You let that maniac think he can try anything with me. I'll dropkick him all the way to the middle of the Pacific. At least I'd try."

He chuckled, admiring her fighting spirit. "So, I take it you have taken self-defense classes."

Estella suddenly looked uneasy. "Not really. I mean, Jeff tried to make me go once but I didn't ever get around to it."

Ben frowned at her. "Women should take self-defense classes. No one wants to be attacked, but if you were, you would have the skills to defend yourself."

"Okay, okay," Estella wrapped her hands around her mug, feeling guilty under Ben's accusing gaze. "I see that now."

Ben sighed. "Sorry. I'm a bit passionate about the subject. When you've seen the number of female assault cases that I've

132

seen, you want everyone to know how to give themselves a chance."

Estella smiled as she took a sip. "You sound just like my brother. Yes, you're right. I'll start taking self-defense classes when—"

"Tomorrow," Ben interrupted her. "I can teach you and Jane the basics and some more. So can Jeff."

"That would be good," Estella nodded. "You're right. We should."

"Plus, I think it would help Jane a little with her anxiety problem. Sometimes it helps having the confidence to know that you're not totally helpless."

"True that," Estella replied, nodding.

"Maybe even teach you both how to shoot."

Estella's eyes went round with shock. "A gun?"

"No, a bow and arrows." Ben chuckled. "Of course, a gun. Wouldn't make much sense teaching you how to shoot arrows now, would it?"

Estella seemed unsure. "I've never really liked the idea of shooting guns. Especially...having to shoot a person in self-defense."

"Of course not." Ben leaned back in his chair. "Look, I can't make you do anything. But knowing how to shoot could save your life."

"I guess you're right."

"If you feel uncomfortable about it, we can stick to basic self-defense. Jeff might say otherwise."

Estella shrugged. "I guess it's about time. Jeff's been trying to convince me to learn how to shoot for a long time now."

"Seems like you have a very smart brother," Ben remarked with a smile. "You should listen to him more often."

"Yeah, don't go telling him that. His head's already pretty big enough as it is."

Ben laughed and finished the rest of the coffee but didn't reach for the pot.

"So can we start tomorrow?" he asked Estella, who was staring into her mug.

"Sure, but you have to talk to Jane about it. We could only do it after church."

"Ah, church. Sure."

Estella noticed the guilty, uncomfortable look that crossed Ben's face. "Let me guess. You've not been to church lately, not counting last Sunday, but you used to go when you were young."

Ben looked away as he shrugged. "There is hardly any time for that stuff."

"First of all, don't let Jane hear you call church 'that stuff.' Then make sure that you're ready for service tomorrow morning."

Ben frowned. "I know. If you and Jane go, then Jeff and I have to go anyway."

Estella chuckled as she got up. "You should want to come though. Might do you some good. I liked the sermon the pastor preached. I'm actually looking forward to it and it made me realize how much I missed going to church, and how close I used to be with God."

A thoughtful look crossed Ben's face.

"What?" she asked.

"Nothing. Well…" He scratched his head. "I kind of feel like something's been missing in my life, too. I used to be close to God when I was a kid, but you know, life happens. Maybe that's what I've been missing."

She patted his arm. "Maybe you'll find out tomorrow." She reached for the faucet to wash her mug but Ben beat her to it and gently took the mug from her.

"Don't worry, go on to bed. I'll wash these."

"Thanks." She smiled at him, then made her way up the stairs.

Ben watched her leave, then he walked to the sink to wash the mugs before moving back to the living room, preparing for a long night.

CHAPTER TWENTY

"Wasn't that wonderful?" Estella remarked excitedly as Jeff opened the door and let them in.

The minister at church had talked about trusting God to make a way when there seems to be no way. Looking at how happy and relaxed Jane seemed now, it was exactly the kind of message she needed to hear. It had lifted her spirit. Of course God had a plan for her. She just needed reminding.

"It was wonderful, Estella," Jane replied with a grimace. "But if I don't take these shoes off this very moment, I might as well say goodbye to my legs."

By the time they got back from church, Jane was starting to wonder why anyone would want to subject themselves to this kind of torture all in the name of fashion. She took them off and went upstairs to change into casual clothes.

She headed back down the stairs to check the fridge and decide what she was going to prepare for lunch. She was surprised when she got down to the kitchen where Jeff was frowning at the box of uncooked pasta in his hand, then at the pot of water he had placed on the stove to boil.

"What are you doing?" she asked after a moment of watching him, her lips already tugging upwards in a smile.

Jeff glanced back at her. "If you have to ask that, then I guess I'm not doing it right at all. Thought I'd start lunch."

Smiling, she walked forward and collected the carton of pasta from him, checking to see that the water was already boiling before dumping it in.

"It's just pasta." He walked to the island and sat down, watching as Jane began rummaging in the fridge for materials to prepare the sauce with. "You've been doing all the cooking lately, and I guess I'm starting to feel guilty."

"Why?" Jane asked, her brows puckering in genuine confusion. "I enjoy it, and it's the least I can do for all you've done for me. It's my way of saying thank you."

"You don't need to thank me."

"But I want to," Jane replied, her back turned to him as she as she started mixing sauce ingredients in the pan.

"There is no way that's Jeff cooking," Estella said out loud from the stairs. She ran into the kitchen and paused when she saw Jane in the kitchen. "Oh, should have known as much. Let me guess; you thought you could get Jane to cook for you and then you'd pass it off as your cooking?"

Jane chuckled. "No, Estella, it's nothing like that."

"Good, because I offered to cook, but he went all macho-like," Estella puffed her chest out theatrically, "saying things like Jane has been cooking this whole time and he wanted to be the one to do the cooking thing today. Probably trying to be romantic."

Jeff cleared his throat loudly, giving Estella a look.

Jane awkwardly opened the cabinets, taking out spices, pretending she hadn't heard Estella.

"I'll set the table," Jeff said, giving Estella one more warning look before walking away.

A few minutes later they were all seated and eating at the table.

"Ben, isn't there something you wanted to talk to Jane about?" Estella said.

"Yeah," Ben said, turning to look at Jane. "I was thinking of talking it out with Jeff first though."

"About what?" Jeff asked.

"I guess it's okay if we discussed it now." Ben took a drink of water and continued. "I was talking with Estella last night and we thought it would be great if we started teaching Jane and her self-defense."

Jeff gave Estella an 'I told you so' look. "I always told Estella she needed to learn self-defense, but she always found a reason not to go for any of the classes I signed her up for."

"Good reasons, Jeff," Estella retorted, glaring at her brother. "You know, like my job and school. I didn't have time then."

"You would have created time if you thought it was important," Jeff replied just as heatedly.

Estella was about to say something else when Jane quickly jumped in. "Alright, that's enough. If we let you two carry on, you'll continue going all day."

Estella paused and sighed. "Sorry. Anyway, I think it's a good idea, and Ben says he has some training teaching self-defense. I think in a way it can help us feel a little bit safer. Considering, you know, everything that's been happening recently."

Jane wondered what else Estella and Ben had talked about. She knew that not feeling totally helpless would help her feel a little better. "I guess after the phone call, I couldn't help but worry a little about what would happen if I should ever come face to face with the stalker. It's not like you can protect me forever. I mean, only God knows how long this is going to take."

Jeff stabbed a piece of pasta with his fork. "I was also thinking it's time we run an ad to see if we can find anyone who remembers Jane."

"We already did that," Estella reminded him.

"Yes, but just in the local paper. I was thinking something with a far wider reach online, and this time using a clearer picture too. We could post it all over social media."

Estella glanced at Jane tentatively. "I don't know, last time I tried to take Jane's picture she was not a big fan of cameras."

Jeff looked at her, as did Ben, and Jane glanced up from her plate to find everyone's eyes on her.

"Jane?" Ben asked. "What do you think?"

Jane finished chewing her bite of pasta and swallowed, thinking for a moment before deciding. "That I want to know who I am so bad at this point I don't really mind. I mean, I don't even know why I think cameras are bad. I don't know my real name, but every day I learn something new about myself. I want to know who my parents are, if I have brothers and sisters, and where I'm from. So yes, I think you should put my picture online and see if anyone recognizes me."

Jeff looked at her, making sure she was fine with the decision before continuing. "Okay, so I guess that is what we'll do."

Now that they were all finished eating, they each brought their plates to the sink. Jane began washing them, glad for something to distract her.

"What if... What if my memory loss is permanent?" Jane asked after a moment.

"The doctors said you'll gradually start to remember things," Estella encouraged her, patting her back, then taking a plate from her to dry.

"But what if I don't?" Jane insisted.

Jeff put away the parmesan cheese, milk, and leftover pasta sauce. As he turned to look at her, he realized she was a little pale.

Jane took a deep breath and squared her shoulders. "I don't know, but the memory loss could be permanent, and I think now is the time to prepare for that eventuality."

"The doctors said—" Estella began.

"I know what the doctors said, Estella. I also know that every time I try to think about who I was in the past, I come up blank except for those few things I've remembered. I can't even remember what my parents look like or if I even have parents." Her voice shook, and she struggled to hold back tears. She lifted her soapy hand and used her wrist to push a few strands of hair out of her eyes. Taking a deep breath, Jane gathered her composure. "What I am trying to say is that maybe I'll get my full memory back before we catch this stalker and maybe I won't. But I'll learn how to defend myself if I should ever come in contact with him."

"Here," Jeff said, taking the sponge from Jane. "Let me finish this."

For once, she didn't argue. She handed Jeff the sponge. As Jane walked up the stairs, Estella and Jeff exchanged a look.

A few minutes later, a knock sounded on Jane's door.

"Estella, I'm fine. Just tired," she called out as she walked to the door to open it, planning on doing her best to assure the other woman.

She was surprised when rather than Estella, it was Jeff who answered back.

"Jane, it's me."

"Jeff?" Jane's hand paused on the lock on the door as she wondered why he was here.

"Can you please open the door? I want to make sure you're doing okay."

If she let him stand out there for too long, he may actually think she was not doing okay. She unlocked the door and opened it to give him a small smile.

"Hey," Jeff said, returning her smile as his eyes searched her face. "How are you doing?"

Jane smiled wider, suddenly feeling embarrassed. "I'm fine. Sorry about that down there. I guess hearing all of you talk about it made it seem too real too fast."

"I'm sorry," Jeff apologized.

"You were trying to help and I can't thank you enough for that. You should come in."

Jeff took a step forward. His eyes took in the neat state of Jane's room and he realized he wasn't surprised. Then he turned to look at Jane who had taken a seat on the edge of the bed, presumably leaving the chair by her bedside for him. Jeff chose to remain standing instead.

He continued talking. "About what you said down in the kitchen—look, I'm not a doctor and I don't know enough about this amnesia thing, but I don't think it's permanent. You'll get your memory back in time."

"But what if I don't?"

"Then you take what you have now and use that to build a better you. I don't know and I can't presume to read the future, or in this case, your past. I know what I see now, and I can tell you that I don't think you'll have any problem becoming whatever you want to be. You even get to have new dreams and

141

forget about some of those things in your past that made you think you couldn't achieve your dreams. You could be a chef, a schoolteacher, even a lawyer if you want."

"A lawyer?" Jane asked, unable to stop the chuckle that bubbled out of her.

"Sure," Jeff said with a smile. "Imagine you in a power suit and heels, facing the jury and explaining why your client couldn't have committed the crime. Trust me, you'd have them eating out of your hands in no time."

This time Jane burst out laughing. "Okay, from the way you paint the picture, you suddenly make amnesia seem like this amazing thing."

"I was trying to say that you are amazing, and I know you can do whatever you set your mind to do, amnesia or not."

Jane went quiet as she looked at him. "Thank you."

"You're welcome."

"And I think learning self-defense from you and Ben would be a good thing. I guess I can admit I've been a little bit scared of going out after the whole boating incident and then the phone call." She grabbed the edge of the bed sheet and started fiddling with it. "Maybe I'll learn enough to take him down with a karate chop when he tries to come out attacking me."

Jeff burst into laughter. "What novel did you read that from?"

Jane smiled. "A movie, not a book. And if the movies are realistic, I could take out a whole squad of men with the proper training."

"You know, now that I think of it, you look like you could take out a whole room of men on your own. Just remember to smile at them first. That should knock them out for a while at least."

It sounded like a compliment, and Jane blushed slightly as she looked away. When she looked back at him it was to see him glancing at the stack of books on her bedside, including her journal.

"Have you ever had to draw your gun?" Jane asked sheepishly.

Jeff went quiet as he looked at her, wondering why she was asking. "Yes, I have," he finally answered.

"And... have you ever had to fire your gun?"

"Do you mean in Afghanistan or working for CPDU?"

"Well... both."

Jeff sat down in the chair beside her. "That's a loaded question. No pun intended."

She raised one eyebrow.

"Okay, that was a bad joke." He sighed. Did she really want to know about how many terrorists he'd hunted, the friends he'd lost, or what he'd faced in combat? Some of the criminals he'd chased here in Maine while working for CPDU seemed like clowns compared to those terrorists. He looked at her innocent face. There was no way she was ready to hear about what it had been like and what he'd gone through in the Marines. The sounds of gunfire, explosions, and his friends' screams still echoed in his mind, and he could almost smell the smoke and desert dust. "Well, most people are scared enough when they see the gun."

He hadn't answered her question. She opened her mouth as if to ask him more about it, then stopped. Jane suddenly looked guilty. "Estella said you were about to take some time off to mourn your father's death before going back to work at CPDU since you just got back from Afghanistan."

"I haven't taken any time off in a long time, mostly trying to log in enough time to climb the ranks." He shrugged. "I've always wanted to be a detective, and from the time I left the academy that was what I worked towards. It meant less and less time with friends and family. I wish now that I spent some of that time with my father. You've reminded me what's important in life, so I know there is no better way I could have spent this time. I'd rather be doing this than be on vacation anyway."

"I bet your father was proud of you."

"Thanks. I wish you could have met him. He could be funny when he wanted to, which was most of the time. He was so smart. Sometimes I wonder if my kids would be impressed with me half as much as I was with him. That is, if I ever have kids."

"I think you underestimate yourself, Jeff." Jane stood, and not knowing why, began to pace around the room. "I mean, you're strong, intelligent and smart. Plus, you are also funny, sometimes even when you don't want or mean to be. Besides, you're a cop. I don't know about you, but what kid wouldn't be proud to say their father is a big, tall, handsome police officer and Marine?"

Jeff glanced at her, his lips curving in a smile. "You think I'm big, tall and handsome?"

Jane hadn't even realized she had called him handsome until he mentioned it, and she blushed deeply when he did. "Um, well..." She wondered what to say as she turned to stare at the wall above his head. Finally, she shrugged. "Well, you are. So, I think your kids would be very much impressed with you."

Jeff smiled widely, oddly enjoying her discomfort. "But you really think that?" he asked as he got up and took a step towards her.

Jane feigned a look of indifference. "So what if I do? It's not like you are the only handsome man around here. Ben is also handsome."

"I know that." Jeff took one more step towards her, his eyes on her face as his lips remained teasingly curved upwards. "But I bet you wouldn't go downstairs and tell him that, would you?"

She looked away, moving her gaze to the dresser.

"By the way," Jeff continued when she did not reply. "I think you're beautiful."

"Thank you," she replied, looking right into his eyes.

Jeff found himself holding his breath and wondering why he had only said that she was beautiful. It was shallow compared to what he really wanted to say. She was a whole lot more than just physically beautiful—she was a bottomless pit of grace, wisdom, kindness, and strength that he found himself drawn to a little more every day. She was killing him and not even trying.

"Jeff," she said his name, clearly confused by the long silence.

He leaned closer to her and took her hands in his. Jane was so innocent, so precious, and it lit a fire in him when he wondered how anyone could ever hurt her. He ran his thumb gently over her knuckles, and she didn't pull away. When she held his hand tighter, warmth filled his heart.

Jane's hands were so small, so soft. Jeff's hands were worn from the desert, and probably still had sand and dust embedded in his skin. His hands could assemble weapons in the dark, had crawled through trenches, had tried to pull his friends free from the rubble and failed...

His hands had killed.

Seeing how different Jane was from him and remembering the pain of his past made Jeff's desire to protect her even stronger.

He heard her expel a soft breath. His heart pounded as his lips were within inches of hers. When she leaned into him, his hand reached to gently touch her face, and he kissed her. She pulled him closer for only a moment, then pushed him away.

"Jeff, no. Stop," she ordered.

Clearing his throat, he backed away, crimson embarrassment creeping up his neck as his ears burned. Clearly, he'd misread her. "I'm so sorry. I shouldn't have done that."

She shook her head, frowning. "I don't think we should be doing this. I should have stopped you sooner."

"I shouldn't have done it in the first place." He clenched his fists and turned away, angry with himself. When he looked in her eyes and realized he'd hurt her, guilt ate at him.

"We don't know who I am yet. *I* don't know who I am. I could be married with three kids. That's beside the point. I don't want to start anything like that until I know who I am and figure out my past, my heritage. My family. If we are going to build something together, I need to have a strong foundation first," Jane said, her eyes reddening with tears. "Or maybe that was my first kiss ever."

"Oh, Jane. I'm so sorry. You're completely right. I'll wait. I won't kiss you again until you ask me to. I promise." He backed away toward the door, guilt and shame overcoming him. Then words quickly tumbled out of his mouth. "I think I'll get to work on the setup for putting your picture online. I'll send Estella to come take a picture with her phone. When we took Christmas photos, Estella always had us take them again and again until she was sure she got it right and everyone was in the right pose, with the right expression and every wrinkle on our clothes at the perfect angle." He knew he was rambling, but his heart was pounding so fast, and his mind was so full of thoughts of her, he couldn't focus on speaking. He needed to stop talking and get out of there.

She looked away, arms hugging herself. "Look, Jeff, I'd really like to be alone right now."

Obviously. Why was he acting like such a buffoon? "Of course. I understand." He paused and looked at her, his eyes once again drifting down from her eyes towards her lips.

What was wrong with him? She had told him not to kiss her and to leave her alone.

Suddenly, he turned around and walked out of the room, closing the door quietly behind him.

He took a few steps away from the door and then stopped in the middle of the hallway and shook his head. These kinds of emotions were guaranteed to distract him.

She needed friends who would help her through this phase, and that was what he would be to her. A friend. She definitely didn't need someone telling her she looked beautiful and then staring into her eyes like some moony teenager. Remembering how he had acted, Jeff groaned and face-palmed himself, feeling as embarrassed as his teenage self would have felt. He hoped it wouldn't be awkward now between them.

How could it not be?

"Don't worry," Estella said behind him, making him jump slightly, causing him to turn around. "I still love you no matter what you have done that's making you look so sulky."

He was surprised to see a camera hanging around her neck. "Where did you get that?"

"It's Ben's." She lifted the camera, smiling as her tone became soft. "Do you know he is an amateur photographer?"

"Well, you got the amateur part right." He chuckled to himself, remembering how much his detective buddies teased Ben about the artsy shots of his backyard and nature. He was surprised when Estella pinched him in the arm.

"I knew you were too much of an ox to recognize good art when you see it. Ben's pictures are unique," she declared reverently, and then glared at her brother, daring him to contradict her.

"That's one word for it." He laughed when she gave him an annoyed look. "I'm just kidding. I don't know anything about photography."

"Of course not. Anyway, I'm planning on taking the picture outside. Some out back in the garden, or on the porch, even in the kitchen as she cooks."

"You know all we need is a simple picture that shows her face," Jeff said. Not that any photo of her could be simple.

"Every photo should tell a story."

"Let me guess; Ben came up with that."

"No, I did." Estella cocked a brow at her brother, then turned around and flounced her way towards Jane's door and knocked.

Jeff watched her go and chuckled. She was something else.

CHAPTER TWENTY-ONE

Later that night, Jane stared at the words she had just written in her journal.

I pushed Jeff away. I wanted him to kiss me more than anything, but something in me felt like it was wrong. The way he held my hands gave me the most wonderful feeling I've ever felt. He was so gentle, and it was so romantic. I think it was the most perfect moment of my life. And I ruined it.

I could be married. Even if I'm not, it's not right for me to get involved romantically with Jeff until I know who I am...right?

I feel so bad for telling him to leave me alone, but I also feel so guilty about kissing him. I feel like both options were wrong. What am I supposed to do?

He must feel so awkward and embarrassed because of how I rejected him. I wish I could have told him how much I wanted him to kiss me. Instead, I probably gave him the impression that I don't like him at all. I wouldn't blame him if he completely avoids me after this.

I've made a mess of things. Oh, God, please help me figure this out. Please bring back my memories so I can move on with my life.

Please give me a miracle.

Quickly reaching for the Bible in the nightstand, she opened it to the bookmark and began to read.

*

"You can take a break now," Jeff said the next day, and the two women fell against the floor, Estella groaning loudly and Jane laughing at her. They had started the self-defense training early the next morning and were using the living room, moving the center table away and pushing the couches back.

Ben and Jeff had just taken them through something Ben called 'exercise to stretch your muscles' but had consisted of pushups, jumping jacks and squats. In other words, tools of torture. Throughout the entire day, Jane had been avoiding Jeff's eyes. She just couldn't bear to look at him right now, and he was being polite by not making much direct conversation with her.

Awkwardness filled the air between them, but Ben and Estella didn't seem to notice.

"You said self-defense training, not evil dictator's boot camp," Estella said, throwing an accusing glance at Ben. Estella reached for her water bottle and took a long drink before she looked at him again. "Now, how does torturing us count as self-defense training?"

Ben held his hands behind his back, getting into teacher mode as he looked at the two women. "Because being physically fit is always an advantage when it comes to self-defense training. Lesson number one: always run if you have the chance. Don't let appearances fool you into thinking you can take on anybody, man or woman. If you are being attacked or assaulted, run if you see an opening. Actually, most self-defense training and tips are aimed at giving you enough of a window to make your escape."

Jane frowned. "But you just proved that we are not really in any condition to outrun a potential attacker. Should we try to incapacitate them before making a run for it?"

Jeff said, "If you think there is a clear chance for it or if you realize your assailant has already overpowered you, then you can use any weapon you find. Which brings us to tools you can use to defend yourself. Anything sharp like keys. Anything heavy: your purse or a piece of rock you find lying around. If it is sharp and or heavy, you can use it. Also, always carry pepper spray or a whistle with you. Anything to disable them for even a moment so you can run."

"I don't know about that. Pepper spray isn't always effective, and you could also hurt yourself while using it. As for whistles, most people would ignore a whistle. Also, a whistle would be a distraction for the victim trying to use it instead of trying to get away or win a fight," Ben argued.

"Well, it's better than nothing, right?" Estella countered.

For the next hour, Ben and Jeff talked about different tips that could be used in self-defense. By the time they finished, Jane could admit she felt more confident with her newfound knowledge.

"Why do I suddenly feel like I can take down a whole platoon of ninjas on my own?" Estella asked, punching the air.

"It's nice to feel confident, but be careful not to get too cocky, or worse, careless. Oh, the stories I could tell," Ben said.

Estella shivered theatrically. "Boy, I bet your ghosts stories were the best at summer camp when you were a kid."

Ben's lips curved in a small smile. "Well, yes. Yes, they were."

Jeff walked back to a small case he had dropped on the table behind him before he started the next lesson. "Okay, before we continue, we need to talk about guns."

Jane stared in horror at the gun in Jeff's hand. Yes, she knew that guns were a part of Jeff's job and that he'd had to use them overseas. She knew he carried one on him at all times. But seeing him holding it in his hand unnerved her.

Jeff noticed her discomfort. "Look, Jane, there is a psycho out there after you, and as smart as it is to have pepper spray in hand, a gun will scare someone a lot more and does more damage. It could give you the chance to make your escape and save your life."

Jane looked from Jeff's face to the gun in his hand. The small contraption looked so large in her eyes, and even though she had no idea why she found the idea of using a gun abhorrent, she couldn't deny she did. This was more than a feeling. She hated the idea of even holding a gun in her hands.

"I'm sorry, but I can't do this. I don't want to learn how to shoot a gun," she said, backing up. "No way."

Estella glanced at Ben and then back at Jane. "Look, I understand why the whole idea of learning to shoot a gun doesn't sound appealing to you. Trust me, even I didn't like it when Ben first mentioned it to me. But really, Jane, this could save your life. It doesn't matter how you feel about it, to be blunt. You need to do this."

At first, Jane felt offended. Then she realized Estella had a point, a very good one.

"I don't know," she muttered, a part of her aware of how annoying and whiny she must sound. "I still don't want to do this."

"Well, Estella is right. You really should do this. It could save your life. But we won't force you," Ben said, replying before Estella could. "Look, the whole purpose of this training was not just to teach you how to defend yourself if you're attacked, but also to help you feel safe and protected. Estella? Do you want to try?"

Estella glanced at Jane for a few seconds, then turned back to Ben. "Definitely. I still want to learn. At least the basics of it."

"Okay. For now, let's get on with the training we were doing before," he instructed them, smiling when Estella groaned theatrically. "Don't worry, you should enjoy this part very much.

I'm going to teach you about the parts you should target to incapacitate an assailant."

Estella laughed gleefully as she rubbed her hands together. "Okay, this should be fun."

*

A few hours later, Jane looked up from her book to see Estella walking towards her.

"What book are you reading this time?" Estella asked, taking a seat beside Jane on the couch.

Jane glanced back at the novel she was reading and read the title. She smiled as she placed a finger between the pages she was on and closed the book. "You know, you should try to read more books. Books are an escape from reality. You can travel across the world without leaving your couch."

Estella scowled at Jane. "I read."

"I said books, Estella. Not fancy magazines with beautifully dressed women that only talk about dresses and shoes."

"I'll have you know that I learn as much from my fashion magazines as you do from your books. Before we keep on rambling about books and fashion, you know what I want to talk about, don't you?"

"You're wondering why I don't want to learn how to shoot."

"But why, specifically?"

"But whoever strikes you on one cheek, turn to them the other cheek also…"

Estella stared at Jane. "Wait, that is a Bible passage, isn't it?"

"I'm not sure. Maybe it is," Jane said, also looking surprised.

Estella's eyes rounded in shock as she looked at Jane. "Wait, did you just remember something from your past?"

Jane looked just as shocked and also excited. "I think I did."

"That's amazing!" Estella cried. "Of course you would start remembering Bible verses. We should tell Jeff and Ben about this," Estella suggested, glancing back to look at Ben.

"It still doesn't really tell us anything about me. Lots of people know Bible verses."

"We can tell Jeff later. Now back to the gun thing—"

Jane lifted a brow. "Do you see why now? Even more than before, I don't want to shoot a gun."

Estella chuckled. "Of course I do. Just thought I'd take a shot. Okay, sorry, that was lame."

Jane couldn't help herself as she chuckled at Estella's more than intended pun. Then she remembered what had happened between her and Jeff—the kiss. She hadn't told Estella yet.

"Okay, I have to tell you something. But you have to promise not to tell anyone," Jane said.

"Yikes. That sounds ominous."

"Nothing like that. It's about Jeff and me."

Estella leaned forward, elbows on her knees. "What? What happened?"

"We kind of... Well, we kissed."

"What?" Estella shrieked, ignoring Ben who briefly poked his head out of the kitchen to see what the hullabaloo was all about.

"Shh!" Jane waved her hands in the air. "Keep it down! I don't want Ben or Jeff to hear us. It's awkward enough as it is."

"Sorry. Tell me everything that happened. I want details."

Jane told her about how perfect the moment had been, how they'd kissed, then how Jane had pushed him away. "I'm just worried it'll always be totally awkward between us now like it was today."

"If he cares about you, he'll give you space until we figure out who you really are. Don't worry. My brother might seem coarse and insensitive, but he's actually really sweet and sensitive, and very respectful. If you asked him to wait, he will. And I know he cares deeply for you. And that's putting it lightly. I've never seen him like this before. You've had quite the effect on him."

Jane smiled, blushing. "I really care about him too."

"So, don't worry. It'll all work out. I think he understands."

Jane sighed, and Jeff walked into the room. Had he heard them talking? Jane wanted to crawl under the couch.

"Well, I've got to...shave my legs. See you guys later." Estella leapt off the couch and scurried out of the room, suppressing a giggle.

Jeff sat on the couch next to Jane as she fiddled with one of the pages in the book she held. "I'm sorry for making such a fuss today," she said. "Using guns just feels so wrong to me, like it goes against everything I was taught. Maybe it's because of how I was raised. I don't know."

"Don't be sorry. We understand. And you're right, it doesn't tell us anything specific about you, but you're making progress. Be sure to tell your therapist next time you see her. Look, I understand that you don't want to learn how to use a gun. We just want you to be able to defend yourself if it ever comes to that. And hopefully, it doesn't."

Jane gave him a sidelong glance.

"Again, I can't force you to do anything. After this is over, you don't ever have to touch a gun again if you don't want to. I'm pleading with you, Jane. Please do this. It really could save your life." He briefly touched her hand. "It would give me some peace of mind too. It would help me worry about you a tiny bit less. You once said you wanted to repay me, and of course you don't have to. But if you really want to repay me in some small way, this would be it. Please."

The way he looked in to her eyes with so much desperation made her insides melt, and she felt herself caving in. He really was worried about her, wasn't he? The thought of him losing sleep over her pained her. And she did want to do something to thank him for protecting her.

He looked at her the same way he had right before he'd kissed her the other night. As she remembered the kiss, she quickly looked away.

She threw her hands up. "Okay, fine. If it'll make you worry less and to show my gratitude for all you've done for me, I'll learn how to shoot. But I won't like one minute of it."

Jeff smiled. "Thank you, Jane." He looked in to her eyes again for a moment too long, and Jane ignored the way it made her heart rate spike.

She shot up off the couch. "Well, I'm going to make dinner."

"Let me help."

"Thanks." Jane didn't bother arguing as they walked to the kitchen. It would be nice to have his company. "So, I meant to tell you I remembered something. It's not much. Just a Bible verse."

She quoted it again and Jeff tilted his head. "You're right, it doesn't tell us anything specific about you. But you're making great progress with remembering more."

"Which of your cases would you say is the most memorable?" She pulled vegetables out of the fridge as Jeff helped her make dinner. It wasn't the first time he helped her cook, and he was learning quickly.

"Oh, that's easy. There was this case of sex trafficking in an Amish community in Unity, Maine a few years ago that my partner Olivia was working on. Up till today that case still stays with me."

"An Amish community in Unity, Maine?" Jane wondered why those words rang a bell in her head. It was a sort of tingle in her memory, and yet the more she thought about it, the blurrier it became. She could almost envision the town of Unity.

"Sometimes I think about going back to that place. It was peaceful there, as if time stands still there. And in a way, it does." He shrugged as he looked at Jane. "You know who the Amish are, right? They dress old-fashioned and don't use anything modern, living like people did a few hundred years ago. They have this set of rules that they all must adhere to. Well, I was not a big fan of them, and I know for a fact that I wouldn't have been able to live by those rules. It seemed too strict for me, especially how they shun people for leaving. As far as their way of life, I could manage it for two or three days. Anything more than that, and I need to get back to the real world."

Jane nodded, not sure she agreed with him, but also not knowing enough about the subject to discuss it with him. She was going to be doing a little more research about the Amish at the library as soon as she could.

She had started to read the Bible more, not only to feed her soul and spend time with God, but to hopefully come across more verses she recognized.

She was definitely starting to get her memory back, but most of it was information she could not use. She still had no idea what her real name was, where she used to live before the accident, or who her parents and relatives were.

As they cooked, she listened to him talk about his time with the Amish, noting the slight sense of déjà vu it gave her to hear some of the things he said, like when he mentioned how they wore head coverings and didn't use electricity, or how they rode in buggies.

It also made fear grow within her, and she didn't know why.

"Everything you're saying sounds so familiar," Jane said. "The town you're describing, Unity—I can almost picture it in my mind."

Jane could envision rolling hills of crops, humble homes dotting the landscape, fragrant wildflowers, and a long, winding dirt lane that ran through the countryside.

Then the small room with the stack of books and one tiny, barred window filled her mind.

The pond.

The barn.

The farm.

It was all in Unity, wasn't it?

"Really? Then maybe it means something. Maybe you've been there. We should go there to see if it triggers any memories for you."

"No!" Jane blurted out louder than she'd intended. "No. I don't want to go there." Had she been held captive in the Amish community in Unity? Why else would she feel so much resistance to visiting a place that might help them find out who she was?

"Why not? It could help us finally find out who you are. Maybe you're from there."

"I said no! I'm not going back there." Jane shrank back, stepping farther away from Jeff.

"Back there?" Jeff asked, concerned, as he slowly stepped forward. "Did you remember something?"

Jane squeezed her eyes shut, the images circling through her mind like pictures on a merry-go-round. They almost connected, but she just couldn't quite put the pieces together. "I think... I don't know. All I know is that place—Unity—scares me. And I don't ever want to go back there."

"You think the Amish kidnapped you? Do you think that was where you were held?"

"Maybe. I don't know. It's still a blur."

Jeff took a few more careful steps until he was close enough to gently touch her arm. "Look, Jane, I know this is scary. But don't you think we should at least drive by to see if it triggers any memories? Maybe we could talk to a few people to see if they recognize you—"

"No, Jeff! I'm never going back there!" Jane cried, and ran up the stairs.

"Jane?" Estella asked in the hallway, but Jane rushed past her as her eyes stung with tears, crashing into her room and shutting the door. She sat down on her bed, palms to her eyes.

The memories of the farm and the room with the window crowded her brain, and tears wet her hands. Was that really the place where she'd been a prisoner? Just thinking about the Amish community made her stomach twist with dread and the hairs on her arms raise, and she trembled at the thought of ever going back there.

Even if the Amish community held the truth about her identity, she'd never go back.

159

CHAPTER TWENTY-TWO

The next morning, the group finished breakfast before continuing their self-defense training. While Estella and Ben carried on their playful banter about how well Estella would shoot, they hardly seemed to notice as Jeff approached Jane.

"Jane, I'm sorry about last night. I didn't mean to upset you," Jeff said, putting plates in the sink.

"It's not your fault. I know you're trying to do the right thing," Jane said, scrubbing a fork a little more vigorously than necessary.

Jeff rested his hand tenderly on her arm, and she stopped scrubbing, looking up at him. She had dark circles under her eyes, and Jeff wondered if she'd slept at all after her fearful reaction to their conversation.

"I'm not going to make you go back there, of course, but if you don't want to go with me, either Ben or I still have to go there and investigate. We need to ask people if they know you and show them your picture."

"Don't expect them to give you much information. The Amish don't like to answer questions from the police. They don't even report crimes." Her eyes widened. "Wow. I didn't realize I knew that. Or maybe I just remembered it."

"See? The Amish community will probably help you remember so much more if you let it."

"No." She continued her ferocious scrubbing, rinsing off the forks and moving on to the plates with determination. Jeff took his hand off her arm and started to turn away.

"Jeff, I'm just not ready. Last night I thought I'd never go back, but maybe you're right. I think I just need some time."

"Okay. Of course. You know, Ben has worked there before. He got to know the people. Maybe they'd be more open to talking to him. He should probably go while I stay here with you. If he goes to see what he can find out, maybe later on, when you're ready, we can all go together."

Jane took in a deep breath and nodded. "Maybe. I don't know. I'm not promising anything. You know, I just remembered something else. The Amish don't wear wedding rings. So..."

She didn't need to say anything else. Jeff could tell from the way she looked up at him in realization what she was really saying.

So she really could be married. Jeff told himself to not think about it. "Jane, this is your past and your identity we are trying to learn about. When you're ready, it's up to you to open up to the answers." He smiled at her, then went back to the table for the rest of the dirty dishes.

*

A half hour later, the four drove to a nearby indoor shooting range and put on their ear protection. Jeff was pleased and impressed with how quickly both women were picking up the tips and lessons he and Ben gave them.

When Jeff first handed the gun to Jane, she'd looked as uncomfortable and disgusted as if she were holding a dead rat.

"Here, hold it like this." He moved her hands around the gun, showing her the correct way to hold it, ignoring the way her hands felt under his and the way it made his heart pound. "See? It doesn't bite."

161

"I keep expecting it to explode or something," she said, holding it stiffly.

"It's not going to explode. It will kick when you shoot it, but this gun doesn't have as big of a kick as the others, so that's why I'm having you shoot it first. When you get used to this one, you can shoot some of the others."

"Okay."

He helped her aim the gun at the target. "You ready to try?"

"No, but let's just do it."

"I like your attitude. Okay, so don't stiffen in anticipation of the recoil. Hold it firmly, but relax." He put his hands on her shoulders. "Take a deep breath if you need to."

She inhaled. "Okay. I'm ready."

"Line up the iron sights so it's level and center. Then squeeze the trigger."

She closed one eye and zeroed in on the target, aiming for the center mass on the black silhouette of a man on the target. She pulled the trigger carefully, and the gun kicked in her hands, startling her more than she'd expected. She grinned and laughed, surprisingly feeling empowered, not afraid like she'd expected. "Wow. That was incredible! Let's do it again."

Jeff chuckled. "See? You did great. Now that you know what to expect, we can really get going. Go ahead and try again."

Jane squared her shoulders and aimed again, then shot several rounds rapidly until the magazine was empty.

She lowered the gun and looked at Jeff, astounded. "I didn't expect to like this."

"You're actually doing really great for a beginner." He took the gun, removed the empty magazine, and replaced it with one he'd already loaded. "Here, let me show you how to load the mags with a speed loader."

Jeff taught her everything he could about loading, handling, and shooting a gun in the allotted time they had. Jane had impressed him with how well she shot.

"Have you shot before, you think?" he asked her. "Because you're a natural. Your aim is great."

Jane's cheeks turned pink, and his insides warmed at the pretty sight. "No, I don't think so. It feels so foreign to me."

"Well, I'm not just saying this. You're really talented. You're doing better than a lot of people I've seen shoot for the first time. I'm so glad you agreed to this."

"Me too. Maybe I won't feel so helpless now. Thanks." She looked away and finished loading bullets into a magazine. She inserted the magazine into the gun and walked back to the shooting area. "Let's keep going."

Jeff grinned and gestured toward the target down the range. "Let's see what you've got."

CHAPTER TWENTY-THREE

After they returned to the house, Jeff approached Ben in the kitchen and explained how he'd told Jane about the human trafficking case in Unity and her reaction to it. "She won't go there, but one of us needs to go there to see if anyone knows her. Since you've already spent time there, I think they'd be more open to answering your questions."

"Maybe. But that was a few years ago, and I'm still a cop. They don't like to answer questions from cops," Ben said.

"It's worth a shot."

"Definitely. Sure, I'll go in the morning."

"Here, take this." Jeff handed Ben a photo of Jane. "Maybe this will finally give us some answers."

"Thanks. Well, it's probably about a two-hour drive from here. I'm going to go to the store to get some snacks for the road," Ben said and pulled Estella's grocery list off the fridge as Jane and Estella walked into the kitchen. "Anyone need anything else not on the list?" he asked, waving a piece of paper around.

"Oh, yeah! Almond milk," Estella put in.

"Almond what? Gross. Why even drink that?" Ben laughed.

"I use it for my cereal and my coffee. It's healthy, and it tastes pretty good, actually." Estella hiked her chin.

Jane laughed. "Never heard of it."

"Oh, Jeff, I just remembered you parked behind me."

"That's okay. Take my car. Here." Jeff tossed Ben his keys.

"See you later." Ben headed out the door.

"Don't forget the almond milk!" Estella shouted at Ben through the window of the kitchen as she waved at him.

Ben nodded to show that he heard her, even rolling his eyes a bit while chuckling. This was his first time getting groceries, and if he was going to be placed on grocery duty again, he was going to grab the list on the fridge and get out. Estella had added tons of items to the list last minute. It was annoying but in a cute kind of a way. As he drove out the gate, he found himself grinning.

They had spent an hour with Estella shooting one-on-one while Jeff worked with Jane. Estella was really impressing him. She showed remarkable improvement for someone who had squealed the first time he handed a gun to her three days ago. That memory had him grinning even more. He knew he was starting to fall for Estella, and apart from sometimes worrying what Jeff would think about that, he did not mind at all. Estella had a great sense of humor, she was kind, not to mention beautiful. He was already thinking of asking her out on a date. It was an idea he had been working on for a while.

He got to the supermarket and quickly went through the list, remembering to also get the things Estella had asked for. As he drove back, he started whistling a tune, gently tapping his fingers on the steering wheel. The road was free, as it usually was in this town, and the car steadily picked up speed until he was driving a couple of miles below the speed limit. Seeing a car in front of him, he pressed down on the brakes to reduce his speed. Rather than slowing down, his car continued at the same speed.

The brakes weren't working.

Panic filled Ben, and he reached for his phone to call the police as Jeff's car swerved out of control.

*

Estella and Jane were laughing as they stared at old baby pictures of Jeff and Estella while Jeff sat in the living room working on his laptop.

"Please tell me that is not Jeff in a dress," Jane said as she burst into laughter and pointed at him.

Jeff scowled at Estella. "Come on, Estella, why did you have to add that one? I thought you said you took out any embarrassing pictures."

"Come on, bro," Estella replied teasingly. "They're pictures of us when we were kids. They are all embarrassing. Besides, it's not a dress. Just a really long shirt."

Jane interrupted their squabble. "I think it's kind of cute."

"Of course you do," Estella muttered with a smile she tried to hide. "I bet you think all his pictures are cute."

Jane heard her but said nothing, just dropped her head quickly before either of them could see her blush. Truth was, Estella was right. Jane did think Jeff's baby pictures were cute.

She glanced at Jeff and he smiled at her, then politely looked away. A small shiver swept through her. A shiver that felt good in a way she wasn't comfortable with.

They were still flipping through the picture album when they heard a car pull up outside the house.

"That must be Ben," Estella said, jumping up excitedly and hurrying to the door.

"Hold on. Let's make sure." Jeff looked outside. "Oh. It's Officer Horton. He's probably checking in."

All three of them were standing at the door when they saw Officer Horton come out the door at the driver's side, and then Ben get out from the other side of the car. They knew instantly something was wrong from the bandage on his head and the way he gingerly held himself up on the car door. Estella was racing towards him, worry and anxiety written all over her face.

"What happened to you?" she asked immediately as she got to him, Jeff and Jane behind her.

"I'm fine," Ben quickly reassured her. "Just some minor injuries."

Now that they were closer, Jeff could see the bruises and cuts on Ben's face. "What happened?" he asked, glancing at Officer Horton, who stayed silent as he waited for Ben to answer.

"Got in a little bit of an accident. I'm totally fine, I promise," Ben quickly added when he saw the look of panic in Estella's eyes. "The paramedic made sure of that before I left. Officer Horton here helped me after the accident. The car is at the car repair place downtown."

"I tried to get him to go to the hospital, but he refused," Officer Horton said.

"I need to be here. Besides, the paramedics said I'm fine."

Estella took a deep breath and looked down to see that in her panic she had reached for Ben's hand and was now gripping it. As much as she hated to, she let go of the hand. "We should go inside so you can rest."

Ben nodded. As the others moved towards the house, Officer Horton signaled to Jeff to stay back. They watched as the two women helped Ben, who was capable of walking into the house on his own but knew better than to refuse the help he was being offered. When they were gone, Jeff turned to look at Officer Horton.

"Let me guess. This was not some ordinary accident, was it?" Jeff asked.

Officer Horton nodded. "I'm guessing Ben is going to give the women a short version of the accident. The two of you will have to decide exactly how much they should know."

"And what happened exactly?"

"Someone punctured the brake lines on your car while he was in the supermarket."

"What?"

"The brakes were sliced so that fluid would leak slowly, so it's not noticeable until it's too late. As the brakes are used, they become less effective due to the leaking fluid. The person did a pretty good job so we think they must have some kind of previous experience, maybe even as a mechanic. We've asked around but no one saw anything suspicious. The security cameras were down for maintenance, conveniently. Still, we'll keep on asking people and see if anyone saw anything at all."

"It was my car. I was the one intended to be injured, not Ben."

Officer Horton gave a heavy sigh. "That's what we suspect. This guy is getting braver in his attempt to cause Jane harm and those close to her. He's probably jealous of you being around her all the time. It means he is more likely to make a mistake. It also means he's unpredictable. I'll be sending a car to patrol here more often and more frequently at night. I wish we could do more than that, but it's the best we can offer right now."

Jeff nodded. "Thanks."

Officer Horton sighed. "Whoever this is, he is one really sick and twisted psycho."

*

Later that night after the women had gone to sleep and it was only Jeff and Ben in the living room, they sat down to talk about whether or not to tell Jane about the car incident.

"I don't know. The only thing it might do is scare her even more." Ben took a sip from the mug of coffee in his hand. "I mean, if I thought there was any advantage in telling her about it, I would tell you to do it. But I don't."

"Neither do I," Jeff agreed. "So, I guess for now we leave them with the impression the brakes failed on their own."

"You mean for as long as it would take Jane to wring it out of you?" Ben asked, smiling a bit.

"All it would take her now is one trip to the library for her to figure it out." Jeff sighed as he leaned against the couch and sipped from his own glass.

"You're lucky she's not a big fan of computers or the internet," Ben said.

"We have no idea how long she was held captive for. That might have something to do with it."

"It's one of the things that makes her special."

"Yeah, it is."

The look on Jeff's face had Ben sitting up and staring at his friend. "Is there something going on between the two of you?"

Jeff shook his head. "No. Honestly, I kissed her, and she told me to stop. She doesn't want to get involved. I was an idiot." Jeff shook his head. "She wants to find out who she is before even thinking about starting anything with me, and she's completely right."

"You know how they always warned us against getting too emotionally attached to a case? Well, even though we're volunteering to protect her, it still applies. It's too late for that, isn't it?" Ben asked calmly, a curious and mildly amused expression on his face.

"Of course not."

"Are you falling in love with her?"

Jeff opened his mouth to reply in the negative, then paused and closed it. Shrugging, Jeff stared at the contents of his glass. "Why does it matter what I want?"

"Well, to be honest, it doesn't matter what you want or how you feel right now. Wait this out. See what she wants after this is over and she can breathe again."

Jeff chuckled. "Dude, you're right. I've been a total idiot about it. Anyway. Enough about me. How are you doing since the car accident?"

Ben frowned at first, then smiled when he understood the reason for Jeff's concern. "I was shaken up. But it was nothing compared to Afghanistan."

Jeff looked out the window, memories of firefights and explosions crowding his mind. "Still. It's no small thing."

"After, when I realized that I had somehow come away with only a few cuts and scrapes, I became at peace. I'm grateful. I thanked God that I survived. Maybe going to church is rubbing off on me in a good way."

"Glad to hear that, man. I think it is for me, too." Jeff said, nodding slowly. God had protected Ben, hadn't He? "When I asked for your help, I honestly never thought it would get to the point where things became this dangerous. Thank you again so much for helping me out with this. I can't think of anyone else I want to be with me on this."

"Really, man, it's the least I can do for you after what you did for me in Afghanistan."

Jeff shifted in his seat and changed the subject. "So, do you still feel good enough to drive to Unity tomorrow or should I go instead? Since you were the one who was assigned there with Derek to protect Maria Mast, you should be the one to go if you're up for it. They know you already, so they'd probably be more likely to talk to you."

"You're right; the Amish don't normally answer questions from police. They probably would talk to me, but I probably shouldn't drive after hitting my head in the crash. The paramedics told me not to drive yet. Sorry, man."

"Do you think you'll be okay here with Jane and Estella alone? What if something happens?"

"Of course. I feel fine. And I would drive if the paramedics hadn't advised against it. Just tell the Amish that you work with me or you used to work with Derek. He's one of them now. That might help. Maybe he could go with you," Ben said.

"That's true. But he doesn't have a phone, does he?" Jeff asked.

"No, not in his house. He probably does at work. Just call in the morning. Now, what do we do about the movie we promised to take the girls to go see?"

Jeff's eyes widened. "I honestly forgot all about that."

"I guessed as much. What do you want to do about it?"

Jeff shrugged. "I don't know. I think we should cancel it. I mean, it's too dangerous now."

"You want to cancel something they have been looking forward to, and what reason do you plan on giving when they ask?"

"I don't know; tell them that it's dangerous to go into town tomorrow. We'll go some other time."

"Dangerous because someone tried to kill me today, right? I mean, you don't think they'll ask you why it suddenly seems dangerous now when yesterday you had to spend almost two hours convincing Jane before she agreed to go. Besides, wasn't the whole point of the trip to make them feel safe and in control, let them know that this stalker was not in control of their lives?"

"That was before said psycho tried to kill you."

Ben was quiet for a few seconds. "I think we should still go see the movie."

"What? That is a dumb idea."

"Hear me out first." Ben raised a finger before Jeff could continue talking. "If we don't go tomorrow because we think it's dangerous, then we might as well lock ourselves in here until they catch this guy."

Jeff thought about it for a long time, finding it hard to think about Jane being placed in any kind of danger. Even though he knew Ben was right. They could not tailor their lives after the whims of this stalker, running into hiding and cowering indoors every time he tried something. It was why yesterday when he looked up to see everyone idling inside the house, he had come up with the brilliant idea that they go see a movie the next day. Estella had agreed instantly. It had been harder to persuade Jane. Which was all the more reason why leaving the house and having a fun-filled day with no incidents was very important. She needed to know there was no reason she had to fear the world outside her door.

"Fine," Jeff grumbled. "But we make sure nothing happens and don't take our eyes off them at all."

"Stop worrying."

Jeff nodded, even though he still looked worried. "I'll stop worrying when we arrest this guy."

CHAPTER TWENTY-FOUR

Jeff left for the Amish community in Unity before Jane woke up that morning to avoid making her feel any worse. Since it was a two-hour drive, he wanted to leave even before Derek's work opened.

On the way there, he called Derek at eight o'clock, hoping they'd be open.

"Hi, my name is Jefferson. I'm an old friend of Derek Turner's. Is he available?" Jeff asked when someone answered the phone.

"Sorry, no. His wife had to have an emergency c-section at the hospital. He'll be out for a few weeks."

"Oh. Wow. I hope everything is okay. I had no idea Maria was pregnant."

"Last I heard the baby was born healthy and she is also doing fine."

"Well, I'm sure Derek wants to be there for her. That's okay. Thank you anyway."

Jeff hung up. Derek, a father? Jeff smiled at the idea. Derek would be a great dad. Then a pang of envy hit his heart. Someday, Jeff hoped to have kids of his own. He hoped he'd be half the father that his own dad had been.

Jeff didn't want to bother Derek after just having their baby, so he'd just have to make do on his own while investigating in Unity.

The familiar yellow street sign with the horse and buggy on it passed by his car window as memories of this place returned to him. He'd been in love with his partner Olivia Mast back then, who'd grown up Amish and had investigated a murder here

173

undercover. He'd asked her on a date at a restaurant only a few minutes away from here, and she'd turned him down.

Now she was married, and Jeff was happy for her. Besides, that had been a few years ago. She probably also had kids of her own by now.

Ben had been assigned to protect Olivia's cousin, Maria Mast, an Amish woman who'd been stalked. Derek or Ben would have probably gotten more information from the Amish about Jane, but hopefully they'd be willing to talk to Jeff instead.

Jeff pulled into the driveway of The Community Store. He'd always thought before coming here that the Amish community would be gated off, completely separate from the rest of the town, but the homes were spread out. Driving by, you wouldn't even know it was an Amish community if not for the occasional horse and buggy clip-clopping down the road or someone walking by in their traditional Amish garb.

Jeff turned off the car, grabbed Jane's photo, and walked into the store. This would be a good place to start.

A teenage boy behind the counter smiled. "Can I help you?"

"Hi. My name is Jefferson Martin. I'm an old friend of Derek Turner's and I'm also a friend of Ben who once worked here protecting Maria Mast." Jeff held up the photo. "Do you know this woman?"

The young man shook his head. "I don't recognize her, but the owner might. He knows everyone. I'll go get him."

An older man with a graying beard came out from the back room of the store. "Hello. I'm Irvin Holt. I hear you're looking for someone?"

"Yes. I'm a police officer for CPDU. I used to work with Derek before he joined the Amish, and I work with Ben Banks, who

174

protected Maria Mast here. I found this woman after she was hit by a car and she has amnesia. We think she might be from here. Do you recognize her? Have any women or girls here gone missing?" Jeff held up the photo.

The older man studied the photo. "Oh, yes. Derek has told me about you. But I'm sorry to say I don't recognize her. A few of the young girls were kidnapped when Maria was being stalked, but they were rescued and returned home."

"Do you know anyone else I could ask? Any information would help."

"Well, Derek and his wife just had a baby and are at the hospital, but you could go to Mrs. Johnson's house down the lane or Mary and Gideon's house, Maria's parents. Although—" Irvin looked out the window. "Looks like they might not be home. I don't see the buggy. You know, Mrs. Johnson's daughter Jill was kidnapped a few years back but also was rescued. Not sure how she will react to a police officer at her door, but you can still ask her. Liz and Simon also live down there." Irvin pointed to the different houses, showing Jeff where to go. "And my son Elijah lives up on that hill." Irvin gave him quick directions.

"You've been very helpful. Thank you so much, Irvin." Jeff shook his hand, then walked out of the store, hopeful he'd finally dig up something useful.

He got back in his car and drove up the lane to Mrs. Johnson's house first. He got out, knocked on the door, and a woman in a white bonnet-like head covering answered.

"Can I help you?" she asked.

"I hope so." He told her how he knew Derek and Ben, and lifted the photo. "I'm looking for this woman. I think she might have family ties here."

"You have some kind of identification?"

Jeff showed her his badge. "I'm off duty right now. That's why I'm not in uniform. I'm just trying to help my friend figure out who she is."

The woman's brows furrowed. "I'm sorry. I don't recognize her. Now, if you'll excuse me, I have food on the stove." The woman closed the door, leaving Jeff standing on the porch.

Well, that went well.

After figuring out the Masts weren't home, Jeff went to the other houses Irvin recommended, but either they weren't home, didn't answer the door, or didn't recognize the woman in the photo.

And Jeff didn't blame them. After all this community had gone through the past few years from the kidnappings to the human trafficking and murders, he could see why they didn't trust strangers.

Hope bruised, Jeff slumped in the driver's seat of his car. Still nothing.

Jeff drove past the store, and Irvin came over, waving his arms to get Jeff's attention.

"Any success?" Irvin asked, resting his arm on the car door.

"No, unfortunately. The people who did answer the door didn't recognize her."

"Have you tried Smyrna, our sister community up north?" The older man's beard bobbed as he spoke, his eyes crinkling in the bright sunlight.

Maybe this wasn't the right Amish community. Maybe she was from a different one.

It could be any Amish community in the entire country.

"No, I didn't realize there was another community in Maine. I'll definitely try it."

"Many of our families originally were from there. Years ago, several families moved here to start this new community. So, I have relatives there. They haven't experienced crime like we have here, so they are more friendly toward strangers. I'll call my relatives Barb and Bill Maas and let them know you're coming if you want."

"Oh, yes, that would be great. Thanks, Irvin." Jeff briefly touched the man's arm. "We appreciate it. It's getting late so I won't go today, but probably one day later this week. I'm going to try to get Jane—the woman in the photo—to come with me. Maybe it'll trigger her memory."

"Happy to help. I hope you find out who she is."

"Thanks. Me too."

*

When Jeff arrived at the beach house, Jane was waiting expectantly to hear what happened.

"I'm sorry, Jane. I didn't find out anything. No one recognized your photo."

Jane's shoulders slumped as Jeff gave her the bad news.

"But there's another Amish community up north, Smyrna. We could try there. Would you come with me?"

"Smyrna?" Jane said the word slowly, searching it for familiarity. "Doesn't sound familiar at all. Well, maybe a little, like I've heard of it before, but it doesn't mean anything to me."

"Well, do you want to go with me then?" Jeff asked.

"Actually, yes. I'll go."

"Good. Well, sorry for the bad news. Maybe the movie will cheer you up."

A few hours later, Estella stood at Jane's bedroom door.

"Jane!" Estella called out as she knocked twice on Jane's door and pushed it open. "Why are you taking so long to get ready?"

Jane sat on her bed, hands twisted in her lap.

"Please tell me you're not still worried something will happen," Estella said.

"No, that's not it. The Amish don't wear wedding rings. So even if I am Amish and I really am married, I wouldn't have been wearing a wedding ring when Jeff found me."

"Really? Why don't they wear wedding rings? Are you sure?"

"Yes. They think it draws too much attention to themselves, that it's vanity, I think. What if I really am married, Estella?" Jane asked, eyes wide.

"What if you're a convicted criminal? What if you're allergic to peanuts? What if you're an alien?" Estella asked dramatically, and Jane made a face at her, then laughed.

"Okay, okay. I get the point."

"Look, we don't know. That's just it. We don't know. So, don't live your life worrying about what you might be or not be. Just live in the moment. That's my advice."

"Well, it's not the main reason why I'm worried. I'm worried that going out with Jeff is a bad idea."

"But all four of us are going out together as friends. It's not like it's a date or anything."

What would she do if she was left alone with him and had nothing to say to him? What if he put his arm around her during the movie? She shook her head, realizing how silly the thought was.

"Jane!" Estella called out when Jane did not reply to her or even look at her.

"I don't want to go to the movies," Jane quickly said, looking down at her hands and not meeting Estella's eyes. Not even when Estella sat down beside her and placed an arm around her shoulders.

"Come on, of course you do. I know you do because this afternoon you couldn't stop talking about it. Is this about the whole stalker thing?"

Jane said nothing, allowing Estella to think that was it.

"Come on, Jeff already promised you he won't take his eyes off you the entire night. Besides, I remember someone telling me she wished the stalker would show up so she could spray him with her pepper spray and punch his throat."

Hearing those words made Jane burst into laughter. She looked at Estella and decided it was time she came clean, at least a little.

"I don't think I can do this, Estella. I don't know if I'll be comfortable in that kind of setting."

"I don't understand."

"What if I don't know the right thing to say, or if I fall asleep and get drool all over my shirt, and when Jeff sees me with drool all over my shirt he thinks I'm gross?"

"Oh, come on. That's unlikely." Estella laughed.

Jane glanced at her friend before sighing. "I don't know. I don't even know if all of this is real. I mean, what do I know about

179

love except from novels? And we both know that's not how it works in real life."

"You'll be surprised how things could work out if you give them a chance to."

Jane shrugged. "I don't know—"

A knock sounded at their door at that moment. "Hey, Jane, you ready?" Jeff asked at the door. "Can I come in?"

"Sure."

Jeff pushed the door open and poked his head in, surprised when he saw Estella sitting beside Jane. "We've got to go soon, or we'll miss the previews."

"Who cares about the previews?" Estella rolled her eyes as she glared at him. "And what would Mom say any time Dad tried to rush her out the door when they went out?"

Jeff cracked a smile. "She used to say, 'I'll come when I'm good and ready, Mr. Martin.'"

Jane chuckled. "That's cute."

"Just do what you have to and come down. Besides, Jane looks perfect as she is," Jeff said sheepishly. "Estella, you look perfect too. Now let's go."

Jane turned to Estella with wide eyes and a grin, feeling her cheeks heat at the compliment.

Estella shooed Jeff out of the room. "We will come down when we are good and ready, Mr. Martin. Until then you may as well go down and pace the floor like Dad used to."

When Jeff was gone, Estella explained, "My mom used to tell my dad that the most important part of any date to a woman was the time she took to get ready for it." Estella smiled sadly. "Used to drive Dad absolutely bonkers, right until she was ready. Then he would stand there with this goofy expression on his face, looking at her as if she hung the stars out at night. Kind of like the look I saw Jeff giving you just now."

"What look? I didn't see him give me any look."

"If you say so," Estella said as she moved Jane's hair from her face and tucked it behind her ear. "You need to stop overthinking things. Come out and have a good time. The rest of it is going to take care of itself."

Finally, Estella finished her makeup and had done their hair. While Estella was all dolled up, Jane had used no makeup at all.

"You look so beautiful," she said to Estella, admiring her friend in the mirror.

"Thanks. So do you. Now, what do you say we go out and have a good time?"

"Thanks," Jane said with a small smile.

"How about I put a little makeup on you. Just—"

"No. No makeup." Jane shook her head adamantly.

"I'm not talking of doing the whole shebang, we definitely don't have time for that. Just a little powder on your cheeks. Some lipstick and a little blush to bring out your color."

"I said no makeup, Estella." She stopped and stared at herself in the mirror. "I don't know. I don't feel comfortable in it."

"Okay, that's weird. You're like...the only woman I know who would feel uncomfortable in makeup. You think it's a sin or something?"

Jane frowned, wanting to say yes but not knowing why she would consider it a sin. Still, she shook her head. "I ... I don't know. I don't think it's something I'll be comfortable doing."

"Have you ever tried it?"

"I don't think so."

Estella shrugged. "Sorry, I don't understand. I know it's not a sin, and the only people that I know who don't wear makeup are nuns."

"I'm definitely not a nun," Jane insisted.

"Yeah, but you keep acting like one. Look, I'm not piercing your ears or your nose or anything. I'm talking about a little powder and mascara. Trust me, you can't even classify that as putting on makeup."

"No. I'm sorry, but I won't," Jane snapped, then paused to take a deep breath when she saw the hurt look on Estella's face. She softened her tone. "I know you're trying to help, but no."

"It's okay. I'm not going to make you." Estella patted Jane's arm. "Now, come on before those men outside break down the door."

Smiling, Jane took the hand Estella held out and walked out of the room.

CHAPTER TWENTY-FIVE

During the movie, Jane and Estella both sighed at the same time and Jeff couldn't resist rolling his eyes, catching Ben doing the same above the heads of the women. After an argument that involved him and Ben begging that they see an action flick and Estella insisting they were going to see a romantic comedy instead, they had ended up seeing a romance movie. Even though he would not admit it to his sister in a million years, the movie was actually kind of nice. The male lead took his shirt off far too often and most of the music made him want to punch a hole in his ear. The best part of the movie, though, was that halfway through, during a suspenseful scene, Jane had reached out and grabbed his hand. She hadn't let go since then, and Jeff was not ready to let go yet.

When the male lead lowered his head and slowly kissed the female lead, the scene slowed down for effect. From the corner of his eyes, he was surprised when he saw Jane look away from the screen.

"Something wrong?" he asked with a small smile.

She glanced at him, blushing a bit and grateful for the dark light in the theatre. "It's weird seeing people doing something like that. It seems kind of personal."

"You mean kissing?" Jeff couldn't help but think about their own kiss and how perfect it had been.

Until she'd pushed him away.

Jane said nothing, blushing even deeper.

"Well, I think they kind of have to put stuff like that in the movies or they won't sell as much. Besides, they kiss all the time in the stories you read."

"Not all the time," Jane said with a small smile. "But yes, they do in some. It's kind of different seeing it played out in front of you."

"Surely, you've seen people kiss in public." He paused, kicking himself for forgetting about her amnesia. "Sorry, I assumed you'd know about that kind of thing."

"It's okay. I honestly don't know if I have," she said, looking to the screen again. She was still holding his hand but didn't seem to notice.

The good feeling it gave him far outweighed the guilty one that told him he should let go.

After the movie, they got ice cream and walked back to the car. This part of Kennebunkport was practically deserted at night, so it was easy to hear the lapping of the water as they walked across a wooden bridge. The moon glittered on the waves and Jane inhaled the salty air, savoring each moment.

"That was so great," Estella said, shifting so she was walking closer to Ben. "Especially at the end when he rode that motorcycle into the church and stopped the wedding."

"Okay, why didn't he park the motorcycle outside and walk into the church as any sane person would?" Ben countered.

"Why would he park his motorcycle outside when he can ride into the church instead?" Jane added, laughing.

Jeff chuckled. "I see you've caught the Estella syndrome."

Jane smiled. "The movie was great, Jeff, and I am really glad I came."

"Next time we come to see a movie, we are watching one where things get blown up and the bad guy has done something worse than trying to blackmail a girl into marrying him."

"Men." Estella looked over her shoulder, rolling her eyes.

"So, Jane," Estella said as they walked. "Books or movies? Which one do you think is better now?"

Ben scoffed. "Like there was ever a debate about that. Books, of course."

Estella couldn't help herself. "Of course you think books are better."

Ben and Estella walked on ahead of them, lost in conversation, as Jane and Jeff hung back.

Jeff turned to Jane. "I'm guessing you were going to say books were better."

Jane smiled, tipping her head to look at the stars. "Like Ben said, there is no debate about that."

"I don't know, there are some things that look better seeing it than reading it." He shrugged. "Like that kiss for example. No way a book can describe a kiss so well that it makes you actually know what it feels like."

"Oh, no, no. You'd be surprised," Jane argued, her mind going back to a book she had read a few days before. On her mind also was the fact that watching that kissing scene had made her uncomfortable because it had made her go over every detail of when Jeff had kissed her like that...and how she wanted him to kiss her again. That desire left her feeling—

She still had no word for how she felt. The best she could call it was "ashamed", and no matter how much she told herself she had no reason to be ashamed, she couldn't shake it off.

"Want to know something?" Jeff asked. "It wasn't as bad of a movie as I thought it would be."

Jane replied honestly, "I guess I think it's nice to see two people who love each other get a happy ending despite everything in their way, even the man's denial of the feelings between them. The real question here is how do you know if you love someone?"

He sighed. "I won't say I'm an expert, but I think the best you can do is be honest with yourself and with the other person. Then both of you can see if there really are any feelings between you and if these feelings are actually love."

"I think I'll agree with that."

Jeff suddenly laughed. "See, this is why I like action movies. You have the bad guy and the good guy. Good guy beats bad guy and that's the end of that. No philosophical debates like the one those two are having right now."

He nodded at Ben and Estella who somehow had moved from an argument between movies and books to discussing the ending of the movie with Ben proposing several different—and in his opinion—more sensible while still movie-appropriate endings.

"Thanks," Jane said a little shyly to Jeff. "For the movie and keeping me safe. Even more than that, I had a great time with you."

"You're welcome," he replied. "Just glad you had fun."

Jane chuckled. "You know you don't have to stay with me around the clock. Ben is around, and I know he'll be fine staying home with me if you and Estella want to go out and do something fun."

"I don't know." He shrugged. "I don't think I'd really enjoy myself if you're not there with me." Jeff slowed to a stop and put his hands on the bridge railing.

"Well, I hope you'll remember that when you get bored of me." Jane stood next to him and leaned on the railing, looking up at him.

"I doubt that would ever happen, Jane."

It sounded like something that should be a joke, but his expression showed it was anything but. He looked down at her intently, as if trying to read her thoughts.

Jane's heart pumped harder. She was too close to him, and she fully realized that when she could hear him exhale. With the moonlight, and the stars, and the water beneath them, it was all too romantic.

She took a few steps back. If she didn't, she might do something she'd regret later, especially if she really was married. Her mind wandered to what could happen if they found out who she was, then found her husband. She'd already kissed Jeff, and if she did have a husband, she'd have to tell him that. How humiliating would that be? Guilt gnawed at her. She chewed her lip, deep in thought.

"Jane…" He was clearly about to say something, then stopped as if changing his mind at the last minute. "Come on, let's get in the car and get home before those two strangle each other."

Jane smiled and nodded, wondering what he'd been about to say. She walked to the car, Jeff following behind her.

CHAPTER TWENTY-SIX

The next morning, the four of them took a road trip to the Amish community of Smyrna in northern Maine.

As they drove onto a gravel lane, a horse and buggy drove by. Jane knew she'd definitely seen a horse and buggy before—and had ridden in one—but this place so far wasn't familiar.

As they passed large homes and barns, Jane stared out the window, nose pressed up to the glass. The sight of sprawling fields of swaying grass was comforting, as comforting as ocean waves, but nothing triggered her memory.

"Anything familiar, Jane?" Estella asked.

"I've never been here. I'm sure of it. The Amish clothing, the style of the plain homes, and the way of life is familiar, but not this town."

They stopped the car at a farm stand in front of a house. Several children played in the yard, and their mother sat behind the stand with two of the older children.

Jane stepped out of the car, inhaling the familiar scent of manure, grass, and fresh produce. She looked around, taking in the house, the horses in the fields, and the long stretch of road.

"Hi," Estella said, walking right over to the family. "We're here with our friend and asking people if anyone recognizes her. She has amnesia, and we think she might be Amish. Come here, Jane."

Estella waved her over, and Jane took a tentative step forward.

"Does she look familiar to you at all?" Estella asked.

The Amish woman took a good look at her and squinted. "No, can't say she does. And I know everyone around here."

"Do you know anyone else who might be willing to talk to us?" Jeff asked.

"So, you're the ones Irvin told us about," the woman said, scratching underneath her prayer *kapp.* "My cousin Irvin said you'd be stopping by. I'm sorry I'm no help. But you could try my brother down the lane that way or the Yoder family that way." She pointed, showing them the way. "Word travels fast here, and I think most of them heard you were looking for this young lady's family. They'll probably be happy to help."

"Thank you. We will try that." Jane smiled at the woman, and they got back in the car. Hope bloomed in Jane's belly.

Maybe someone here could help her.

After a day of talking to families in Smyrna, they hadn't gleaned any new information. The people were friendly and willing to talk to them, but no one recognized Jane, and no one had ever gone missing from that community.

Though there were several barns, there were none that she'd recognized, and there was no pond there either.

Defeated, Jane barely said a word the entire way home. In an effort to cheer her up, Estella suggested that they take her out to eat to get her mind off it.

"That actually sounds really fun," Jane said. "Let's do it."

*

After they'd gotten dressed and had done each other's hair, Estella reached out and took Jane's hand. "Come on, let's head downstairs and watch them make fools of themselves when they see us."

Jeff and Ben looked up to see Jane and Estella walk down the stairs. Smiling, Estella took Jane's hand, and they walked toward the door, the men stumbling over themselves to quickly get the door open for them, completely flustered.

"Told you," Estella said with a wink at Jane after they were seated in the car. Jane couldn't help herself as she laughed out loud.

Jane, Ben, Jeff, and Estella walked up the stairs at Alisson's Restaurant in Dock Square, Kennebunkport, to the second-floor dining room. The blue walls, beams stretching across the ceiling, and wooden tables and chairs gave the restaurant a charming look. The busy restaurant was buzzing with chatter.

Jane studied the menu, having no idea what she wanted to eat. Every single item on the menu sounded delicious, and she wanted to try them all.

"Made a decision yet?" Jeff asked, leaning in close to her.

Jane shook her head. "How can you choose one single thing when almost everything here sounds so good?"

Jeff chuckled. "How about you pick one today and when we come back another time you can try something else?"

Jane smiled and nodded. "I'd love to come back here."

After dinner, as they made their way to the car, still laughing and talking like they did almost throughout the entire dinner, Jane felt a sharp pang of pain in her stomach. She held back a groan as she wondered if she had indulged in too much of the chocolate cake they'd had for dessert. The pain subsided for a few seconds, and she sighed in relief. Then it came back sharper. This time she doubled over as she groaned.

"Jane." Jeff reached for her shoulder. "What is it?"

"My... stomach," she moaned, the pain so much now she couldn't hide it anymore. She suddenly felt something rise in her throat and managed to run to a nearby bush just in time, her stomach retching. Estella patted her back.

Jane turned away, thinking it was over, and Jeff helped her into the car. They barely pulled out of the parking lot when she grimaced and clutched her stomach.

"Something's not right," she cried. "This is not just a stomachache."

"What's happening? What's wrong with her?" Estella demanded.

Ben glanced at Jeff in the rearview mirror as he drove. Ben immediately pushed down on the accelerator and spun the wheels around, turning the car back towards town as he sped to the hospital.

CHAPTER TWENTY-SEVEN

Jane opened her eyes to see Estella sitting on a chair beside her. At the foot of her bed, Jeff sat on another chair, his head resting lightly against the back of it. From the small rise and fall of his chest, she guessed he was sleeping. She remembered Ben driving to the hospital and Jeff carrying her in, shouting at the nurses that it was an emergency.

After that she couldn't seem to remember anything. Her throat felt dry, and she groaned a little as she felt a small pain in her abdomen, but it was nothing at all like the one she had felt before.

Jeff heard Jane stir and he was on his feet in a flash, the sudden movement also waking Estella. They stood beside her bed. Jeff reached for the glass of water on the bedside table and poured her a cup, holding it up so she could drink from the straw. When she was done, she lifted a hand and nudged the cup back.

She was about to talk when Estella spoke. "You shouldn't try to talk for now."

Jeff nodded as he sat behind her. "Ben and I got suspicious and rushed you down here. The doctor said the food you ate at the restaurant was poisoned. It was some kind of homemade concoction." He paused as shock washed over Jane's face. "I know, it's horrific. Whoever did this to you is..." Jeff stopped, scrubbing a hand over his face. "Anyway, we were able to get you here in time and they pumped your stomach. The doctor said you're going to be fine, but they want to keep you under observation." He stopped as a look of anguish crossed his face. "What was done to you was so brazen and cruel. I don't know how it happened. The stalker must have snuck into the kitchen dressed as a cook or a waiter and put the poison in your food before it was brought to you. It was busy, so I guess no one noticed. I feel so…"

He stopped when he felt a soft hand grab him and squeeze gently and lifted his head to look at Jane who slowly shook her head. "This is not your fault, Jeff. What, were you supposed to go stand in the kitchen while they were cooking my food?"

"Well, I should have."

Estella sighed. "He and Ben have been kicking themselves all night even though I told them that you would not want them to blame themselves." Estella choked up as she lifted her hand and swiped it across her face to clean the tears about to drop. "I was scared, Jane. I swear I don't know what I would have done if the stalker had succeeded in taking you away."

Jane shook her head. "I'm… I'm fine," she managed to say even though her throat hurt. "And that's…all that matters."

The door opened, and Ben walked in with three cups of coffee in his hand, stopping when he saw Jane sitting up in bed.

"How are you doing?" he asked.

Jane nodded with a small smile to show she was fine.

Jeff patted Jane's hand. "I knew you were a fighter."

Estella couldn't resist rolling her eyes. "You should have seen Jeff last night, acting like a baby, running up and down the halls, hounding the doctors and nurses."

Jane managed to laugh a bit, not finding it hard at all to believe that. Then she smiled even more when Estella suddenly leaned down and hugged her, whispering in her ear, "I'm really glad you're fine, Jane. You have no idea how much."

Hugging her friend back, Jane closed her eyes, thankful.

Jeff sat by Jane's bed, the magazine in his lap long forgotten as he watched her sleep. The sight of her chest rising and falling peacefully filled his heart with joy. He could still remember the fear that had gripped him when she'd been rushed into the ER. He was still kicking himself for being so stupid and letting his guard down.

Before Jane had gone back to sleep, she warned him not to blame himself for what just happened. It was hard not to do exactly that, considering that this was not the first time Jane's life had been put in danger. She had almost died, and that was what Jeff couldn't forgive himself for. It was time he admitted it to himself that he was not good enough to protect her.

Jeff froze when he saw Jane blink before her eyes finally drifted open.

"Hey," she said with a croaky voice.

"Hey." Jeff grabbed the bottle of water by her bedside, moving his chair closer to her and presenting the straw to her.

Jane took a few sips, smiling gratefully at him. "Why are you still up?" she asked when he took the straw out of her mouth.

"You surely don't expect me to sleep, do you? Nobody comes in here without me interrogating them and watching their every move."

Jane was about to reply when she remembered what had happened the last time she was in the hospital and decided it was a good idea he was awake to keep an eye on her.

"Then I'll keep you company," she said with a small smile.

Jeff shook his head immediately. "I don't think that is a good idea. You should rest a little bit more."

She looked around the room. "Where are Estella and Ben?"

"Home, getting some rest. Are you hungry or anything?"

Jane smiled as she shook her head. "Don't worry about me; I'm fine."

Jeff sighed. "I guess food is not something I should even be talking about right now. You know, because of what happened." He looked away; his eyes downcast. "I can't believe I allowed that to happen."

Jane reached over across the edge of the bed and took his hand. "No, Jeff. This is not your fault."

Jeff shook his head stubbornly. "It is one hundred percent my fault. If I had given you my food instead when you said mine looked better, none of this would have happened."

"Why?" Jane frowned as she looked at him, trying to figure out how that worked. "I don't understand; is there something in your digestive tract that makes you immune to poison?"

Jeff's brow puckered in confusion. "No..."

"Then what difference would it make if you were the one who got poisoned and not me?" Jane asked, oddly angry at him. "Let me to tell you what difference it makes. It would be me sitting in that chair right now worrying about you."

She had a scowl on her face as she stared at him, and Jeff chuckled.

"What's funny?" she demanded to know, her ire at him still apparent.

"Sorry. You're right. I guess what's done is done, and nothing can change that." Jeff stared at her, silent for a little bit. Finally, he took her hand and held it in his, glad when she curled her fingers around his and held on.

"I'm sorry about what happened last night," he said in a heavy voice, lifting a hand to her lips when she tried to say something. "I know you are going to say I should not worry and all that stuff, but I am truly sorry. Sorry because you had started to feel safe again, laugh and smile. You were so carefree and happy at dinner. Then this monster took it all away."

"Not everything," Jane replied, shaking her head. "They weren't able to take the best parts away, like my new memories and spending time with my closest friends."

Jeff listened to her, nodding slowly to her words. When she was done, he looked at her, in awe of her strength and the spirit of hope she carried. What kind of life had she lived before that made her this steadfast and brave? It seemed like he was more scared for her than she was for herself. Her bravery wasn't stupid. She understood the risk and was ready to do anything to protect herself. She also wasn't ready to allow the fear of those risks stop her from living life.

She was magnificent. Even lying on a hospital bed in the dull hospital gown, her beauty was still radiant.

"The doctors said that you should be ready to leave sometime tomorrow afternoon," he finally said, his hand brushing her hair away from her face. "But we are not going back to our house."

"No...?" Jane looked confused. "Why not?"

"Because the perpetrator seems to have a pretty good knowledge about this area. Makes it hard for us to spot him or to track him down. Makes it easier for him to attack us." Jeff sighed as he looked at her. "I talked to Ben, and we decided a change of scenery would be good for you. It might help you recover and will hopefully throw the assailant off his game enough that he eventually makes a mistake."

"Where did you have in mind?"

"We're moving to Ben's house," Jeff replied. "He's letting us use his beach house. Hopefully it'll throw off the stalker and he won't know where you are, and we will make sure we aren't followed. There's a fence and Ben has good security cameras. Plus, it'll be good for you to get a change of scenery. There were people renting it for their vacation, but they're leaving."

"Alright, when do we go?"

Jeff hesitated. "As soon as they let you out of here. So, I've been wanting to ask you something. You know we didn't have any luck finding someone who recognized you in Unity. And I know you said you don't want to go back. But maybe if you just reconsider…"

"No. Jeff. Please. Drop this. Please, just leave me alone. I'm just not ready." Jane pulled the covers up higher and looked away.

Jeff stood up. Before walking out, he said, "I'm sorry. I just want to get you some answers. I'll give you some space. Forget I asked."

Chapter Twenty-eight

When Jeff said Ben had a beach house, Jane didn't realize that it was actually more like a mansion. The beautiful, massive house near the water was stunning. Jeff and Estella's house was also beautiful, but theirs was a normal-sized house while this one was much larger. Jane's stunned reaction when Jeff drove them to the house was so funny and priceless, he laughed.

They'd taken the long way to the house, driving down streets that were out of the way just to make sure they weren't being followed. Finally, when Jeff was satisfied, they'd arrived.

"There's no way we were followed. You're safe here, Jane," Jeff said as they got out of the car.

They went inside, and Jane marveled at the huge, beautiful house. It had high ceilings, white walls, and elegant furniture, with a massive window overlooking the water. Jeff showed Jane and Estella the room Jane would be staying in, then went back downstairs.

Jane walked towards the balcony in her room that overlooked the beach, lifting her head and taking a deep breath. It was dark out, but there was still enough light for her to see the waves roll and break as they reached the shore.

"It's so beautiful," she said, glancing to her side when Estella also joined her at the balcony.

"I know, right?" Estella agreed. "Too bad I only get one more week of this before I have to head back to work."

Jane whirled around. "One more week? Already?"

Estella nodded. "They've been so kind to me at work, but I can't be on vacation forever. I've been working there for years, and I've been saving my vacation days, just like Jeff." She suddenly pouted as she leaned against the metal railings of the balcony. "This would be a nice place to go on a romantic walk with someone special."

"So is your house." Jane chuckled as she leaned against the railings and looked at her friend. "And who do you want to go on long romantic walks with?"

"I kissed Ben," Estella suddenly blurted out.

"What? When?" Jane asked, gripping her friend's hand in shock.

"It happened when you were in the hospital with that whole food poisoning thing. Ben took me home and we were talking. I was shaken up. He made me tea and then sat with me in the living room. He was so sweet and really tried to make me feel better. One thing led to another and I suddenly found myself kissing him."

Jane looked at her friend, a wide grin on her face. "And did he kiss you back?"

"Oh, yes," Estella squealed.

"I'm so happy for you," she said, patting Estella's hand.

"I'll have you know that man knows how to kiss."

Jane blushed deeply, scandalized by Estella's remark. Her shock was tinged with humor since she knew Estella was just being her honest self.

Estella frowned. "But things have been so busy that he and I haven't had the chance to be alone or say anything about the kiss or anything, so we haven't talked about it. It's really awkward."

"Not at all?"

Estella stammered a bit. "I mean, we've talked and stuff like that. About the move and other things. We haven't talked about the kiss. I don't know, maybe it was a mistake…"

"No…no…" Jane quickly interrupted her friend. "I'm sure it's nothing. Maybe Ben is waiting for the right time, trying to keep things professional. I mean, you guys do have to sit down and talk about it. Maybe on one of the long walks you were dreaming about," Jane added with a small smile.

She was relieved when Estella returned her smile.

"Yeah, I can see that now." Estella paused, a gleam in her eyes. "Why do I get the feeling a horse would look perfect in this scenario. I would be on the beach…"

"…dressed in white," Jane added with a smile. "And he would be dressed in a black tuxedo."

"Yes," Estella joined in excitedly.

Jane laughed with her friend. Shaking her head, she turned back to admire the beauty of the scenery before them.

Jane had been writing in her notebook for about an hour, and her arms were starting to ache. For a moment she thought about taking Ben up on his offer to lend her one of his old laptops. She admitted that she loved the feel of the pen in her hand, the way the words seemed to flow out of her and onto the pages of the books.

She stopped and leaned back, closing her eyes briefly as she rested her head against the headrest of the chair. In her head she played out what she was going to write in the next pages, the scenes almost as vivid to her as if she was living them. A small noise startled her, and she opened her eyes to see Jeff standing at the other end of the table and reaching for the phone he had forgotten on the table.

"Hey. Sorry, I just came to get this."

"Oh, no problem." Jane sat up with a small smile on her face as she realized she had been so busy the last two days she hadn't seen much of Jeff in that time. "Sorry if it seems I've been too busy these last few days. It's that I've been really excited about my writing."

"Oh, no worries. I've been kind of busy myself." Jeff glanced at the phone in his hand. "See you later."

Maybe she wasn't ready to show it to anyone yet, but she had been hoping he would be a little curious and interested in what it was she was writing. He had been before they had kissed, often remarking that he would one day like to see what it was she kept on writing in that journal of hers. Even though she told herself it didn't really mean anything, she still felt hurt.

She looked at the floor. This was silly. He probably just had a lot on his mind, and why would he care about her writing anyway?

"Have you eaten?" she asked.

"No. Don't worry, I'll order a pizza or something for lunch."

"How about I make you lunch?" Jane stood up.

He shook his head as he stared at something on his phone. "You don't have to, Jane. I said I'll order pizza or something. Besides, I don't want to take you away from your writing or anything. Would hate to stop you just as you're getting into your groove."

Then as if to take the sting out of his words, he smiled at her. He turned around to leave, stopped and walked to the window behind her and checked to make sure it was secured from inside the house.

Was he mad at her? She thought back on the last few days, trying to figure out what she could have done to make him act like that towards her. Nothing came to mind, and as she glanced at the journal in front of her, she realized she no longer felt like writing. Staring at the book for a few more minutes, she finally gave up and got to her feet as she headed out the door.

"Where are you going?" Jeff asked, standing from the couch and looking surprised.

Jane didn't reply. She opened the door and walked out and to the beach. She headed toward a cluster of rocks and sat down, gathering her skirt under her as she sat cross-legged and stared out into the ocean.

She didn't need to look back to know that Jeff would now be sitting on the lounge chair on the porch. It was where he had sat down the day before when she came out here on the beach to take a break. Even with the distance between them, she still felt his eyes on her. He was still protecting her, still playing the part of her knight in shining armor.

Only this time it suddenly made her feel helpless, and she wished she didn't need him. That they could spend time together because they both wanted to and not because Jeff felt obligated to protect her. Would Jeff even want to spend time with her if he didn't feel like he had to?

She heard steps behind her and turned around.

"Hey, you," Estella said as she walked toward Jane, a glint in her eye. "What are you doing?"

"Just thinking," Jane replied, not sure she was in the mood for company.

"Alright, what is it?" Estella asked.

"What is what?" Jane asked, surprised at how easily Estella had read her.

"I know that look. It says you're worried about something but angry at the same time..." she trailed off and glanced back at Jeff sitting on the porch, his eyes scanning the beach. "Okay, what did my stupid brother do this time?"

Jane spluttered, telling herself to calm down before she asked, "Why would you think Jeff did anything?"

"Because you look worried and mad about something at the same time. That would take a really big idiot to make happen— my brother. Right?"

Jane couldn't help but smile at Estella's weird, yet somehow accurate, reasoning. "It's just—"

"Just what?" Estella prompted her when she stopped talking, sitting down next to her.

Jane glanced back at Jeff before turning to Estella and leaning towards her. "I think Jeff is mad at me about something."

Estella frowned. "Why would he be mad at you?"

Jane looked away as she shook her head. "I don't know. He's been avoiding me. Yesterday he barely said a word to me. Today, I offered to make lunch for him, and he refused. Then there is the fact that he is sitting over there when he could just sit here with me..." Jane trailed off as she realized how she sounded. "It sounds really stupid when I say it out loud. Sorry. I guess maybe it's all in my head after all. It's probably nothing."

Estella shook her head and sighed. "Anyone else and I may have said that, yes, you're imagining things. It's you, and I know you're not prissy or anything like that. I don't know why Jeff would act like that. Maybe he's got something on his mind. Don't worry, I'll have a talk with him and—"

"No." Jane shook her head vigorously. "Don't tell him I said anything. Like I said, it's possible I imagined the whole thing."

"I doubt that, but if you say don't talk to him then I won't." Estella glanced at her brother, glaring at him all the way from where she sat until Jane tugged at her dress. Ben looked over at them and walked over to them from where he stood about fifteen feet away. "Just give him time. He can be a bit dense at times," Estella concluded.

"Hey," Ben said quietly. "Sorry. I hate to interrupt, but I couldn't help but overhear you. But there's something I want to tell you, if that's okay. It's about Jeff."

"Of course," Jane said, motioning for him to sit beside them. Ben sat beside Estella.

"Like you said, Jeff can be dense sometimes about certain things. Even though he's a bit prickly sometimes, Jeff has the best heart of anyone I know. He'd do anything for someone he cares about. Do either of you know about when he saved my life in Afghanistan?"

Jane shook her head.

"Well, I know he saved your life and that's how he got shot in the leg, but he doesn't talk at all about what happened in Afghanistan," Estella said. "Not even to me."

"That's understandable. A lot of us still don't talk about it, and he's too humble to tell anyone. He risked his life for me, and he got shot in the process. We were ambushed, and there was an explosion and a firefight. A beam from one of the buildings fell and buried some of us in the rubble. He and the others who could pulled as many out as they could, but they couldn't save everyone. While he was carrying me to safety, he got shot in the thigh. He could have been killed. But he kept on carrying me and didn't put me down until it was safe."

"Wow. I had no idea my brother was such a hero," Estella said in disbelief.

"I was barely conscious, but I remember it. I owe him my life. That's why when he called and asked for my help, I jumped at the chance to come here," Ben explained, his eyes glistening with unshed tears. "He still blames himself for not being able to save them all that day, but they were already gone. There was nothing he could have done."

"That's incredible," Jane murmured, picturing the scene in her mind, seeing Jeff bravely carrying his comrades to safety through the gunfire, smeared with desert dust, not giving a second thought to his own life. He truly was a hero.

"He is a hero, but he'd never let on to it. Even so, sometimes his people skills aren't the best. So, I know he's being a dolt right now, but just remember he has a good heart, Jane." Ben smiled at her. "He'll see the light and come around."

Jane nodded as she looked back out at the ocean in front of her. She still couldn't push Jeff out of her mind, especially not after what she'd just learned about him.

It made her even more drawn to him.

CHAPTER TWENTY-NINE

For the last few days, Jeff had been trying to keep his distance from Jane, and it had been getting harder and harder. Yesterday he had watched her walk to the beach and sit on her favorite rock, lost in thought as she stared out at the ocean. It had taken all he had not to walk up to her and ask her what was on her mind.

The truth was that he was falling for her, and she'd made it clear she didn't appreciate his advances. So, to prevent himself from getting any closer to her, he had to keep his distance while still protecting her.

The most important thing right now was finding Jane's family, and Ben had gone to see if Jane's data came up in any of the missing persons' reports. They'd run DNA tests, but the results hadn't given them anything. They hadn't been able to find any of her relatives through it.

It was a long and tedious process, but with Jane's memory still not back, it was the only chance they had. Jeff hoped it turned up something.

He heard a noise from the stairs and turned around.

"Is Ben here yet?" Estella asked, her eyes on the door.

Jeff shook his head. "No. But he's almost here. A few minutes at the most."

She sighed as she walked into the kitchen and began to putter around. Their post on the internet had gotten them no leads, and the search was getting more and more frustrating, something he tried to hide from Jane since he knew how sensitive she got about her amnesia.

The truth was that without anything from Jane's memory to help them, it was hard to streamline their search towards a particular region or place. They still hadn't gotten a hit on any of the police bulletins they put out or any reports of someone looking for a woman that fit Jane's description anywhere. No one had reported her as missing and endangered. Since she didn't have fingerprints or DNA on file, it could be very hard to ID her by description or picture.

"Why are you still up?" Estella asked, interrupting his train of thought as she stood at the other side of the table with a mug of tea in her hand.

"You know I have to wait until Ben gets back until I can sleep. I hope that's decaf," he said, gesturing toward her mug.

She shrugged, glancing at the door again before she walked forward and sat down on a chair. Before Jeff could figure out why she was so concerned with who was going to come through the door, she asked him a question that surprised him.

"So why are you ignoring Jane?"

"I'm not ignoring her, I'm just giving her space." Jeff sighed. "She refuses to come to Unity with me even though it could give us answers about who she is. If she was with us, people would be a lot more likely to recognize her than just a photo."

"I know. She's talked to me about it. This is really hard for her."

"I feel bad about it, but really, if she just showed her face there, I really think we'd find out who she is. I've been pressuring her to go, but I just want what's best for her."

"It could traumatize her all over again. We have no idea what she went through. What if going there makes her remember something horrible?"

"I know. It's a chance she'd have to take. If she ever chooses to. She asked me to stop asking her and to leave her alone, so I've been giving her space. Maybe it was wrong of me to push her. But if I couldn't remember who I was, I'd do anything to find out."

Estella peered at her brother over the rim of her mug. "She's not you. Ever thought of that?"

Jeff looked at the floor. "I really shouldn't have pushed her."

"I know. You just want what's best for her."

"Ugh. This is an impossible situation."

"When she asked you to give her space, I don't think she meant for you to completely ignore her for the past few days. I have to tell you, Jeff, she's really hurting about it."

Jeff felt a pang in his chest at Estella's words. "She's hurting?"

"Of course she is hurting. Someone she thought was her friend, someone she thought she was having feelings for, suddenly decides not to talk to her anymore."

Jeff sighed as he placed his head in his hands. "I was trying to be helpful. I thought it was what she wanted. Also, by keeping my distance, it helps me protect her better."

Estella grimaced. "Okay, now I am totally lost. How?"

Jeff lifted his head back up. "Twice now her life has been put in danger when she was with me. It's like I'm blind to some of these things, and I think it is because I'm too close to her. Too emotional about this case and it's making me sloppy. You know, like how they say that doctors can't treat their family members or something like that."

Estella stared at her brother, blinking several times as if she was finding it hard to comprehend what he said. After a few moments, she lifted her cup of tea and took a sip before setting it back on the table. "Alright, so you're avoiding Jane because you think your feelings for her are getting in the way of you doing a good job."

Jeff sighed. "I'm bad news for her. She got poisoned on my watch, and I couldn't do anything to stop it."

"You did everything you had to do to stop it," she corrected him gently, pity in her eyes as she saw his anguish. "You realized what it was and took her to the hospital on time."

Jeff looked away from his sister, suddenly realizing how dumb his actions had been. "I really messed up, didn't I?"

"Big time, brother."

"I didn't know she was going to notice it. I mean, I tried to be as polite as I could be and—"

"Polite?" Estella's voice rose. "Polite is apologizing for walking in on someone in the bathroom. Polite is not what you try to be with real friends, much less somebody you have feelings for. Yes, Jane noticed your attempt at being 'polite'"—she said this with air quotes around the word and an eye roll—"and as I said before, she was hurt by it. Now if it was me you tried the whole polite thing with, then you can be sure it would take you a while and a lot of effort before I started being polite with you again."

"Can you please drop the polite thing?" Jeff begged, shaking his head when he saw her lips flash a smile.

"Just saying that Jane would forgive you if you're ready to pull your head out of the sand for one second and apologize to her."

"You know, you're starting to annoy me."

"So, you're going to apologize to her?"

Jeff nodded. "Yes."

She was about to say something else when they heard a click at the door and the lock opened.

"Ben's home," she said, eyes shining with excitement as she glanced down at herself before looking at the door.

But Jeff's mind was already somewhere else, and the more he thought about it, the more he agreed that his sister was right.

CHAPTER THIRTY

Jane hadn't slept well at all, tossing and turning several times throughout the night. Even the sound of the ocean outside her balcony that used to sound so soothing and relaxing felt harsh and grating to her ear. By the time the sun started to rise, she still had her eyes open and could not go back to sleep. Rather than get out of bed, she remained in it as she let her mind wander without settling on any particular train of thought.

Finally, she started to think of her writing, her mind going over the work she had done the day before and plotting out what she was going to write today. Thinking of her book finally calmed her down. Soon her mind was racing as she began to feel inspired to write. She lifted her head and glanced at the table beside her bed before she realized she had forgotten to bring her journals to her room with her.

For a moment she thought of going downstairs to get them. The possibility of seeing Jeff with that courteous smile on his face and the way he ignored her made all the inspiration she was feeling a few seconds ago go down the drain. Finally, she admonished herself and got to her feet, telling herself all she was going to do was head downstairs and grab her journals then come right back. Mind made up, she got to her feet, slipped her feet into her slippers and went to the bathroom to brush her teeth and splash water on her face.

She had no plans to talk to Jeff. But on the off chance that he did stop to talk to her, then she didn't want her morning breath to be the reason why he didn't.

Face cleaned and mouth minty, she headed down the stairs. It was easy to see that the living room, especially the couch in the corner that Jeff loved to sit in was empty. Jane told herself the small feeling of disappointment she felt was imagined and not real. She climbed down the last step and turned to walk into the dining room and was surprised to see Estella crouched down on the floor and looking at something. Before she could say anything, her eyes first drifted to where she kept her journals. One of the journals was missing.

"Jane!" Estella whirled around, surprised to see Jane standing behind her.

Jane already had an idea what she would see when she looked at what had kept Estella's attention on the floor, but she was still hurt and surprised when she saw her missing journal open to one of her entries. From the look of guilt on Estella's eyes it was clear her friend also knew she had messed up.

Estella quickly got to her feet, the journal in her hand. "I didn't know you were awake."

For a moment, Jane said nothing, not entirely sure what she should say or how to react to Estella's invasion of her privacy. Estella beat her to it.

"I'm really sorry for reading your stories, Jane." She looked embarrassed as she stood there holding the journal. "I had no idea you were behind me... No, no. That is no excuse for what I did, and I promise if there was a way to undo it, I would."

Jane said nothing, and it was clear that her silence was unnerving to Estella.

"I promise I wasn't intentionally trying to read the book or anything like that. I was clearing the table when the whole stack fell over and this book fell open. I guess I saw the first line and I became interested in the story you were writing..."

Estella trailed off, no idea what else to say. Then Jane finally sighed as she took a step forward.

"Estella, this was really personal and private. It's my journal. I didn't want anyone to read it." Jane crossed her arms.

Estella quickly covered the distance between them. "And I promise I wasn't trying to spy on you or anything like that. I thought it was a story. I didn't realize it was your journal."

"Well, it is a story, but I wrote it in my journal. What else did you see?" Heat flooded Jane's cheeks as she remembered the private thoughts she'd recorded in the journal about her feelings and experiences. She'd wrote about her fears, her hopes, and her wildest dreams. She didn't want to share those with anyone yet.

Jane took the journal from Estella's hand.

"All I saw was a few pages of the story. That's it, I promise," Estella said, reaching for Jane's arm. "Jane, I'm so sorry. I didn't mean to intrude. I shouldn't have done that."

Embarrassment overcoming her, Jane turned and ran to her room, closing the door. She thumbed through the pages, her heart pounding as her eyes skimmed over her secret thoughts that covered the pages. Had Estella really only seen the few pages she'd mentioned, or had she read more? Had Jeff or Ben seen it?

So much of what Jane had written had been about Jeff. She'd crawl under her bed in embarrassment if Jeff had seen what she'd written about him.

A soft knock sounded on Jane's door.

"Jane? It's me. Can I come in?"

Jane ignored her. Tears pricked her eyes, and she worried that if she spoke, she'd come undone.

"Okay, well... I'll go, but I want you to know I'm truly sorry."

Jane listened to Estella's footsteps as she went back downstairs.

A few hours later, Jane awoke to someone hammering outside. Yawning, she realized she'd fallen asleep on her bed holding her journal.

Now that she'd had time to think about it and sleep on it, her reaction to Estella reading her story felt silly.

Jane shook her head. Estella was her best friend, maybe the only best friend she'd ever had in her life. She should trust her.

Jane rubbed her eyes and meandered downstairs. Estella was cleaning the kitchen when Jane walked in.

"Estella…"

"Oh, Jane. I feel terrible about what happened."

"I know you would never intentionally try to spy on me," Jane said as she took a seat at the table and opened the journal to the last page she had written. "If you say you didn't read anything else beside the few pages of that story, I believe you. Even if you did, you're my best friend, and I shouldn't be so afraid to tell you things I wrote about."

"Like your feelings for my brother?" Estella looked at her intently, her eyebrows raised.

"Maybe."

Estella laughed. "I already know about that."

Jane chuckled. "But when I write about it, it's so much more detailed than when I talk about it. I guess I'm better at saying what's in my heart on paper than by speaking. About the story— in a way, I guess I have been too scared of what anyone who read it would think, and that is why I haven't shown it to anyone. Now that you've read it, I can ask. What do you think?"

Estella's eyes rounded in excitement. "Are you kidding me? It was amazing. I mean, the first sentence on that page alone had

214

me curious and eager to continue reading. I had no idea you wrote that well."

Jane blushed a bit, embarrassed by Estella's praise. "I've had the idea for a while now, and I have been writing steadily ever since. I know, it's not like professional or anything like that…"

"I don't know about professional," Estella interrupted her, "but I was amazed by what I saw. Actually, if I want to be honest, the first page may have opened accidentally, but I opened the second one myself."

Jane smiled. "Alright, that sounds like a really good compliment, and I'll take it."

Estella nodded. "And if you're still confused about if the story looks professional, you can get Ben to help you."

Jane looked down at the journal, her finger tracing the gold decal emblazoned on the cover. "That was my plan when I first started. Write something down and ask Ben if he thought it was any good. Then I started writing, and I guess I became too scared he would think it was no good, so I didn't show it to him."

Estella laughed as she hugged Jane quickly. "The Ben I know is no fool, and only a fool would think that story is no good. Just as a warning, if you don't want me to read that story from the beginning then you better hide those books very well."

Jane chuckled. "Then I guess I have to remember to conveniently forget them here tomorrow morning again."

The two women burst into laughter, and they were still laughing when Jeff walked into the room.

A few seconds of awkward silence followed as Jeff and Jane avoided looking at each other. Unable to take it any longer, Jane grabbed her journals and then, holding them close to her chest, turned around.

"I'm going to go work on my book," she said quietly to Estella and headed towards the stairs.

Estella glared at Jeff, nodding towards Jane in a gesture that told him now was the time to do something. Jeff looked away and pretended not to see anything.

"Idiot," Estella muttered as she shook her head and followed Jane up the stairs.

Back in the living room, Jeff decided he had little reason to argue with that assessment. He really was an idiot.

CHAPTER THIRTY-ONE

Ben smiled at Estella, noting the pink on her cheeks as he looked down at her. It was almost midnight, and they were the only ones still awake, Jeff and Jane somehow deciding to spend most of the day in their rooms like they had the day before.

He had been very busy the last few days, going to the station to look at photos of missing persons and talk with some of his buddies about Jane's case. An idea had popped into his head the day before that he was testing out. He needed more time before he was ready to share it. For now, though, he was having the best time of his life with Estella in his arms.

"I wonder what Jeff would think if he came down here and saw us like this," Estella said, snuggling closer to Ben.

Ben chuckled. "I have no idea how he would react, but I'm going to guess that he wouldn't exactly be jumping for joy."

"Why not?"

Ben looked down at her, one eyebrow raised. "Well, you're his sister—"

"His very grownup sister who is a woman and is old enough to decide what she wants for herself," Estella added, scowling at no one in particular.

"Yeah, but you're still his little sister. Trust me, he won't be exactly pleased at first."

"But he won't have a choice but to be happy for me."

Ben nodded, his lips curving in a small smile. "I guess he won't have a choice. I know he would be anyways."

They kissed briefly before breaking apart, and she settled deeper into him.

"You talked to Jane yet?" Estella asked him. "Did she show you her stories?"

"Yeah, she showed them to me yesterday before dinner." He paused when she turned around to look at him.

"What do you think?"

Ben smiled at the excitement in Estella's voice. "She's definitely got a talent for words and is very creative in her scenes."

"I knew it!" Estella exclaimed. "That is what I was telling her. She's, like, really good."

Ben nodded. "That she is, and that is what I told her. She asked me to give her some tips, and I pointed out some things she may want to take note of. She's supposed to show me the first draft when she is done with it today."

Estella had a goofy smile on her face. "Can you believe my friend is an amazing writer?"

Ben chuckled.

"I mean, she cooks, she writes, she's funny." She suddenly grimaced. "Sometimes I wish I could wrap the truth around a rock and hit my brother on the head with it."

"So, he's told you about that too?"

Estella scoffed. "Like he needed to tell me before I knew. He's my brother." She paused and stared at him. "Wait, he's told you about the thing with him and Jane."

Ben shrugged. "Well, from what he's told me, there's nothing between him and her yet—"

"Because he won't do anything about it," Estella said.

Ben chuckled as he looked in the direction of the steps. "Thank you for announcing that to the world."

"Sorry," Estella replied with a sheepish smile. "He just annoys me sometimes."

"Yeah, and no matter how annoying he is, at the end of the day it has to be his decision."

Estella sighed. "I know."

"Don't worry. Jeff may be smart in some things and dumb about others. But I know that even he knows a good thing when he sees one, and he won't let it slip out of his hands." He smiled and leaned towards her. "I know I didn't."

Estella blushed as she looked at him, unable to stop herself from wanting to kiss him again.

"So, I'm the best thing in your life?"

"Didn't know I'd need to say it out loud, but if you want me to then I will. Yes, Estella Martin, you're the best thing in my life." He paused, his hands reaching for hers as he closed his fingers around her palm.

With her arms around Ben, Estella still couldn't help but think of her brother and best friend. "He better not let her get away."

Ben hugged her harder. "He won't."

*

The next day, Jeff looked out the window and saw Jane standing on the rocks, her hands folded as she stared out at the ocean. His first thought was that he really did miss talking to her. She'd been spending a lot of time in her room. Of course, it was not lost to him that ever since the day he had replied to her offer to make lunch for him so cruelly, she had started to keep herself locked away in her room. While that made it easy for him to keep his space from her, it also meant that he couldn't apologize for acting like an idiot. Even now he felt reluctant to go out there to her, not sure what he would say.

She was wearing a sleeveless dress, her arms wrapped around herself. She was probably chilly out there in the wind. Hesitation forgotten, Jeff jumped to his feet and quickly grabbed a jacket from inside the closet by the door. He made his way across to her.

"Hey," Jeff greeted her when he got to the rocks, coming closer until he was standing a few feet away from her.

"Hey," Jane replied sullenly, not bothering to look at him.

"I brought you a jacket." He lifted the jacket and presented it awkwardly to her. "It's windy out here."

"Don't worry about me; I'm fine." Jane looked stubbornly ahead.

"I can see you shivering from where I'm standing, Jane. There is no way you can convince me that you're not cold."

"I said I am doing fine. You can worry about something or someone else." Jane heard the sulkiness in her voice but couldn't stop it. Hating him even more for making her feel that way, she took a step forward and sat down on the rocks.

"Alright, if you're going to be stubborn about it..."

Jeff threw the jacket around her shoulder, arranging it so it covered her arms. Jane immediately shrugged it off, looking away when Jeff made an exasperated noise low in his throat. He picked up the jacket and again placed it around her shoulders. Once again, Jane shrugged it off, this time going as far as to get up from where she was sitting and moving away from the jacket and the frustrated man who watched her with a shocked expression on his face.

"What's wrong with you?" Jeff asked, about ready to bundle her into the jacket.

For a split second, Jane considered not answering that question. Then she gave up as she whirled around and pointed an accusing finger at him.

"What's wrong with me? What's wrong with *you*?"

Jeff frowned. "What does that mean? I saw you out here feeling cold and brought you a jacket. How—"

"No," Jane interrupted him. "You don't get to do that. You don't get to ignore me like I was the plague or something, treat me like I somehow wronged you, then not even talk to me long enough for me to find out what I may have done. You don't get to treat my offer to cook lunch for you like I was offering to feed you worms and then show that you had no interest in me and what I was doing. You don't get to do all of that and then come out here trying to play the hero. I don't need a hero."

Jeff stared at her, shocked as much by the vehemence behind her words as he was by the actual words themselves. He had no reply to her accusation since everything she said was true. Looking at her standing in front of him, so close he could reach out and touch her face and yet so far, he felt like they were standing on opposite sides of a chasm, Jeff knew he had truly messed up.

"Jane..." He took a step forward, stopping when she took one back away from him. He took a deep breath, deciding that this was a case where he could only hope the truth would set him free. "I was trying to give you space. In the hospital, you asked me to leave you alone."

"Oh...I'm sorry. I said I wanted you to leave me alone, but I didn't really mean ignoring me completely. I just wanted you to stop bugging me about going to Unity for five minutes."

"I guess I took it literally."

"I'm sorry. I really didn't mean it like that."

"I'm sorry too, Jane. I didn't mean to hurt you. And I shouldn't have pushed you so hard about going to Unity."

"Well...About that. I've really been thinking about Unity the past few days, and I talked to Estella about it. She had some really good points. I've decided to go with you. I want to go to Unity with you to find my family."

Her family. That was a heavy word. It hung in the air like humidity.

She continued, "I know it could trigger terrible memories for me, but it's a chance I'm willing to take. If I never go back, I might never know who I am. But if I do go back, then there's a chance I might. I'll never know until I go there."

Jeff wanted to throw his arms around her and twirl her around. Instead, he smiled in admiration and patted her arm. "Jane, I'm so happy. That's great news."

She beamed and nodded. "I know you and Estella will be there to help me."

"Good. And of course, I'll be with you every step of the way." Jeff patted her hand, and she held it tightly.

Did she have a family in Unity, maybe parents or siblings? Grandparents?

A boyfriend? A husband? Children?

Jane pulled her hand away, shame creeping up her neck. She'd made the huge mistake of letting this go too far.

Jeff said, "Of course we will. But there's another reason I was avoiding you. I was scared that me being close to you was putting you in danger."

Jane paused, her lips curving in a frown as she stared at him. "What?"

"I said—"

"I heard what you said. I am trying to figure out how it even makes any sense."

Jeff sighed, turning around to look at the ocean. "Two times now your life has been put in serious danger. That time at the boat and the second time was when you got poisoned at the restaurant. Two times when I was there and couldn't do anything to help you. Two times when I was there and couldn't even see enough to know that you were in danger."

"Jeff..." Jane said, taking a step towards him as she recognized the look on his face. Anguish, pain, and self-loathing. He was blaming himself yet again, only this time he was not blaming himself so much as he was blaming the relationship between them. Somehow, this was even worse to Jane. "Of course you were there for me. I mean, the fact that I am standing here is proof that you were indeed there for me."

"I don't know, Jane, it seems the way I feel about you blinds me to things I should see, precautions I should take..." He trailed off as he stared out at the ocean. "I thought that if I took a step back, I'd be able to protect you better. I swear, I had no intention of hurting you."

Jane heard all he said, but her mind grabbed a hold of one phrase and wouldn't let it go. "The way you feel about me?"

Jeff turned around to look at her, deciding that it was now or never for him. "Yes, Jane, the way I feel about you."

"And how do you feel about me?" she asked, her voice quiet.

"How do I feel about you?" Jeff shrugged. "It's kind of hard to put it in words. I know you make me happy, make me smile at even the silliest of things. I know you are smart and beautiful. I love that you are kind and sweet and yet have this brave little core inside of you that makes you fearless in the face of things that would have made so many other people scared. You're quick to see the good in other people and willing to give of yourself to make them better. You make me better. You make me see the world differently."

Jane's breath hitched, her heart beating faster at his words.

He was not done yet. "You know my flaws. I can't put it in exact words how I feel about you. The best thing I can say is that I think I'm falling in love with you."

Jane's hand rested on her heart as she looked at him, no idea how to respond to something so beautiful and true.

"Jeff..." she stammered and then stopped, really having no idea what she was going to say.

Jeff stood still as he waited for her reply. "Jane, please say something," he said quietly when she stood and stared at him.

"I'm trying to think of a way to respond to that and show you that I feel how you feel," she said quietly.

She took two steps, covering the distance between them in an instant, then rose on her tiptoes and kissed him.

If Jeff was shocked, it was hidden by the fact that he had wanted this for a long time. He curved his arm around her back and held her, returning her kiss as he lowered his head, so she didn't have to reach so high. Her lips on his were soft and undemanding, and yet he gave her everything he had to give, pouring the whole of his feelings and emotions inside that kiss.

Of course, Jane kissing him said a whole lot more. He knew she was not the kind of person to bestow this kind of honor on just anyone. That she took a step forward and kissed him was her own way of telling him she had feelings for him too. It was a first step on a journey Jeff was hoping continued for a long time.

Finally, they broke apart, each reluctant to let go of the other.

"I can't believe you decided not talking to me was the best response to the fact that you had feelings for me," Jane said, a small smile on her face.

"I guess I'm a little smarter now," Jeff replied with a crooked grin.

Jane chuckled. "And so, we're clear on it, I want to say that I'm falling in love with—"

Her confession was suddenly interrupted when from one end of the property, Jeff heard someone screaming and running at them. Then he saw the knife in the assailant's hand and immediately stepped in front of Jane, using one hand to guide her behind him.

"Get away from her!" the intruder screamed, running full tilt toward Jeff.

Jeff watched carefully, his eyes on the knife in the outstretched hand. As soon as the intruder came close enough, Jeff delivered a chopping blow to the knife hand, causing him to drop it. Jeff kicked him, and he stumbled to the ground as Jeff picked up the knife.

"Quick, run inside and get Ben!" Jeff instructed Jane, giving her space to dash behind him toward the house. Jeff stared at the enemy, noting that he looked about thirty, tall and lanky with dark, curly hair.

"You have no right to kiss her," the young man insisted as he got up. "She's mine..."

Before Jeff could process that last statement, the intruder lunged at him. Jeff easily sidestepped the attack and then tackled him to the side, quickly jumping on him, forcing him to the ground, and twisting his hand behind him. Ben and Jane ran towards him, Ben's pace much faster than Jane's. By the time he got there, it was clear Jeff already had the intruder subdued. The intruder struggled against Jeff to no avail and finally gave up. Jane stood behind Ben.

"Jane, I think we've got your stalker," Jeff said.

Chapter Thirty-two

Jeff glared at the man who was now handcuffed in the back seat of his car, secured so he couldn't escape or try to hurt anyone. He looked like he was in his early thirties, and a bruise was on his head from where Jeff had tackled him. He had a tattoo on his arm and a look of loathing on his face aimed at Ben and Jeff. Mostly Jeff.

Jeff slammed the car door shut.

"Look. We don't work for this town's police department, so you know we probably won't get the chance to interrogate him alone once he gets to the station. This car ride is our only chance to question him ourselves with no one else around," Jeff said to Ben quietly. "We're the ones who know this case the best. We were the ones protecting Jane from him."

"Well, let's go then." Ben briefly went inside to tell Estella and Jane they'd be back soon.

"What's your name?" Jeff asked the man, getting in the driver's seat.

The man just chuckled, setting Jeff's blood on fire.

"Look, man. You're going away for stalking and attempted murder. We'll know your name soon enough."

"Nonsense," the man spat. "I'm not a stalker. I'm passionate. And my name is Tobi. Tobi Mitchell. It was all a misunderstanding."

"Yeah. Sure."

When Ben got in the car, Jeff read Tobi Mitchell his Miranda rights and asked him if he understood.

"Yes, I understand," Tobi said with an eye roll, as if he'd been through this before.

"Are you willing to answer our questions?" Jeff said and drove out of the driveway.

"Yes," Tobi said from the back seat. Since Tobi agreed to answering their questions, his Miranda rights were waived and the questioning became legal.

"How about you explain exactly what you found hard to understand about the fact that Jane didn't want you stalking her?" Ben said.

Tobi smiled, his face going soft in a perverted mockery. "My Jenny."

Jeff glanced at Tobi in the rearview mirror, trying not to pull over and grab him by the shirt collar. "Is that her name?"

Tobi looked at him in the mirror with a scowl. "That's what I call her."

"Do you know her real name?" Ben asked him.

He shook his head. "I don't know. She didn't want to tell me her name, so I gave her one instead. I don't care what her name is, I know that she is Jenny to me." He smiled again, a dreamy expression on his face. "My pretty Jenny. She had the face of an angel. I only wished she wouldn't argue with me."

"Is that why you tried to kill her when you ran her over with your car?" Jeff demanded, trying to keep his cool.

"I didn't try to kill her," Tobi shook his head. "It was all a mistake. I would never hurt my Jenny. I promised to take her home with me. She did not want to come home with me. Even when I begged her. She wouldn't come home with me."

"You tried to kill her," Ben said.

Tobi shook his head violently, as if rejecting the notion that he could have ever harmed the object of his obsession.

"It was a mistake. I wanted her to keep quiet and take her hand away from the door. It's not my fault. See, she made me so mad. She opened the car door and started to run. I knew she would call the cops. I couldn't have that. I had to scare her and stop her."

"So, you ran her over with your car," Jeff concluded, gripping the steering wheel tightly to keep from punching the guy. Anger pumped through his veins. It was a good thing he was driving right now and not sitting in the back seat with that scum. He wasn't sure if he would have been able to restrain himself.

Tobi groaned as if in pain when he nodded. "It was a mistake, and I swear I went back for her. When I got there, she was gone. That was when I knew that someone had found her before I could get her back."

"What did you do next?" Ben asked.

Tobi turned to Ben. "I drove to the hospital. I knew she'd show up there sooner or later."

"So, you decided you'd finish the job when you tried to smother her with a pillow." Jeff's fury showed in his voice and his body vibrated with anger.

"No. I didn't even go in the hospital. I didn't want to risk her seeing me. I waited until you left with her," Tobi said.

"But Jane said the man dressed as a doctor who attacked her had dark, curly hair. You have dark, curly hair. So, Tobi, let's try this again. You tried to kill Jane by smothering her with a pillow at the hospital, didn't you? You followed us there!" Jeff slammed the steering wheel and looked at the rearview mirror, pinning him with an intense stare.

Tobi threw his hands up. "I told you, I love Jenny! I wouldn't try to kill her. I had to get her back from you. See, she belongs to me. She was mine, and you took her from me."

"She was never yours!" Jeff shouted. "But you wanted to scare her, didn't you? So, you cut off her oxygen by covering her face with a pillow? You could have killed her!"

Ben touched Jeff's shoulder, signaling to Jeff that he needed to calm down. Jeff took a deep breath as he lifted a hand in surrender. Ben nodded, understanding the other man's anger. He turned back to face Tobi.

"Since she was no longer yours, you decided no one else was going to have her. Is that right?" Ben asked.

Jeff gave Tobi dagger eyes in the mirror again, clenching his fists so hard that the veins on his arms practically popped out.

"Okay, okay!" Tobi raked a hand through his disheveled mop of hair. "I did go in the hospital and shove a pillow in her face. I had no intention of killing her. I was angry that she left me like she did."

Jeff had to turn his eyes away from the criminal and focus on the road before he did something he'd regret.

"Just like when you tampered with the boat? You were trying to scare her? Get back at her?" Ben asked.

"What boat?"

Jeff shifted in his seat to briefly glare at Tobi. "Come on, Tobi. We know you put a hole in the boat. We know about the notes, cutting the brakes, and about the time you tried to poison her in the restaurant."

"The notes..." Tobi stammered. "I wanted her to know I was thinking about her. I wanted her to know I have not forgotten about her. I was watching over her."

Jeff scoffed. "And the accident with the boat?"

A cocky smirk covered Tobi's face. "Okay, okay. I had to do it. It was too easy. It was sitting right there!"

Jeff took a deep breath to keep himself from shouting at Tobi. "She can't swim. You could have killed her."

"No," Tobi adamantly shook his head. "I know she can't swim and that she's scared of the water. She told me when we met. Come on, I left the life jackets in it. I'd never let her die. I love her. If you guys had let me have her, I wouldn't have had to do what I did."

"She's terrified of the water. How could you do that to her?" Jeff demanded.

"How did you know the women would go on the boat alone without us?" Ben asked, ignoring Jeff.

"I didn't. That was lucky for me. I just wanted to scare Jenny to show her I still had power over her." Tobi smirked at Jeff, and all Jeff wanted to do was knock it off the perpetrator's smug face.

"And what about cutting the brakes on my car and almost killing Ben? You knew that was my car, but Ben used it to go to the store. You were trying to kill me instead, weren't you?" Jeff asked.

Tobi shook his head. "Whoa! I don't know anything about cars. I wouldn't even know how to do that."

"You've been telling the truth for the most part until now. Why stop now?" Jeff asked. "You wanted me out of the picture so you could have Jane to yourself. Ben drove the car that day instead."

"No, man. I didn't cut anyone's brakes, okay?" Tobi's eyes filled with desperation. "Look at my job history. I never did any type of mechanic work. I don't know anything about cars."

Ben touched Jeff's shoulder again. "Don't let your emotions cloud your judgment."

Jeff gave him an icy stare. "I'm not."

Tobi was a selfish control freak who wanted Jane all to himself. Who else would have done it?

"Maybe we're missing something," Ben said.

Jeff glanced back to Tobi, ignoring Ben. "Moving on. So, you say you love Jane. Then why did you poison her at the restaurant?"

"Poison her?" Tobi frowned. "No. I didn't do that. That's crazy. Why would I poison Jenny? I love her."

Tobi looked even more confused as he stared back and forth between Ben and Jeff. "I would never try to kill Jenny. I told you that."

"You tried to kill her when you ran her over with your car," Jeff pointed out, his voice rising again. When Ben glanced at him, he took another deep breath.

"That was a mistake, okay?" Tobi suddenly screamed. "But I never tried to poison her."

Ben stared at Tobi until he cowered and looked away. "But someone poisoned her, and from what we know, you are the only one who has a grudge with her. You are the only one who has been stalking her."

"Ha. That's not true." Tobi let out a humorless laugh, leaning back in his seat, looking cocky again.

Ben frowned as they pulled into the police station parking lot. "What do you mean, that's not true?"

"I've been watching all of you with my binoculars." He looked annoyed as he added, "I try to see inside, but I can't because of all the curtains on the windows. I saw an old man on the other side of your house. He's there watching like me. He pretends as if he's wandering the beach. I know he's not. He's been there for two days, and I see him watching my Jenny as if he wants her. He's an old man, and I am not scared. I can take him. If he tries to do anything to my Jenny, I know I can beat him."

Ben and Jeff glanced at each other with raised brows just as the local police officers came outside for Tobi, communicating silently to each other. At this point, Jeff felt as if they could read each other's minds sometimes.

Was it true? Could Jane really have two stalkers after her, or was Tobi just making up stories?

After they took him inside the station to be questioned, Jeff asked Ben, "You think he's telling the truth?"

"I don't know. What I know is that he's had plenty of reasons to lie to us before now and he doesn't seem to mind that much of what he's told us puts him in a lot of trouble. As I said before, I don't think he's a killer. Just a controlling stalker who wants what he wants."

"Come on." Jeff shook his head. "You know what it means if he is telling the truth?"

"You mean that Jane has two stalkers after her?" Ben asked incredulously. "That's rare."

"I don't know how else to interpret what he told us."

If Tobi was indeed telling them the truth, it would mean Jane and Estella were alone, thinking they were safe when they actually were not safe at all.

Jeff's blood ran cold. "We have to get back to the house."

They raced toward the car, got in, and sped off. Jeff dialed Estella's cell phone to warn her.

Hopefully she'd answer.

CHAPTER THIRTY-THREE

"Why do you look like someone who is still worried about something she knows has been taken care of?" Estella asked as she walked into the living room with two cups of tea.

Jane smiled as she turned around in her chair. "I don't know. It all feels kind of surreal to me. Almost as if it's truly not over."

"You want me to take a guess at why you still feel this way?"

Jane smiled as she collected the cup Estella handed to her, knowing Estella was going to give her opinion either way.

"I think a part of you was thinking that once we caught your stalker, everything would magically become okay. You'd get your memory back and all the boxes would fit in their place."

As Estella spoke, Jane had to admit she had gotten this one spot on. From the moment Jeff tackled the man who had attacked them on the beach, the first thing she had realized was that not only did she not remember him, she also had no memory of ever meeting anyone like him. Even though she knew from what the doctors had told her that it was very rare for her to suddenly get all her memories back, a part of her had been hoping that her recovery would at least start when she came face to face with her stalker.

"So, you don't recognize him at all?" Estella asked.

Jane shook her head. "Not really. I mean, when I look at him, I do get this small sense of déjà vu. But I don't think I know him well."

"Like you're seeing a familiar place but can't name it."

Jane nodded. "I don't know. I guess I really was expecting that once we caught him, I'd get my memory back."

"Don't worry too much about it. You were already getting your memory back before we caught him, right?"

"Yeah." Jane nodded, thinking how passages of her Bible had started to feel familiar to her. "But I can no longer wait for my memory to come back."

Estella puckered her brows in confusion. "What do you mean?"

"There is no reason for me not to venture out into the world now. I may not remember what I knew about it before, but the weeks I've spent with you and Jeff have taught me that there is a lot more I can learn from it."

"You know you've taught me and Jeff a lot too, right?"

Jane chuckled. "I doubt I had anything to really teach you guys."

"Are you kidding?" Estella sat up, her eyes fixed earnestly on Jane's face. "Forget about the fact that you taught me to cook or that you taught Jeff how to appreciate a book. I'm talking about how you've been a good friend to us. Reminding us of things we've forgotten. You helped us find God again."

"I'm sure you'd have gone back to church eventually. God will always find a way to bring His children back home."

"Yeah, and you were the way." Estella beamed with pride. "You don't even know how much I've learned from watching you pick yourself back up every single time you've been knocked down. The courage you show every day, teaching yourself new things even while you've dealt with the confusion of not remembering all the things you used to know. You really have no idea how much you've taught me in these last few weeks. If you did, trust me, you'd be prouder of yourself than you are now, but of course you'd be humble about it."

Jane's mouth was hanging open when Estella finished her speech, and her cheeks were tinged red as she stared at her friend. "Okay, why do I feel like I'm going to start crying anytime now?"

Estella chuckled, her voice sounding shaky. "Well, you better. I'd hate to be the only one crying."

Suddenly, they heard a knock on the door. Jane glanced at it in surprise.

For a moment fear gripped her heart before she reminded herself that she had no reason to be scared. Still the pounding in her heart didn't stop.

"You think Ben and Jeff forgot their key?" Estella asked as she frowned and got to her feet.

Jane shrugged, also getting to her feet. "They'd have called first."

Estella moved towards the door. Through the peep hole, she saw a man standing on the other side who looked to be in his fifties or sixties.

"Who is it?" she asked, stopping in front of the door.

"Hello there. I'm really sorry for bothering you like this. May I please borrow your phone?"

Estella frowned. Nothing about the man screamed danger, but she was still reluctant to open the door, considering what they had gone through.

The man noticed her hesitation and continued, a little bit of fear in his tone this time. "I need you to help me call the number on this card. The nurses at the home said I should give it to someone if I ever get lost. I went for a walk and... This doesn't look familiar." He looked around, confused.

Estella's eyes widened as she realized he was probably from the nursing homes or assisted living center down the street. They were all over town. She released the latch on the door and glanced out, the chain that held the door still in place. The man smiled gratefully as he held up a business card with the name of the nursing home that was down the street.

"Who is it, Estella?" Jane asked as she came to the door and peered around her friend.

Estella's phone rang on the kitchen counter, and Jane ran to it and answered when she saw that it was Jeff calling.

"Hello?"

"Jane? Listen. You have two stalkers. We got one, but there's still another one out there. Don't let anyone in the house. We're on our way," Jeff said in a panic.

Jane felt her face drain of color as dread seeped through her veins, plummeting in her stomach.

"I think he's lost," Estella said as she prepared to push her hand through the door and collect the card in the man's hand.

"Estella!" Jane screamed, whirling around. "No! Jeff said don't let him in!" She dashed to the door, trying to get it closed again. "Help me close the door."

The moment she looked into the man's eyes through the narrow opening of the doorway, her body had locked in fear as she stared at him.

She remembered.

Not everything, but enough to know who he was.

"Jane, he's just an old man who's lost," Estella said, confused.

"No!" she screamed before Estella could reach for the business card. "It's him!"

Dragging her friend back, she tried to slam the door shut, but the man kicked the door with a surprising amount of strength. It fell open, pushing Jane and Estella into the house. Jane sprang to her feet, helping Estella up, and they both ran into the house.

"We need to get into the bedroom!" Jane pulled Estella along.

Suddenly a shot rang out in the room. Jane and Estella fell to the floor, screaming in fear as they ducked behind the couch in the living room.

"Cecilia!" the man screamed with a deep, booming voice.

Jane's eyes widened as the name triggered another memory of her cowering in a dark room, this man calling her Cecilia over and over again, even though she hated it.

"No, my name is Lucy!" she shouted, then gasped, realization sending chills over her body. "Lucy. My name isn't Jane or Cecilia. It's Lucy."

Estella quickly glanced at her friend with wide eyes, but when the man took a step closer to them, Estella's eyes darted back toward him.

"For five years I took care of you, and you don't even remember who I am. I'm your father," he spat.

Jane shook her head, rejecting the man's claims. If he was truly her father, why did the sight of him fill her with so much fear? "No, you're not," she retorted.

"Come on, Cecilia. Don't you remember me? These people must have brainwashed you. I'm here to take you home. Come on."

Again, that name. It, like everything about this man, filled Jane with fear.

Estella shouted over the couch, "My brother is a cop, and he will be back any second! If you know what's good for you, you'll get out of here right now."

The man laughed. "Your brother? You mean the fool who allowed Cecilia to get poisoned? The same man that left you two alone here at home? He's not here now, and he can't protect you now." The man walked towards the couch. "You betrayed me, Cecilia. You abandoned me when all I ever did was love you."

"I don't want your so-called love," Jane spat out as she looked to Estella, trying to figure out what to do. If they moved away from their position, they would be exposed to the man and his gun, not that the couch would be much protection from gunfire. If they stayed where they were, he would get to them and shoot them.

"You ungrateful brat. I should have left you to die. All those times you were sick. All those times when it would have been easier to abandon you. I loved you like you were my own daughter. And you are."

He was already so close Jane could hear him breathing. She looked over at Estella, pointing in the other direction away from the corner where the man was coming towards them, and signaled to Estella to get the phone and call for help.

He stopped as he cocked his gun. "I tried and tried to make you my Cecilia. I taught you all the songs she loved, gave you her books, and loved you like you were my own daughter. You didn't love me like a daughter should love her father. 'Honor thy father and live long.' I taught you that."

"You're not my father!" Jane screamed as she pushed Estella to make a run for the bedroom.

Instead of following Estella, Jane turned around and jumped over the couch, intending to tackle the old man and give her friend a chance to escape. Her plan failed miserably when the man threw her to the floor.

"I am your father, but you never became the daughter I wanted." The man lifted the gun and pointed it at Jane.

Estella launched herself at the man. He grunted as Estella grabbed the hand holding the gun and pulled it away from Jane. It went off, the sound deafening.

"Get Jeff's gun!" Estella shouted as she wrestled with the man.

It was in the safe on the wall behind her. She scrambled to open the safe, shaky hands pressing the code to unlock the door. She heard Estella cry out in pain and quickly grabbed the gun. By the time she turned around, trembling hands pointing it at the man, he had subdued Estella and was holding his gun to her head. Jane's stomach clenched.

"Drop the gun now, or your friend gets a bullet in her head," the man ordered.

"Don't shoot her. I'll do it." She crouched to the floor.

Estella stomped on the man's foot and threw her head back into his face at the same time, and when he stumbled back, she roundhouse kicked him. The man yelled in pain as he fell, his gun clattering to the floor. Estella kicked it, and it skittered under the couch. He grabbed her feet, and she lost her balance.

"Shoot, Jane!" Estella urged Jane as she rolled away from the man and ducked for cover.

"No, wait, please! Cecilia, don't do this!" the man cried, crouching on the floor and holding his hands up.

Jane pointed the gun at the man, trying to remember what Jeff and Ben had taught her and Estella. Her hands shook as she held the gun, and she tensed, knowing she could never actually shoot a person, even if he was one of the vilest men alive.

The man was already struggling to get back on his feet.

Just in case she really did have to shoot, Jane frantically searched for the safety. Where was it again? Her mind reeled, her heart pounding. Then she remembered what Jeff had taught her. She flicked the safety off, lifting her gun at the man again.

"Stay back or I'll shoot!" she shouted.

"Oh, come on, Cecilia. I know you won't," the man sneered.

Jane pulled the trigger, aiming for the wall, and the gun recoiled in her shaking hands. The man smiled in triumph. "That was a warning shot," she said, her voice sounding much shakier than she'd intended.

"Oh, Cecilia. You don't know how to use that, do you?" He snickered. "You're nothing without me."

Jane's mind filled with memories of him abusing her, taunting her, and degrading her during the years he'd stolen from her. She remembered how he'd starved her when she'd refused to agree that she was his daughter, and the times he'd tortured her mentally and physically.

Jane inhaled deeply, calming her shaking hands, staring at the man before her

"Look! Jeff and Ben are back!" Estella cried, pointing to the window. "Now you're done, mister."

As he looked toward the window, distracted, Jane struck him in the head with the gun and all of her strength. "You're wrong. You're nothing to me."

He collapsed and fell to the floor with a satisfying thud, unconscious.

"Are you okay?" Ben yelled as he ran inside the house, handcuffing the man.

"I'm fine," Estella assured him. "We're okay."

"What happened?" Jeff asked, and Estella and Jane ran to him. He wrapped his arms around Jane.

"Estella fought him off and took his gun. She distracted him and I knocked him out. You were incredible, Estella," Jane said.

"You're shaking. I'm shaking too. Are you okay?" Estella asked, laying a hand on Jane's arm.

Jane took a deep breath. She was shaking, adrenaline still coursing through her. Instead of the fear she expected, she felt calm and empowered. "Actually, I'm more than okay. It's over. We're safe now."

Estella took a step back, and Jeff pulled Jane close to him. She sighed in relief, smiling, and taking in the familiar scent of him. She held onto him tightly.

"I'll never forgive myself for letting this happen, Jane," he murmured. He pulled back enough to look at her.

"Lucy," she told him. "My name is Lucy."

CHAPTER THIRTY-FOUR

Lucy sat on her favorite rock, staring out at the ocean. Finally, she knew her real name. She'd come to really like the name Jane, but Lucy felt so much more right to her. She still didn't remember her last name, but it was a start.

On the journal opened on her lap she had written her name over and over again. She still didn't have all her memories yet, but she had enough that she had been able to corroborate George Merin's story when he finally started confessing. He'd admitted that her name truly was Lucy and that she was from Unity, but said he didn't remember who her relatives were or her last name.

At first, Merin had refused to answer questions from the police, but once he realized he was going to prison, his delusions began to clear. He gave in and told the whole story of how he'd kidnapped her and held her captive in his basement, which had not been in the Amish community.

After Jane had escaped, even though he was still sick, he was intent on finding her. He'd listened to the police communicating with a police scanner, and had heard them talking about a Jane Doe who had been brought to a local hospital. Once he found out which one it was, he'd quickly tracked her down, then followed them from the hospital to the beach house.

He even admitted to sneaking into the busy restaurant kitchen dressed as a waiter and sneaking poison into her food and how he'd gone through great lengths to do it. He'd followed them to the restaurant, sat at the table near them dressed in a disguise, then stopped a waiter in the back of the restaurant. He'd asked him where the bathroom was, using his confused, elderly man act. Merin knocked out the waiter and stole his uniform, then went into the kitchen and poisoned her plate. He had a background in chemistry and had used his own homemade concoction.

Merin had played the part of a confused, elderly man more than once. The first time had been at Jeff's house, when Jeff and Ben had almost arrested him, but they had believed the story of him being a lost nursing home resident. Merin had even called someone and hired them to pick him up right after Ben and Jeff had called the nursing home to come get him, then he had called the nursing home to tell them it had been a false alarm so they wouldn't drive to Ben's house.

He had played the part of a confused old man again at Ben's house, when he had broken in and attacked Jane and Estella.

By the time Merin had told the whole story, Lucy had already gotten many of her memories back and knew what had happened to her anyway, and Merin's statements corroborated with her memories.

Lucy heard footsteps behind her and turned her head to see Jeff, who sat down beside her.

He gave a heavy sigh. "Well, it's over, Jane. I mean...Lucy. I just got a phone call. Merin committed suicide less than an hour ago. He hung himself."

"He's dead?"

Jeff nodded. "And Tobi stalked many other women beside you. He killed some of them. Those families finally get closure now, and you were one of the few who survived. He's going away for life, Lucy. They'll never hurt you again. You're safe now."

At first, peace washed over Lucy like a wave breaking on the sand. Then realization set in. She didn't need Jeff to protect her anymore.

But she still wanted him to.

"Wow. That's a relief." She wrapped her arms around herself and looked out over the ocean.

"Now you can stop worrying about being in danger and finally focus on finding out who you are."

"Can we go to Unity in the morning? I want to get it over with. You know, in case it goes badly. Merin said I'm from Unity, but he doesn't know who my family is. They could have moved by now, or they might even be…" She paused and took a deep breath. "I don't want to be disappointed again. Anyway, I just want to get it over with."

And she was scared of finding out what type of family she had…including a boyfriend or husband.

She was scared of never seeing Jeff again and living a life that wouldn't seem like her own.

"Of course. We can go in the morning, first thing."

"Thank you, Jeff, for everything. I'll never forget what you've all done for me, no matter what."

She stood up and walked straight to the house before he could see her tears.

*

Jeff, Ben, Estella, and Lucy got up at dawn and left right away for Unity. Even though the stalker and kidnapper had been arrested and Ben and Jeff no longer had to protect Lucy anymore, the four of them wanted to see this through to the end together and offer their support.

The entire drive, Lucy's stomach was twisted with anxiety. What if they uncovered nothing? What if they uncovered everything?

She didn't know which she was more afraid of.

What if she had to live out the rest of her days married to a man she didn't remember? What if she had children and wouldn't even know their names when she saw them?

Estella sensed Lucy's anxiety, and for once she said nothing, as if knowing all Lucy needed was silence to think right then. Instead, she'd occasionally pat her arm or squeeze her hand, and that was just the right amount of comfort Lucy needed.

As Jeff drove, he'd glance back at Lucy in the rearview mirror every few minutes, and Lucy avoided his eyes, staring out the window or trying to focus on the pages of her book, distracting herself. At her feet was her few possessions packed into a bag, just in case they really did find her family and her home.

Home. Family. Those were heavy words.

After reading the same page eight times without comprehending a word, she eventually threw it on the seat next to her with an annoyed sigh. She just couldn't focus.

And with no distractions, the ride seemed like an eternity.

When they approached the community, Lucy sat up taller in her seat. That yellow sign with the buggy on it looked familiar. That pizza place. That old bowling alley.

The shops faded away, and picturesque farms whizzed by Lucy's window. She gaped at the horses and cows in the fields, and the lush green grass that spread out as far as she could see. In the other direction were the woods, the tall trees swaying in the breeze.

As they turned onto the dirt lane, Lucy's eyes locked on the Community Store.

"Stop!" she cried. "I know this place."

"Really?" Estella asked, grabbing Lucy's hand.

The car stopped and Lucy got out, running into the store. She turned slowly, staring at the shelves stocked with dry goods, flour, and tools. There was even a sign for fresh donuts.

She remembered devouring them, the warm powdery sugar sticking to her chin.

"Can I help you?" an elderly man behind the counter asked.

"Hi. I think I'm from here. This all seems so familiar. Sorry, I'm just taking it all in."

"Oh, you're the girl from the photo," the man said. "I'm Irvin Holt."

Jeff, Ben, and Estella followed Lucy into the store.

"This is all familiar," she told them. "I remember it."

"Wait a minute," Irvin said, walking out from behind the counter and closer to Lucy. Peering at her, he squinted. "You do look familiar now that I see you in person. You look a lot like Lucy Yoder, a girl who left the Amish a few years back. Might have been four or five years ago, I can't remember."

"Lucy Yoder?" Lucy repeated slowly, savoring the words like candy. "Yoder." Was that her last name?

"*Ja*. Elizabeth and Bob Yoder live just down the road a bit, down that way. It was their niece who left the Amish those years ago. Maybe a few minutes of driving if you're in a car. They live a bit farther out than the rest of us." He gave Jeff more detailed directions, and they got back in the car.

Lucy could hardly contain her excitement as they left the store parking lot and drove to the Yoders' house. She bounced on her seat like a child, hands pressed up against the glass, not caring one bit about making fingerprints on the window.

247

When they pulled into the driveway of a tall, tan house with no shutters, Lucy sat still. There was a greenhouse, a dog scampering in the yard, a buggy in the driveway, and—her breath hitched at the sight of a pond and a large red barn.

"The barn. The pond." Lucy's hands covered her mouth as shock washed over her. She blinked a few times to make sure she was seeing clearly. "That's it."

"So you weren't held captive there?" Jeff asked from the driver's seat.

She remembered running around in the yard with that dog, the wind whipping at her hair. She remembered riding a brown horse bareback through the fields, tending the plants in the greenhouse with an older man, and helping an older woman in the kitchen inside the house make homemade noodles and shoofly pie.

She'd laughed here and had friends here. She'd had a good life here.

"No. I must have gotten confused and thought this was where I was kept by my kidnapper. But I was wrong. This was home," she said breathlessly before bolting out of the car and running right up to the door.

Her heart pounded as hard as her feet slamming the wooden steps as she bounded up the porch to the front door. She knocked. Waited.

Finally, the door creaked open, revealing a woman's kind, wrinkled face. She wore a long blue dress and her gray hair was mostly covered by her prayer *kapp.* "Hello there, may I help—"

Lucy tried to think of something eloquent to say, but she never got the chance.

The woman's eyes widened, then traveled over Lucy head to toe. The woman gasped, her eyes filling with tears. "Lucy? Lucy!"

The woman threw her arms around her niece, squeezing tight with surprising strength for her age.

"Oh, I knew you'd come back, my dear. I knew you'd come back."

Lucy smiled through her tears, hugging the woman—her aunt—back.

"Bob! Bob, come here quick!" the woman hollered.

Lucy saw a man wearing a black wide-brimmed hat coming out of the barn and walking toward them.

"Bob, it's Lucy!" Aunt Elizabeth called.

Uncle Bob took off his hat, dropped it, and ran as fast as his feeble legs could carry him. He took a moment to look at Lucy, then he threw his arms around her and Aunt Elizabeth, who was still hugging her.

"We're so happy you're back. We've been praying for this every day since you left," he said, his voice cracking with emotion.

"Come inside," Aunt Elizabeth said, then waved at Ben, Jeff, and Estella, who'd been watching quietly. "And you too. Come in. We have a lot to talk about. I'll put a kettle on."

When they opened the door, the smell of freshly baked cookies wafted to Lucy's nose, and she took a good look around the cozy home. A large kitchen with a huge table took most of the space, and there was an open living room with two couches and large sunny windows.

Lucy remembered baking in the kitchen with Elizabeth and her children, her cousins, packing food to bring to church or talking to neighbors. They would sing as they worked, and Lucy remembered how long it took to sweep the floors of the big house.

Aunt Elizabeth bustled around the kitchen, putting some homemade sliced bread on the table and a kettle of tea. "Help yourself," she said. "Have a seat, everyone."

After introductions were made, everyone sat down. Jeff explained everything to Elizabeth and Bob from how they'd found Lucy to how they'd come here looking for answers. Bob and Elizabeth listened intently, shocked and horrified at many of the things they heard. Both of them were in tears by the end.

When he finished, Bob said, "So you all probably want to know more about Lucy and her family. Lucy, I am sorry to tell you this, but you may not remember that your parents died in a buggy accident when you were sixteen. We raised you after your parents died," Uncle Bob said, his kind eyes smiling above his long gray beard.

Lucy couldn't remember much of her parents. She didn't cry because she felt as though she'd never known them. Maybe one day she'd remember them.

"We've missed you so much," Aunt Elizabeth said, patting Lucy's hand.

"I do have to know one thing. Why didn't anyone report that Lucy was missing? Is it because the Amish don't report crimes?" Jeff asked. "Not to sound insensitive."

"No, not at all. If we had known she'd gone missing, we would have reported her. We had no idea she was missing because she'd gone on Rumspringa. That's a time when Amish youth explore the outside world. When Lucy didn't come back home, we assumed she'd decided to not be Amish anymore," Aunt Elizabeth said.

"All that matters now is you're back," Uncle Bob said.

"So, you're the only family I have?" Lucy asked tentatively. "Do I have children or a...a husband?" Her heart pounded, and she braced for the answer.

"Oh, no, dear. It's only us," Aunt Elizabeth said with a chuckle. "You always said none of the men here interested you at all, despite our hopes."

Lucy let out a breath she'd been holding. *Well, that's a relief.*

"She's safe now," Jeff said abruptly. "Her kidnapper died, and the other stalker is going away for a long time. So, Jane—I mean, Lucy—do you want to stay here? I mean, now that you've found your family, we figured you might want to stay."

Lucy looked at Jeff, then Estella, then Ben as they waited for her answer.

How could she leave them after all they'd been through?

But she'd found her home. She should stay and find out more about who she really was. All she knew was that she was from here and that this couple were her aunt and uncle. She wanted to know who her friends were growing up, what school she'd gone to, what her church was like. There was so much left to discover, and she'd barely begun.

She couldn't leave here.

"I'm sorry. You know I appreciate everything that each of you has done for me. But I need to stay here and relearn who I am. This was and is my home, and there's so much I can learn about myself here. I hope you understand."

"Of course, we understand, Lucy." Estella said the new name with a smile as she patted Lucy's hand. "As long as you're happy. That's all we want."

Tears stung Lucy's eyes, tears of both guilt and gratitude. "Thank you." She looked to Jeff, who gave her a smile, but she could easily see the hurt in his eyes.

Would he invite her to go back to the beach house with him?

"Well, then, we should leave you to it," Jeff said, looking away from her and standing. Ben and Estella also got up.

Her hope diminished as they all went outside to say their goodbyes.

"It's been an honor," Ben said, shaking Lucy's hand.

"Thank you, Ben." She let go of his hand and pulled him into a hug.

Estella had tears in her eyes as she hugged Lucy.

"Does this mean you'll disappear forever?"

Lucy smiled as she hugged Estella back. "No. Don't worry, I'll find a way to talk to you regularly."

"Promise?" Estella demanded, her gaze earnest as she looked at her friend. "Even if you only write me letters, which is so old school."

Lucy chuckled, mostly to stop herself from bursting into tears. "I promise."

She needed this. Already she was starting to miss these people she had come to call friends in the past weeks. While she was curious enough about her past and roots, she realized that somehow, she had formed a new family with these three people, and leaving them was like ripping a part of herself away.

"Thank you for everything you did for me," she said softly, feeling her eyes sting with tears. "You have no idea how grateful I am to you."

"It's been fun," Ben replied in his usual affable manner. "Loved every minute."

She nodded as she looked at him. Dashing her hands across her face, she wiped away her tears.

Then she turned to Jeff. He had that forced smile on his face, and Lucy wondered why she hated the sight of it right now. As if he was pretending to be happy to see her go. She stopped in front of him, hoping once more to hear him ask her not to leave.

"I bet you're glad you're staying," Jeff said instead with a hint of regret. "For a moment there, I was scared we wouldn't find your family."

Lucy swallowed. "Thanks for your help. Truly, I'll never forget it. I don't know how to express how grateful I am. You've been a good friend to me."

For a second, Jeff's face held an odd expression, then he regained composure. "And it's been great knowing you." He turned to smile at Estella. "God knows the thought of eating Estella's food doesn't exactly fill me with joy."

"Idiot," Estella muttered under her breath as she glared at her brother, clearly wishing he would stop his macho display. "I'll go grab your bag, Jane. I mean, Lucy."

Estella dashed off to the car, and handed Lucy her bag, then gave her one final hug. Thanking Estella again, Lucy took a step back from them and joined her aunt and uncle.

Waving goodbye to her friends, she watched them get into the car. It seemed almost unreal, as if they were going in slow motion. As the car drove down the driveway, Lucy began to cry, a huge lump filling her throat and emptiness overtaking her heart.

"Come on inside, dear," Aunt Elizabeth said, a gentle hand on her back, guiding her back into the house.

As Lucy walked to the staircase and went upstairs, the memories of the bedroom she'd shared with her cousins rushed to her before she even saw it. There was her twin bed with the colorful quilt she'd made with the help of her aunt and her old dresses hanging in the closet. She opened the closet and ran her hand along the garments, then saw a white prayer *kapp* on the top shelf. She took it down and turned it over in her hands.

"That was yours. We kept all your things," her aunt said. "We knew you'd come back."

Lucy stared at the head covering, then moved closer to the mirror above the dresser. She pulled the prayer *kapp* on to her head and studied her reflection.

Yes, this was so familiar, but was it truly *her*?

"Well, I'm sure this is a lot for you to take in. Do you want a moment alone?" Aunt Elizabeth asked.

"Actually, yes, if you don't mind. I'm sorry."

"Of course, dear. I'll just be in the kitchen. Come down when you're ready."

Her aunt left and slowly shut the door, and Lucy sank on to the bed. She took a deep breath as she realized she'd been foolish. Jeff wasn't going to ask her to come back with him to Kennebunkport.

He was letting her go.

*

Jeff walked away from Lucy, his hands held stiffly by his side. It felt like part of him was being torn away. Only the pain was concentrated somewhere in his chest. And his stomach. And his whole body and soul.

254

I did the right thing, he told himself, wondering why, then, he felt like he'd just made the dumbest mistake of his life.

They all got in the car and Jeff drove down the lane.

Ben said, "I've got to say, Jeff, letting her go like that was the dumbest thing I've ever seen you do."

"What do you mean?" Jeff asked.

"You could have at least asked her if she wanted to come back with you."

"But she needs to be home. It'll help her regain her memories. She needs to be with her family. This is what's best for her."

"Well, you could have at least told her how you feel," Estella said, "Now that we know she's not married after all."

Jeff shook his head as he gripped the steering wheel tighter. "No. She's a grown woman. If she wanted to come back with us, she could have said so. I outright asked her. She's finally found her family, her home. She can finally learn about herself and find out who she really is. I won't take that away from her. I won't make her choose between her home and me. This is best for her."

*

The more time Lucy spent in Unity, the more she remembered leaving the Amish community temporarily as a teen to explore the outside world a little.

During her excursion away from the Amish community, she had been kidnapped by George Merin. Merin had lost his only daughter to a hit and run driver, a daughter who resembled Lucy so much that even she had been shocked when she saw the photos of her. For five years she had lived in the basement of Merin's farmhouse, far removed from the nearest town. For the first six months of captivity, he had locked her in a basement with thick iron bars on the doors and windows. Then he'd started to allow her short periods of freedom, sometimes letting her come upstairs or even go out in the backyard, which was fenced in.

She'd found his daughter's stash of books and soon devoured them. When she was done with those, he'd gotten her more books, happy to indulge her as long as obeyed him.

Merin often told Lucy about his dead daughter and called her Cecilia, her name. For a long time, Lucy had held out hope that he would make a mistake and she could leave. He was as careful as he was methodical. The first time she had tried to escape, he'd left her in the basement for days without food or books. The next time he let her out again, Lucy had been too relieved to feel the sun on her face and didn't make an attempt to run away.

For years, they had lived like this until one day Merin fell sick. He'd let her stay upstairs with him and Lucy had taken care of the elderly man, guilt forcing her to stay and help the man who had kept her captive for years. He'd convinced her for years that she was unable to escape even if she tried.

One day she realized that she really could walk out the door, now that he was so sick and unable to stop her. Soon he would be back on his feet and she'd miss her chance.

That day, as Merin took a nap after she had given him his medicine plus a little extra to make him sleep longer, Lucy ran out of the house she had been forced to call home with a man she'd never accepted as her father.

The desire for freedom had been ignited within Lucy, and she had kept on running.

She ran until she got to the highway and continued for many miles on foot. Tired and hungry, she had accepted a lift from a nice-looking young man who promised to drop her at the nearest police station.

That young man was Tobi Mitchell. At first, he had been kind and jovial, keeping a steady stream of conversation going, and even managing to make Lucy smile a time or two. There was something off about him that made Lucy wary, though, even to the point of not telling him her name when he asked. Then they got to the next town. Instead of him dropping her off like he'd promised, he kept on driving, not stopping when she begged him to.

Scared for her life and not ready to become anyone's captive ever again, Lucy had opened the door to his car and jumped out. She was running away from him when he slammed his car into her. That was when Jeff had found her and taken her to the hospital.

Every day she remembered new things. It was kind of disorienting sometimes. Other times she was glad to have her memories back.

Or at least she was trying to convince herself that she was happy and not disappointed that Jeff had agreed with her decision so eagerly. The same Jeff who had claimed to be falling in love with her. The same Jeff who liked to hang around with her, make her laugh, and talk to her.

The same Jeff who had been the first to tell her how happy he was that she was staying here. It was as if the moment she stopped needing him he had seen no reason to want to be with her.

Lucy sniffed, surprised to find out she had been crying. She shook her head and used the back of her hand to clean the tears away from her eyes. She was not going to cry for him anymore.

Maybe it was all for the best that Jeff had abandoned her. Better now than after she fell in love with him.

Only Lucy was almost sure it was already too late for that.

Chapter Thirty-five

"We're almost home," Uncle Bob said as he drove the buggy down a backroad after running errands in town.

"When I first came back here, this didn't look like what I thought it would," Lucy said as they drove past a pizza place, a bowling alley, and a few shops.

"There's the Unity Community Store, owned by our friends, the Holts. Maybe Irvin would give you a job there if you want," Aunt Elizabeth said.

A job there? It wasn't how she'd pictured her career, but maybe it was a start.

"That's our friend's house, where the Kulp family lives, and Simon Hodges lives down there, and Derek and Maria Turner live down that way. They are all about your age. Maybe you'll all be friends again like when you were kids," Uncle Bob suggested.

"It would be nice to have new friends," Lucy said, but her heart ached for the friends she'd left behind.

"Well, they won't really be new. You've known them since you were babies." Uncle Bob chuckled. "You even took baths together."

"Here we are," Aunt Elizabeth said as the buggy rumbled to a stop.

"Come on inside, dear," Uncle Bob said, collecting her bags from the back. "Your cousins and our grandchildren are all excited to see you."

Just then several children burst out the door and came running to meet them, ages ranging from toddlers to teenagers.

Their parents, her cousins she'd spent her teen years with, followed behind.

Lucy looked at all of them and the house again.

Suddenly images bombarded her mind. Playing tag in the front yard, doing chores inside the barn, playing jump rope in the driveway with her cousins.

"Come in, come in!" they shouted, taking her hands and pulling her.

They all went inside, and Lucy went up to her room. Many of the younger girls followed and crowded around Lucy, asking her a dozen questions at once. She could barely get a word in edgewise.

"Were you kidnapped?"

"Did you like being an Englisher?"

"Do you miss it?"

"Girls, come help me prepare dinner!" Aunt Elizabeth called, and the girls scampered away, leaving Lucy alone.

She sank into the bed, closing her eyes as the memories flooded her mind and stung her eyes with tears.

"Thank you, Lord, for bringing back my memories," she whispered. Her eyes wandered to a shelf across the room, filled with books. She knew those had been hers as well.

She couldn't wait to explore the rest of the community to see how much she could remember.

But still, Lucy had the strange feeling that though this had been home once, after all she'd been through, it might take her a while to feel at home here again.

Lucy heard a soft knocking sound and looked up to see Aunt Elizabeth in the doorway.

"I thought maybe you'd like to see the house you lived in with your parents," she said. "The girls are making dinner, so we could go now if you want. If it's too soon, I understand."

"No, I do want to see it. It might help me remember them. When I found out they died, I didn't even cry because I can't remember much of them. Maybe seeing the house will help me remember."

"You know, Lucy, they left the house to you when they died. It's yours. All this time, we've been maintaining it for you, hoping you'd come home. If you want to move there when you're ready, you can, but I certainly am not asking you to move out. We love having you here."

"Wow, thank you for telling me. I'll think about that."

"Ready to go?"

Lucy nodded and walked out of the house with her aunt. They took a short walk down the lane and stopped at a gray house with a large yard.

As soon as Lucy saw it, memories dripped back into her mind. She'd expected a rush, but it was a steady, slow stream. She remembered playing outside with her parents as a child, taking buggy rides to church, and planting the garden with her mother.

"You were an only child. A miracle baby, actually. Your mother was told by doctors she'd never be able to have children, but then you were born a few years after they got married." Aunt Elizabeth pulled out a key, and they went inside.

The smell of the house was familiar. Seeing the different rooms each brought their own memories, and tears coursed down Lucy's face.

"I remember them," she cried. "I remember their faces. Their smiles." Aunt Elizabeth wrapped her arms around Lucy and wiped away her tears.

"They loved you so much, Lucy. They called you Lulu."

"Lulu." Lucy laughed through her tears. "That's funny."

"After they died in that buggy accident, you were never the same. You became quiet after being such a social butterfly. Withdrawn. After you moved in with us, we could see signs of depression. When you were old enough, you left for Rumspringa. I'm so sorry we never reported you missing. We thought you liked the outside world better. Maybe that you'd found a job and a place to live. We had no idea. After you left, you didn't contact us, as young Amish people often do when they jump the fence. So, we had no idea what had happened to you." Now Aunt Elizabeth's eyes filled with tears. "Maybe if we'd reported you missing—"

"No, don't blame yourself. I don't blame you, and I don't hold it against you. You had no idea. Besides, who knows what would have happened?"

"Thank you, Lucy. You're right. The Lord does not want us to live in regret."

Lucy took a deep breath and walked slowly around the house, taking in every inch. Could she really make a life for herself here?

Could she call this place home?

*

Lucy sighed as she sat down in the swaying grass of the field and stared down at the miles of green stretched in front of her.

This field was her favorite spot in the whole Amish community.

On her lap she had a journal open and a pen between the pages. Every day for the past few weeks she had come here to write down her thoughts, spending hours alone, pouring her mind and heart onto those pages.

Lucy didn't know for sure, but it had seemed like she'd regained most of her memories as she continued to live here, more and more coming back each day. She was grateful for the pleasant memories of her childhood and living with her aunt and uncle—but some memories here, like the ones of her parents' death, were hard to process.

Life in the Amish community had quickly settled into a routine. Her uncle and aunt were prominent members of the Amish community and knew everyone, so Lucy had quickly made many friends.

They had been extremely accommodating of Lucy, showering her with kindness. Some of it was probably guilt from the fact that for years they had been unaware that she had been held captive.

Getting to know her extended family had turned out to be quite an enjoyable experience. While the Amish lifestyle wasn't exactly exciting, touching base with her roots had been more than worth it.

She loved church, gathering with the women in the kitchen to prepare the meals, and helping Irvin Holt in the community store. She loved the times she spent babysitting her uncle's kids. Two weeks ago, she had started assistant teaching at school, and she quickly fell in love with that role too. All in all, she was enjoying her new life so far.

But something was missing. She longed for more.

When she stopped and really thought about it, she knew her heart wasn't here. Maybe it had been long ago, but it wasn't anymore.

It wasn't the lifestyle. For some reason she really had no problem with it, and while she wouldn't mind seeing a movie again or saying no to wearing something other than the stifling clothes she had on, those were luxuries she could easily do without. In fact, she loved how the simple life drew her closer to the Lord.

It was not for a want of the pleasures of the world that she had found herself slowly growing bored with her life. She missed the world outside and the friends she had made in the little time she had found herself free to explore the world—Estella with her always cheerful demeanor, and Ben with his easy smile, always ready to lend a helping hand or ear.

Then there was Jeff. Lucy refused to think too much of him or why he hadn't come to see her. She thought he would have come to visit at least once by now. Even Estella had come to see her a few times.

Did he not want to see her?

Even still, this wasn't only about him. It was simply that she was no longer the naïve dewy-eyed girl who had left this place all those years ago.

She had seen a lot, lived through a lot, and now it was hard to lock all those experiences and knowledge away.

The sound of leaves rustling to her left had her sitting up and looking in that direction, and she was surprised when she saw Aunt Elizabeth and Maria Turner, who was holding her newborn baby, walking toward her. Lucy quickly got to her feet.

"Sorry, I lost track of the time. Is it time to start preparing supper?" Lucy asked.

Elizabeth nodded. "Don't worry. I think Susan and Mary can take care of it for now."

She smiled at the baby and asked Maria, "May I hold baby Robert?"

"Of course. It'll give my arms a break," Maria said, passing her the baby. The little boy had been named after Maria's first husband who'd been killed in an accident. Maria was married to Jeff's friend Derek Turner, who'd worked at CPDU with Jeff and Ben before joining the Amish to marry Maria. Maria had been a dear, sweet friend to Lucy during this transitional period of her life.

"Gabe told me to give this to you." Aunt Elizabeth handed a note to Lucy. Lucy didn't open the note; she tucked it into her sleeve. She already had a pretty good idea what the note said.

Gabe was a young man in the Amish community, and for a while now he had made no attempt to hide the fact that he was interested in courting her. Lucy had tried to turn him down at first but didn't want to offend him. Gabe had simply interpreted her soft rebuttal as an invitation to try harder, but now she had no idea how to get him to stop.

"You know you need to tell him you don't think of him that way, right?" Maria said. "He'll be heartbroken, but you shouldn't lead him on."

"I don't know how to do it without hurting him."

"So what if he gets hurt? He'll get over it. Imagine how much more hurt he'll be the more you keep leading him on," Maria told her.

"But I'm not leading him on," Lucy countered. "Not on purpose, anyway."

"Sorry, that came out wrong. I was trying to say that the longer this goes on the more hurt he'll be when it ends."

Lucy sighed. "I know. I'll make sure he understands."

They stared out over the field.

"Are you happy here?" Aunt Elizabeth asked.

The question took Lucy by surprise. "What do you mean?"

"You know your Uncle Bob and the rest of us are so happy to have you back."

"I know that," Lucy interjected, still not getting where Elizabeth was going with this.

"You've been here long enough to realize that it's not all it seems to be and starting to question yourself. It's why I am asking if you are truly happy here."

Lucy stared at her aunt, unsure how to answer. "I have all I want, and it's good to be back among family..." She paused as her breath left her in a sigh. "But I feel like I don't belong here. I'm guessing you already knew that, or you wouldn't have asked."

"Call it a woman's intuition," Aunt Elizabeth said with a smile and a shrug.

Lucy looked away. "I should be content here. I have a job at the store and I'm teaching at the school. I have family, people who truly care about me."

"Maybe because the things that make you happy are not here. Or should I say...the people. Or person, to be exact." Maria gave a wily smile as she glanced at Lucy.

"How did you know that, Maria?"

"It was a guess. I know a woman in love when I see one. You, young lady, are hopelessly in love with a man who isn't here.

265

Otherwise, you wouldn't be moping around all the time, sighing like you do." Maria waved her hand in the air.

"Am I that obvious?" Lucy shook her head, chuckling. "And I don't sigh."

"Oh, yes, you do." Maria laughed.

Aunt Elizabeth added, "But it's not just that. My dear, the reason why we separate ourselves from the world is so that we are not corrupted by its influences. Makes it easier to say no to its temptations. You, unfortunately, found yourself in a situation where you had no choice but to be influenced by the world. You still managed to hold on to your values and keep to the teachings you've learned."

"You're saying that the influence I had while out there is what's stopping me from being happy here?"

"Yes and no." Elizabeth smiled when Lucy frowned. "You were happy out there. You found something that brought you joy. That in itself is not a sin. That you did it without actually losing your values is really impressive."

"It also means you can choose to go back out there and find your happiness again," Maria added.

Lucy was shocked to hear Aunt Elizabeth and Maria advising her to leave the Amish community. "Why are you saying this?"

"Because this is a decision you have to make now, when it's easier for you to leave without burning any bridges here. A few years from now and it may not be so easy again." Aunt Elizabeth reached out and took Lucy's hand. "Think about it, pray on it, and search your soul. This place is wonderful, and if it's God's will that you stay here, then I am sure He'll make it possible. If not, then maybe He has a destiny for you outside this community."

"You haven't been baptized into the church yet, so you wouldn't be shunned if you left," Maria added. "You could still come visit anytime."

Lucy nodded, already thinking about their words. Suddenly swamped by emotions, she looked down at the sweet baby boy in her arms, and wiped away a tear. Maria put her arm around Lucy's shoulder.

"Thank you. This really helped me a lot." Lucy looked down at the grass.

"What's wrong?" Maria asked.

"I thought that by now... I thought Jeff would have come to see me."

"Well, maybe you should go see him. Go ask him yourself. Don't wait and let life pass you by. Seize the day!" Maria said with gusto, punching the air.

Lucy laughed. "Wise advice. You know what? I think I might do that."

"Come on, let's get back to the kitchen before Susan burns something," Aunt Elizabeth said, patting Lucy's shoulder.

Lucy chuckled as they headed to the house.

CHAPTER THIRTY-SIX

"I already told you, Estella, I don't want to talk about this anymore," Jeff said.

Estella groaned as she stared at her brother, feeling like she wanted to strangle him. She knew he could be so stubborn. She hated it when he went out of his way to prove her right.

"Exactly why don't you want to see her? It is clear you miss her."

"I don't miss her," Jeff insisted as he walked out of the kitchen and into the living room.

She followed him. "Sure you do. I can see it written all over your face."

"Yeah, in what color ink?" He stopped and turned around to look at her. "Look, it's been six months. Maybe I was in a little bit of a bad mood when she left, but I've gotten over it."

"Is that why you blew up on that rookie you work with for making a mistake on a report?"

Jeff rolled his eyes. "I knew Ben would tell you about that. The guy had it coming. It wasn't his first mistake that morning."

"Yeah, his first mistake was that he was not Lucy."

Jeff sighed. "It still sounds funny to me when I hear you call her that. It's like I can't stop thinking about her as Jane."

"You know her name is not the issue here. Jane, Lucy—She is still the woman you fell in love with."

"Whoa!" Jeff raised his hands. "Who said anything about love?"

Estella's smile was tender. "Look, I know you think that if you tell yourself that you don't love her enough times, maybe you'll really start to believe it. I also know that is not how love works."

"Just because you found love with Ben doesn't mean we all are going to find it, too. She went back home, back to the Amish community. If you haven't noticed, they are not exactly big on one of their own being in relationships with people that don't belong to their community. And I don't plan on joining the Amish. I wouldn't look good in a straw hat."

Estella looked unimpressed. "And you think the only way you can be with her is if you join them?"

"No. I don't want to be the reason why she has to give them up yet again after she just found them."

Estella sighed, finding his reason noble and yet stupid. "How about you talk to her about it, then let her make the decision? She's a big girl."

Jeff shook his head. "I talk to her about it and I'll only be sowing seeds of doubt in her mind. She's fine where she is, back with the people who love her. I'm fine the way I am."

Estella looked around the living room, her eyes falling on the small pile of books arranged haphazardly on the corner, probably by Lucy. On top was an old Bible, one that used to belong to their mother, the one Lucy had loved so much.

Estella knew she had to help Jeff, and she knew exactly what she had to do. She would be breaking a promise she made to a friend but was sure this one time her friend would forgive her for it.

After Lucy had left, Jeff had felt it appropriate to give her space to be with her family and deal with the recovery of her memory. The only thing Jeff could do about it was act like he was happy for her when he was anything but.

How could he stand in the way of her being with her family and discovering herself?

He still remembered bursting into that room and seeing Merin with her. He remembered the way he'd forced himself to be calm. Then the bone-crushing sense of relief that filled him when he held her in his arms, safe and alive.

But most of all the startling realization that she didn't hold a piece of his heart, but had the whole organ in her hands.

He knew how important it is to know your roots, and how precious family is. Even with the loss of his father and mother, he still had uncles and aunts. He had cousins and nieces. Most of all, he had Estella. It would be extremely selfish of him if he deprived Lucy of her chance to get to know her own family.

It would also be completely dishonest of him if he claimed to be happy about her decision.

"I'm planning on getting myself a new couch next weekend for my new apartment. Would you help me move it in?"

Jeff frowned, Estella's words breaking into his thoughts. "Why don't you call Ben for that? I'm sure he'll be more than happy to help."

"Because this is big brother stuff," Estella said, hands on her hips as she glared at him.

"It wasn't big brother stuff when you cooked pork chops for Ben last week," Jeff grumbled under his breath as he picked up his latest read from the coffee table, a spy novel he had gotten from a beachside bookstore a few blocks away. Jeff had passed that small brick building a thousand times without ever considering going inside. Now he stopped there at least twice a week to pick out a new book, which meant that he thought about Lucy at least twice a week.

At least.

No, he thought about Lucy every single day. Every minute of every day.

He missed her even more when he stopped at the bookstore, or prayed at night before going to bed, and when he got ready for church Sunday mornings...

"Okay, okay. Sorry I didn't invite you to our little cookout." Estella smiled and sidled up to him, looking all innocent. "How about you come help me move my new couch this Saturday and then I cook dinner for you?"

Jeff glanced at her, for some reason not trusting her smile. Then again, he had nothing to do this Saturday except sit at home doing nothing.

And think about Lucy.

"Alright, but I get to pick what we have for dinner."

Estella smiled. "You don't worry about that. I can assure you that you'll have no problem with the food."

CHAPTER THIRTY-SEVEN

Jeff walked up the steps to Estella's apartment and knocked on the door. He was a little bit late, but since he was doing her a favor in helping her move her new couch, he decided she was going to have to deal with that. Of course, this was Estella he was talking about, and her idea of dealing with it may differ greatly from his.

Well, if she gave him attitude, he was going to turn right around and walk away. Ben could help her move her couch instead.

And speaking of his friend, Jeff still almost didn't believe his sister was dating Ben. They'd finally told him last week.

"I know you're dating," Jeff said when they'd told him. "I've known for a while now. I have eyes. You guys aren't exactly stealthy about it."

"You're not mad?" Estella had asked. Ben just looked nervous, wringing his hands.

"Of course not. You're perfect for each other. But I do have one thing to say about it. Ben, if you hurt her, I will break your kneecaps."

Ben just blinked. "Understood."

"Come on, man. Relax." Jeff clapped him on the shoulder. "I'm just messing with you. But seriously. You better not hurt her."

The two of them were complete opposites. Estella with her bubbly in-your-face personality and Ben with his calm, quiet and gentle nature. Yet the two of them seemed almost perfect for each other.

He didn't mind it though. He knew how happy Ben made her. He saw it with his eyes anytime he saw either of them alone or together, and heard it when they talked about each other.

Jeff wished Estella would stop trying to force him into becoming as happy as she was.

He'd convinced himself that his attraction to Lucy had been generated purely by the circumstances, his need to protect her and keep her safe. She'd just admired him for protecting her. It would explain why the instant she stopped needing him to protect her he had stopped being anything more than just a friend to her.

Estella answered the door. "Hey, Jeff," she said, even more chipper than usual.

He looked at her skeptically. "What's going on with you? What's the matter?"

Estella shrugged, feigning innocence. "What do you mean?"

"You look really guilty."

"Nice one, Sherlock, but you're wrong. Everything's fine." Estella rolled her eyes sarcastically. "Just come in."

What was she hiding?

Still suspicious, he followed Estella into her living room.

"So, where is the couch?" Jeff suddenly paused, as the smell of something tantalizing wafted from the kitchen and into the living room.

Estella didn't cook that well. Not even close.

For a moment he denied the reality he was considering. Then he heard her voice. He turned around to confirm what his nose and ears had just told him.

Lucy decided everything was going perfectly as she closed the oven. Now all she needed to do was allow the vegetables to simmer before they would be ready to serve. She heard voices in the living room and was curious about who Estella's friend was. Curious enough that she slowly made her way to the living room.

She froze when she saw him turn around. Her eyes widened as she realized the trick Estella had played on her. On both of them, judging from the look of surprise on his face.

Lucy forced her lips into a smile. "Hello, Jeff."

Jeff stared at her, his mouth opening and closing several times as if he wanted to say something but couldn't find the words.

One look at him was enough to make a mockery of her idea that she was getting over him.

She wasn't over him. Not even close.

"Jane..." he said, immediately remembering that was not her name and shaking his head in apology. "Sorry, Lucy."

Lucy smiled. "Don't worry about it. It took even me a while to get used to it."

"Are you just here visiting?" Jeff didn't move from where he stood.

"I've realized I don't belong with the Amish. My relatives could see it too. They encouraged me to do what I thought was best." She smiled. "Funny enough, it was the simple things I missed. Eating popcorn and watching a movie with you all. Playing in the ocean and the feeling of the sun on my face at the beach. I guess what I missed most of all was the possibility of the world outside the community that I still want to see."

"So, you left?" Jeff asked, nodding in understanding. "For good?"

Lucy grabbed the edge of her apron and started to pull at it. "I promised my aunt and uncle I'll come visit from time to time. I wasn't baptized yet, so I wasn't shunned. Yes, I left the Amish for good."

"How long ago?" Jeff turned around to glare at his sister. "And why am I just finding out now?"

Estella raised her hand in surrender. "Don't look at me. I wasn't the one who was too stubborn to drive there and pay her a visit."

"You went to see her?"

"It was my idea to have Estella visit me," Lucy interrupted the siblings squabbling. Any other time and she would have smiled at the familiar sight of them arguing with each other. "I made her promise not to tell you. I thought it would make things more awkward. It was a promise she clearly didn't mind breaking."

"Again, not my fault you happen to be here when Jeff was supposed to help me move my couch."

"Really?" Jeff cocked a brow at his sister.

"Okay, maybe it was my fault, a little. I got tired of hearing the two of you whine to me how perfectly happy you are when I know you are not." She glared at them in turn. "Now you don't have to drive to Unity to see her, Jeff. Lucy, you don't have to keep on tiptoeing around me when I mention his name. You're welcome. Both of you."

Jeff and Lucy stared at their feet, unwilling to admit that Estella was right.

"Now," Estella continued, "I'm going out with Ben to give the two of you the chance to convince yourselves you are nothing but friends. When I come back, I can promise that whatever decision you come to, I am going to stand by it. By the way, I think I smell something burning."

Estella flounced out of the living room and into the foyer where she got her purse and headed to the door.

Lucy ran into the kitchen to save what was left of dinner. Jeff stood there, shaking his head and wondering what had just happened. A few minutes later, Lucy walked back into the living room.

"The chicken is still okay, but nothing else is."

Jeff smiled. "Is that your way of saying dinner is ready?"

Lucy shrugged. "Should I set the—?"

"Why didn't you want Estella to tell me you were around?" Jeff interrupted her.

Lucy looked away, shrugging her shoulders as she refused to meet his eye. "Nothing. I didn't want to—"

"See me? Is that it? You didn't want to see me?"

"Of course not. Why would you say that?"

"I don't know." With each statement he took a step closer to her. "Look, I know you don't need me anymore, and I understand that you wanted to go home. I'm glad you did. I hope it helped you find yourself and regain your memories. All I know is you didn't want me to know you were here when you came back."

"I thought it would be too hard," Lucy said in a small voice that made Jeff visibly deflate. Tears began to form in her eyes, and she stubbornly wiped them away with the back of her hands. "I waited and waited for you to come and see me in Unity. Even when I said I wanted to go back to Unity, you have no idea how scared I was. I wasn't sure if I was doing the right thing, and I was looking for a reason to stay here. That reason never came. You never asked me to stay. I thought you didn't want me here."

"Lucy…" Jeff's voice came out ragged as he stared at her, surprised to hear what she was saying.

She looked at him. "You think I didn't want to see you when I came back here? I didn't want to see that look in your eyes, that look that told me you were keeping your distance from me."

For several moments Jeff looked at her. "Remember what we were talking about before that creep Tobi attacked us?"

Lucy looked away, hating that she had cried in front of him. "Yes, but don't worry. You don't need to apologize. I know it was a mistake."

"No, it wasn't." Jeff took a step closer, stopping when she looked at him. "I was scared that after we caught your stalker and kidnapper you'd realize you didn't need me anymore."

Lucy frowned. "I don't understand. You think that because I needed you to protect me I wouldn't have feelings for you?"

"No, I thought that now that you don't need me anymore maybe you would start to want something different from what you thought you could have. I wasn't trying to keep my distance, Lucy. I didn't know how I'd deal with the possibility of you not having feelings for me. So, it was easier to not ask."

"Jeff—"

"But I don't think I care about that anymore. See, I've spent the last six months without you, and even though I'm angry at Estella right now, I can't deny that she was telling the truth when she said that I've been miserable."

"Jeff—"

"I'm sorry for how I acted when we left you in Unity, sorry I didn't fight for you harder. I'm sorry for not coming to see you. Sorry for making you ever think that you had a reason to stay away from me. I'm sorry I ever made you think that I was not your friend...or something more."

Lucy's mouth opened again to interrupt, but Jeff kept on talking.

"I know that I have to prove myself to you again and win you back. I don't care how long it takes, but I'm going to prove to you that you can trust me. I'm going to prove that I am your friend, Lucy, and that if you'll let me, I want to be even more than that—"

"Jeff!" Lucy stomped her foot.

Jeff kept right on talking. "...because even having you in my life as friend is far better than not having you at all."

Those words, the look in his eyes as he stood there and poured his heart out, the sincerity she saw in his eyes and heard in his words. If he didn't already have her heart, she would have given it to him right then and there.

But he did already have her heart, and she needed to let him know. She had to show him that he didn't have to prove his love to her. He had already done that a million times over.

"Jeff, that time on the beach, before Tobi attacked us, do you remember what you were telling me?"

Jeff nodded. "Yes, how I had feelings for you and how I was falling in love with you."

"And do you remember my reply?"

Jeff frowned. "Are you talking about the kiss?"

Lucy blushed as she rolled her eyes. "Well, yes. I did kiss you, and then after I said—"

"I don't know. I think that is when Tobi jumped out at us."

"I said I think I am—"

"Okay, okay. I remember. You were saying you were falling in love with me, too," Jeff finished for her. "I heard it, but I thought you'd changed your mind about it."

Lucy smiled as she took a step towards him. "You're right, Jeff. I have changed my mind about that reply."

Jeff's eyes fell. "Oh… I understand." Then he squared his shoulders. "And I don't mind. Like I said, I want you in my life anyway. If that means I am your friend and nothing more, then so be it."

"You know, maybe if you allowed me tell you what I think before you jumped to your own conclusion, you would have understand exactly how I feel."

Jeff smiled apologetically. "Sorry."

"As I was about to say before you oh so sweetly interrupted me, I have changed my mind. I don't think I'm falling in love with you Jeff. I know I'm already in love with you."

Finally silent, Jeff stood there, stunned.

Lucy continued, "You're kind and gentle, and you took me into your house, a stranger. I'm not saying this because I am that stranger. I am saying this because you are the kind of man to do that for anyone. You carried Ben through gunfire to safety and took a bullet for him. Yes, I know about that. You make me laugh and bring out a side of me I didn't know existed. You're brave, ready to put yourself in danger for me. More than all of these, I know I love you because the world is indeed miserable when you're not in my life."

Jeff sucked in a breath as he took a step closer. He stood looking down at her, wondering if this was a dream. "I want to say so many things, express in words how I feel. I don't have the words, Lucy. Don't have anything to say except tell you I love you, too."

She placed her hand on her chest as she looked into his eyes. "You told me once that you wouldn't kiss me until I asked you to. I'm asking you now. Please, kiss me already."

"Well, you took long enough to ask." Jeff laughed out loud, then lowered his head and kissed her. As he did, Lucy felt it again, him telling her in another way how much he loved her.

EPILOGUE

Lucy stared out into the ocean in front of the beach house, not really thinking about anything in particular, but enjoying the scenery. It was hard to imagine that Ben and Estella had finally gotten married. She had been ecstatic when Estella had asked her to be her matron of honor. The ceremony had been lovely, and she and Jeff had driven them to the airport for their two-week honeymoon in Hawaii.

Lucy thought it was so romantic. When it came to Estella and Ben, everything those two did was romantic.

She heard a noise behind her and didn't turn around as she felt someone wrap his hand around her shoulder.

"I knew you'd be out here," Jeff said behind her.

Lucy smiled and looked up at her husband. "And I knew you wouldn't be able to stay inside long before you came to check on me."

He bent down and kissed her. "It's a habit."

She chuckled and kissed his cheek as he sat beside her. "I know. Sometimes I still can't believe this was where it all went down."

"Sometimes I still can't believe how comfortable you are here."

"Well, Dr. Wellington is helping me with that. Then I've got you, too."

Lucy patted his knee as they looked out at the ocean. It was now over a year since the kidnapper and stalker had been arrested.

In that time, she'd written her first book based on her life story. It had been difficult to write about what had happened to her, yet also therapeutic. Putting the memories on paper also helped her put them behind her and move on. It also helped her remember even more, and she continued to remember more every day.

Ben had been helping her look for a literary agent, which was so much more of a time-consuming, frustrating, and lengthy process than she'd ever imagined. She'd already received several rejections, but Ben kept reassuring her that was normal and to keep going. In the movies, people got publishers so quickly, but Lucy was realizing that wasn't the case at all in real life. Hopefully, it would all be worth it in the end.

She'd also continued therapy to help her deal with the memories and the psychological scars from her time in Merin's basement. Finally, she was starting to heal and through it all, the one constant thing by her side was Jeff.

Every day she thanked God for him. Every day she fell in love with Jeff more. Every day she watched with joy as he also fell deeper in love with her. She remembered the day he got on one knee and asked her to marry him. There had been no hesitation as she said yes, tears running down her cheeks as she hugged him. It was a decision she had never regretted for a second. She leaned back onto him and sighed.

"Have I told you how much I love you today?"

Jeff chuckled. "I think that is my line."

"Yeah, thought I'd return the favor today."

"Well, you stopped Estella from biting my head off when she heard I forgot to call ahead and confirm their reservation for the seventh time. I think that's the most romantic thing anyone's done for me."

Lucy chuckled. "How about this, Jefferson Martin? I love you so much sometimes I think this is a dream I'll wake from someday."

Jeff's eyes went soft. "It's no dream, my love. All of this is real."

"I know."

The sunset draped the sky and ocean listlessly with fire-like hues.

Jeff said softly into her ear, "And Lucy-Jane Martin, I love you too."

Lucy closed her eyes, taking in the sounds of the sea, the breeze, the gulls, Jeff's breathing, and how he held her. She loved how he was the only person in the world who called her Lucy-Jane.

Home. This place was home. Jeff's arms were her home.

She wanted to remember every detail so she could tell their children about this moment. She smiled, knowing their future held many more memories like this waiting to be made.

And those memories she would remember forever.

****

NOTE FROM THE AUTHOR:

I hope you enjoyed this story.

I would appreciate an honest Amazon review because reviews are actually very important. They help other customers know more about my books. Your opinion matters! https://www.amazon.com/Amnesia-Romance-Covert-Police-Detectives-ebook/dp/B07SDSFV3J

Thank you! Please feel free to email me at ashley@ashleyemmaauthor.com. I'd love to talk with you!

Don't forget to visit http://www.ashleyemmaauthor.com/to download some of my free eBooks and you can even join my Advanced Reader Group.

ABOUT THE AUTHOR

Ashley Emma knew she wanted to be a novelist for as long as she can remember, and her first love was writing in the fantasy genre. She began writing books for fun at a young age, completing her first novel at age 12 and publishing it at age 16. She was home schooled and was blessed with the opportunity to spend her time focusing on reading and writing.

Ashley went on to write eight more manuscripts before age 25 when she also became a multi-bestselling author.

She owns Fearless Publishing House where she helps other aspiring authors achieve their dreams of publishing their own books. Ashley lives in Maine with her husband and children, and plans on releasing several more books in the near future.

Visit her at ashleyemmaauthor.com or email her at ashley@ashleyemmaauthor.com. She loves to hear from her readers!

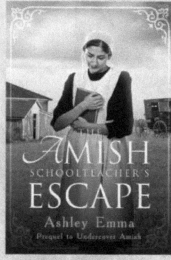
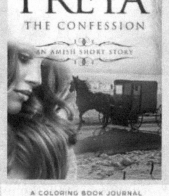

Check out my author Facebook page to see rare photos from when I lived with the Amish in Unity, Maine.

https://www.facebook.com/ashleyemmaauthor/

Join my free Facebook group The Amish Book Club where I share free Amish books weekly!

https://www.facebook.com/groups/theamishbookclub/

LOOKING FOR SOMETHING NEW TO READ? CHECK OUT MY OTHER BOOKS ON AMAZON!

Click here to check out other books by Ashley Emma

Coming soon:

Freya: The Rescue (Book 3)

Amish Safe Haven

Amish Twin Sisters

Princess and the Amish Pauper: the Amish Fairytale

Series

The Amish Beauty and the Beast: the Amish Fairytale

Series

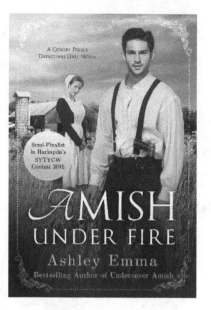

AMISH UNDER FIRE

After Maria Mast's abusive ex-boyfriend is arrested for being involved in sex trafficking and modern-day slavery, she thinks that she and her son Carter can safely return to her Amish community.

But the danger has only just begun.

Someone begins stalking her, and they want blood and revenge.

Agent Derek Turner of Covert Police Detectives Unit is assigned as her bodyguard and goes with her to her Amish community in Unity, Maine.

Maria's secretive eyes, painful past, and cautious demeanor intrigue him.

As the human trafficking ring begins to target the Amish community, Derek wonders if the distraction of her will cost him his career...and Maria's life.

http://a.co/fT6D7sM

FREYA: THE CONFESSION (Book 2 in the Freya Series)

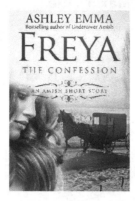

Adam Lapp expected the woman who killed his brother accidentally with her car to be heartless and cruel. He never expected her to a timid, kind, and beautiful woman who is running for her life from a controlling ex who wants her dead.

When Freya Wilson asks him to take her to his family so she can tell them the truth, he agrees.

But when Freya meets his parents Hannah and Aaron Lapp, along with the widowed Mariah, will she have the courage to say what she came there to say, or will she crumble?

Will she find hope in the ashes, or just more darkness and sorrow?

Bonus: Includes an excerpt from Amish Under Fire, the sequel to Undercover Amish!

https://www.amazon.com/Freya-Confession-Amish-Short-Forgiveness-ebook/dp/B076PQF5FS

ASHLEY'S AMISH ADVENTURES: AN OUTSIDER LIVING WITH THE AMISH

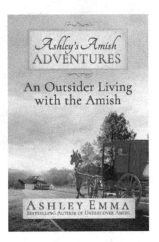

Ever wondered what it would be like to live in an Amish community? Now you can find out in this true story for young adults and middle grade readers.

This unique journal's rare photos literally show you the places you are reading about--even what the inside of Amish homes look like. Come along on the fascinating journey as twenty-year-old Ashley learns everything she can about the Amish.

*

"Highly recommended." -Amazon Top 500 Reviewer

https://www.amazon.com/Ashleys-Amish-Adventures-Outsider-community-ebook/dp/B01N5714WE

ASHLEY'S AMISH ADVENTURES: ATTENDING AN AMISH WEDDING

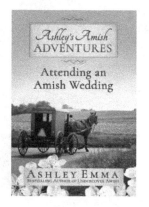

Ever wondered what it would be like to go inside an Amish home, make Amish friends, or go to an Amish wedding? In this sequel to *Ashley's Amish Adventures: An Outsider Living With the Amish*, you can now experience it all for yourself in this true story for young adults and middle grade readers.

Because of this journal's rare photos, you will literally get to see the places you are reading about as you read.

*

"This is the second one that I have read in the adventure series. It was interesting to me as I was able to learn more about the manner in which the Amish live... Highly recommended."

--USN Chief, Ret..VT Town, Amazon Top 500 Reviewer

https://www.amazon.com/Ashleys-Amish-Adventures-Attending-fascinating-ebook/dp/B01MTT0Y3B

FREYA: AN AMISH SHORT STORY (Book 1 in the Freya Series)

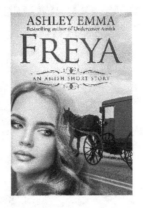

Click here to get my free book, Freya: an Amish Short Story!

After Freya Wilson accidentally hits an Amish man with her car in a storm, will she have the courage to tell his family the truth—especially after she meets his handsome brother?

https://www.amazon.com/Freya-Amish-Short-Ashley-Emma-ebook/dp/B01MSP03UX

HAVE YOU ALWAYS DREAMED OF BECOMING AN AUTHOR?

"...The list of places to promote your book along with the step-by-step publishing and marketing checklist is well worth the cost of this eBook."

---Nicole Cruz, www.nicolecruzproofreader.com

You no longer have to wait for permission from an agent or a publishing house in order to become a successful published author. With the right tools, mindset, and skills, you can do it on your own!

In *Fearless Author*, I will show you how I launched my own bestselling books.

When you use the Book Launch and Marketing Checklist included in this book, you won't even have to take notes unless you want to. The checklist will summarize the steps you need to take and will tell you in what order you need to take them.

Download the printable version of the Book Launch and Marketing Checklist when you visit http://www.ashleyemmaauthor.com!

*

"I read nearly every book on self-publishing, and I can say that this one has information the others don't have. If you want to be sure you are up on the latest, become a Fearless Author now!"

-Ray Brehm - bestselling author of Author Inc, Author Your Success, and The Author Startup

Click here to buy Fearless Author:

https://www.amazon.com/Fearless-Author-step-step-self-publishing-ebook/dp/B06XJGRRT1

Next is an excerpt of *Amish Under Fire*, book 2 in this series, The Cover Police Detectives Unit Series. These books can be read in any order.

http://a.co/fp5V3qt

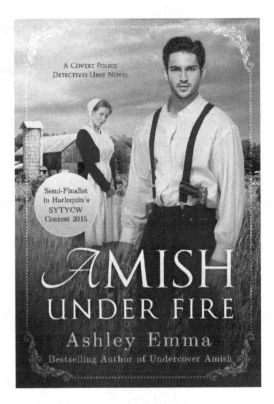

EXCERPT OF AMISH UNDER FIRE

Maria Mast waited in line at her bank in Portland, Maine, wearing a nametag printed with the word *Kate.* She was wearing a retro waitress uniform of which she couldn't wait to change out later. She removed the nametag and tucked it away before anyone else could see it. The back of the dress advertised Miss Portland's Diner, and now she cringed at the thought of people knowing where she worked. She should have thrown on a jacket to hide the words on the back of her dress before entering the bank.

Kate was not her real name. Maria had to lie to her boss about a lot of things, but she was grateful for Karen—the benevolent woman who had given her a job and hadn't asked too many questions.

Her boss hadn't pried too much when Maria had shown up for her interview with bruises on her arms. Karen neither pestered Maria about why she didn't talk to anyone about her personal life, nor did she ask why Maria hadn't made friends or trusted anyone. Karen even pretended not to take notice when Maria would nervously glance up every time she heard the loud rumbling of a diesel truck pulling into the parking lot.

Even if Karen could have seen the gun concealed under Maria's uniform skirt, Maria wondered if her boss would have even pressed for information about that.

Maria wasn't sure if Karen truly didn't want to pry or was just oblivious, but she was thankful regardless.

The bank teller beckoned to her. Maria slid her cash toward the woman wearing round spectacles. She heard the doors open and screams erupt throughout the busy bank just after depositing the money.

She whirled around. Two armed masked men dressed in all black entered the building.

"Everybody on the floor!" the first criminal shouted while the other stomped over to the tellers, demanding cash.

Maria lowered herself to the floor along with everyone else. Her heart fell into her stomach, anxiety constricting her throat and chest. Maybe nobody would get hurt if everyone did what the men said.

Or maybe she would die here, today, after surviving everything she had already been through. Though she was only twenty-five, she had already withstood more hardship than some people did over an entire lifetime.

What about her son, Carter? Would she ever see him again?

She considered the gun strapped to her leg under her dress. What if she accidentally hit an innocent bystander?

A man had been waiting in line a few people behind her. He was wearing some type of law enforcement uniform with a gun on his hip. The man's hand automatically went to his gun.

"Hey, are you a cop?" one of the robbers asked before the man could even get the gun out of his holster. "You shoot and I'll kill somebody." The bank robber aimed his massive gun at a sobbing bank teller. "Give me the gun, or she dies."

Was that fear that flickered in the robber's eyes? Would he really kill the woman if that man didn't give him the gun?

The man in the uniform reluctantly removed the pistol from its holster. He dropped the magazine and emptied the chamber before slowly handing it to the bank robber. Defeat and indignation darkened his face as he sank to the floor beside the others.

The gunman forced the weeping bank teller to hand over all of the cash available.

"That's all the cash we have," the harried teller with the spectacles cried when the bank robber demanded more cash.

"There's got to be more. Isn't there more?" he shouted.

"No, I swear, that's all of it."

The other gunman grabbed a little girl by the wrist, wrenching her away from her mother as she screamed in terror. He locked her under his arm and held the gun to her head.

"If you don't get us the rest of the cash, I'll blow a hole through her head," he screamed at the teller, much more confident than the other robber.

Maria's muscles tensed with every word he shouted. She had to do something.

Her heart pounded harder with each passing second as her fingers reached up to her knee where her M&P Shield was secured in its holster. She slid it out, rested her forefinger along the side of the gun, and clicked off the safety.

The man in the law enforcement uniform caught her eye, looked at the gun, and gave her a nod. His eyes communicated to hers behind black-rimmed rectangle glasses. When she hesitated, he nodded again and jerked his head ever so slightly to the robbers.

Somehow she knew he had a plan. He would help her. All they had to do was create enough of a distraction for it to work.

"Look, the police," the man shouted, his outburst making the two gunmen turn to the window in a panic.

In the two seconds he gave her, she aimed for the torso and fired, hitting the first gunman by the door in the shoulder.

The man with the glasses lunged toward the other gunman who held the girl, knocking her out of the way. After they moved, Maria hit that gunman in the arm.

Two other men who had been in line leapt into action, swiping the weapons from the two robbers and restraining them as their screams of pain filled the air.

The hours spent at the shooting range had paid off. She had traded some of her paintings for shooting lessons, and her instructor had told her she was a natural.

The man with the glasses looked over at her, admiration in his eyes.

The rest of the people in the bank turned to her, thanking her. Especially the girl's mother, who ran to her crying, throwing her arms around her in a hug.

What if this was reported on the news? What if her face got on TV?

After all her hard work, he would find her. This time, Maria didn't know if he would let her live.

She had to get out of there. She pried the hands of the girl's mother off her and made a beeline for the door, then slammed into someone.

Two strong hands steadied her as she looked up into the face of the handsome Glasses Man.

He let her go and said, "I'm Agent Derek Turner from CPDU. I don't usually wear a uniform, but I was on security duty today for an event. It's a good thing you were here. Are you law enforcement? Why are you carrying a concealed weapon?"

"No, I'm not in law enforcement at all. I took lessons at a range. Look, I have a concealed weapons permit." Maria pulled the permit out of her wallet and handed it to him. "I just want to be able to defend myself."

"I thought maybe you were in law enforcement. That's why I gave the signal to shoot the criminals." He paused. "You saved that girl's life. What's wrong?" he asked. His dark hair was gelled stylishly above a short, stubbly beard, and as he looked into her eyes, she felt as though he could see all of her secrets.

"Everything." She ignored the people thanking her and tried to dart out the door, but two officers blocked her way.

"Wait, miss. We need you to give a statement to CPDU. We need to take you there," one of them said.

Realization that she couldn't get out of this situation washed over her. Panic began to grow within her as she realized this could get her on the news or in public records.

And Trevor might see her on the news and figure out where she was.

Yes, she had saved the little girl's life, but had she just ended her own?

***

"Here's your sandwich, ma'am," Maria said, setting a plate down for a customer in a booth at the Miss Portland Diner. "Is there anything else I can get you?"

"That's all. Thank you," the customer said.

Maria's shift was over. She went out back and hung up her apron, looking forward to going home and taking a hot shower. Today had been one of those days with several difficult customers. To top it off, she'd spilled a drink on one unforgiving patron and she'd mixed up a few orders. Her mind had been clouded since the bank robbery.

She couldn't wait to eat dinner with Carter. Maybe she'd make some popcorn and they would watch a movie afterward.

"Bye, Karen," Maria called out, grabbing her purse and keys.

"Goodnight, dear," said her boss with a smile.

Nobody from the news had contacted her so far since the shooting yesterday. Maria had told CPDU that she didn't want to be in the news or in newspapers; she wanted to keep a low profile. They assured her they'd keep her information confidential from the press, like where she lived and worked.

If only Maria had listened to her cousin Olivia Mast when she had first started dating Trevor, maybe she wouldn't be on the run now. Olivia had warned Maria that Trevor seemed controlling, which could lead to abuse.

Olivia, who had left the Amish to become a detective, was like Maria's sister because Maria's parents took her in when her family was killed. The two girls grew up together in the same house like sisters. When Olivia had left the Amish and was shunned, Maria was devastated when she could no longer talk to Olivia. But after Maria left the Amish, they rebuilt their friendship until Trevor made Maria stop talking to Olivia.

Maria opened the diner door and headed outside toward her car.

"We're live. Ms. Mast!" A female news reporter with a cameraman hurried over to her. "Can you tell us what you were thinking when you took down those bank robbers to save that little girl?"

How had they found out where she worked? Had CPDU told them after all?

Maria put her head down and walked faster toward her car, key ready in her hand.

"What you did was so brave, but we want to know more. Where did you learn to shoot? Why were you carrying a concealed weapon?"

"This is America, isn't it?"

Both anger and fear roiled within Maria. She unlocked her car and got inside. Did this news reporter have any idea how much she was endangering Maria?

Now it was too late. The damage had been done.

Maria would have to move again.

***

"I need everyone in the situation room, please," Captain Branson of the Covert Police Detectives Unit in Augusta, Maine, bellowed.

Several special agents, bodyguards, detectives, and police officers looked up from what they had been doing.

"Now!"

Everyone started moving more quickly at Branson's sharp tone. Agent Derek Turner had just sat down at his desk to make a few reports from an arrest he had made earlier that day. Now it would have to wait. When Branson said "now," he meant now. All the officers, analysts, bodyguards, and agents milled into the situation room.

Branson cleared his throat as everyone quieted down. "We have received some information on a sex trafficking ring in Portland. We think it might be the same ring that moved from Boston to Portland that we tried to shut down four years ago."

Derek remembered the case well. CPDU had managed to arrest several of the traffickers, but most of them, along with the boss of the trafficking ring, had relocated themselves along with all of the girls they had kidnapped. The trail had gone cold.

He didn't understand how these men could kidnap and profit of off young women. Anger and grief roiled in Derek's stomach, but he clenched his fists and tried to focus on what Branson was saying.

"We think the ring has returned to Portland, possibly after relocating to Boston. We received a tip from someone at the Maine Mall. They suspect that there are young men who are luring in teenage girls by flattering them, spending time with them at the mall, and then offering to drive them home or to a movie. Instead, the men just bring them to the trafficking headquarters. Four girls have gone missing this month at the mall alone." Branson pointed to four photos that had been hung up, all of men in their twenties.

Derek studied the photos, and one of the agents passed copies around the room to everyone.

"We have identified these three men from mall security footage talking to teenage girls multiple times, but we have not located them yet. Garret Fletcher, Ryan Thompson, and Trevor Monroe. We need to be on the lookout for them. If you see any of them, do not arrest them."

"What?" spat one of the newer agents who was known for speaking his mind. "You don't want us to arrest them?"

"No. We need to follow them so that they can hopefully lead us to their temporary headquarters if they are indeed working for the ring." Branson tugged on the belt that was snug under his round belly. "I will assign four agents to go undercover on a mission. We think the traffickers might be keeping the girls temporarily somewhere in Portland. We are trying to pinpoint the location. I am assigning four men to pose as potential 'buyers' while gathering information undercover." Branson made air quotes, making no effort to hide his disgust.

Rage against the traffickers boiled Derek's own blood within him, but he listened intently as Branson continued. He couldn't wait to get to work locating these men and the trafficking headquarters.

Derek tried to listen as Branson continued speaking, but he slowly tuned Branson out. Memories were taking over his mind. The blood on the white carpet of his apartment, the blood on the walls, Natalia's bruised body lying skewed and broken on the floor...

He had been too late to save her. He'd been working when the murder occurred, trying to locate the very traffickers who had been in his own home that night, targeting the love of his life.

The obscene message written on the wall in her blood had been enough evidence to tell them this specific ring had committed the murder out of revenge after Derek had arrested several of their traffickers. Witnesses had also seen the traffickers in the apartment building on the night of the murder.

But they had disappeared, and CPDU hadn't had any significant clues to their whereabouts.

Until now.

"Cristman, Hughes, Rogers, and Smith, I will tell you the details of the mission privately," Branson concluded. "Everyone else is dismissed."

Everyone stood up, and Derek silently chided himself. The meeting was over, and he had zoned out. He hoped he didn't miss any important information. He'd ask one of the others about it later.

Wait. He hadn't been chosen to go on the mission. He was one of the best field agents in the unit. Why hadn't Branson chosen him? Derek's heart hammered. Had he done something wrong? Perplexed, he maneuvered his six-foot frame through the people leaving the room and walked up to the captain.

"You're wondering why I didn't pick you for this assignment," Captain Branson said gruffly, turning to Derek and looking up at him.

"Yes, sir. I'm just wondering why."

"These are most likely the same men who killed your wife. They know what you look like, so you can't work on this case and go undercover. The other thing is the mission will take place on the fourth anniversary of your wife's death. I didn't want you to be distracted, that's all. You are human, just like the rest of us. Distractions can lead to fatal mistakes," Branson said, sidling past him. "Remember two years ago?"

Derek nodded solemnly. He had been so distracted by grief that he had almost let a suspect escape custody. "That was then. I won't make the same mistake again."

"I know you want the same thing as everyone else, which is to catch these guys. So I need you to do something else."

"Yes, sir." Derek slumped and looked at the floor, but he accepted his captain's decision. If Branson thought this was best, then Derek would comply.

"A woman just walked in here, Maria Mast, the woman who shot those two bank robbers. She claims her ex-boyfriend is abusing her. He is one of the traffickers we saw on the mall security footage who is kidnapping teenage girls, Trevor Monroe. Maria is Detective Olivia Troyer's cousin."

Olivia and her husband Isaac had been temporarily transferred to work on a case.

"Go talk to her and get as much information from her as you can. Let's arrest this trafficker," Branson said, tugging on his belt once more, his bald head gleaming in the light from the ceiling. "See if she can help us find out where the headquarters is. She might know where Monroe is. Report to me afterward. Go."

Branson turned to the four agents he had picked and began discussing the details of the mission.

Derek respected his boss and his boss' decision, but when he saw that his friend Agent Chris Hughes was one of the chosen, Derek could not deny that he felt a twinge of jealousy. They had worked together for a few years now. Hughes was good in the field, but Derek knew he was even better. Even though he was only twenty-nine, Derek already had more experience than many of the other agents, thanks to his service in the military.

This didn't seem fair. Now Derek was stuck gathering information and pushing papers while his coworkers got to do the really important work. At least he would get to see how the brave woman from the bank robbery was doing. He was glad to help her with her problem ex. This work was important too.

He walked to the front of the building to take the woman into his office. He stepped into the waiting room and said, "Maria Mast?"

A young boy held a coloring book and the woman's hand, his brown eyes glancing around behind his round glasses, taking in CPDU with fascination. Derek smiled, and then he looked at the boy's mother.

The young woman walked toward him. Her long hair was highlighted a lovely shade of honey blonde, falling in loose curls that framed her beautiful face. She wore a simple gray sweater dress that might as well have been a ball gown; it looked so wonderful on her. As she walked, her black heels clacked on the marble floor. She appeared to be a few years younger than him, maybe in her mid-twenties. However, her brown eyes held fear, hurt, and secrets beyond her years that intrigued Derek. And where had she learned to shoot and handle a weapon so well?

Speak, you fool, he told himself when she looked at him expectantly. His mind drew a blank.

If you liked this sample...

Get Amish Under Fire

here: http://a.co/fp5V3qt

ACCESS YOUR FREE BONUS AMISH VIDEOS HERE:

Use this secret link to instantly access your 3 free Ex-Amish Interview videos!

http://ashleyemmaauthor.com/free-videos-entry/

CPSIA information can be obtained
at www.ICGtesting.com
Printed in the USA
BVHW031141020320
573830BV00001B/14